ASCENT®

CENTER FOR TECHNICAL KNOWLEDGE

Autodesk® Revit® 2026 Architecture Conceptual Design and Visualization

Learning Guide

Imperial Units - Edition 1.0

ASCENT - Center for Technical Knowledge®
Autodesk® Revit® 2026 Architecture
Conceptual Design and Visualization
Imperial Units - Edition 1.0

Prepared and produced by:

ASCENT Center for Technical Knowledge
11201 Dolfield Blvd, Suite 112
Owings Mills, MD 21117

866-527-2368
www.ASCENTed.com

Lead Contributor: Cherisse Biddulph

ASCENT - Center for Technical Knowledge (a division of Rand Worldwide Inc.) is a leading developer of professional learning materials and knowledge products for engineering software applications. ASCENT specializes in designing targeted content that facilitates application-based learning with hands-on software experience. For over 25 years, ASCENT has helped users become more productive through tailored custom learning solutions.

We welcome any comments you may have regarding this guide, or any of our products. To contact us please email: feedback@ASCENTed.com.

AS-RAR2601-CDV1IM-SG // IS-RAR2601-CDV1IM-SG

Contents

Preface

As architects and designers start a project, they frequently think about the overall massing of a building or the area of the footprint. The Autodesk® Revit® software, using its powerful Building Information Modeling (BIM) engine, includes tools for creating mass elements that can be modified into many shapes. You can then apply walls, roofs, and floors to them to continue designing. You can use space planning tools to set up areas for rooms and colors to mark the different areas. For presentations, you can create, embellish, and render perspective views.

The objective of *Autodesk® Revit® 2026 Architecture: Conceptual Design and Visualization* is to enable users who have worked with the Autodesk Revit software to expand their knowledge in the area of conceptual design, including massing studies, space planning, visualization, and rendering.

Topics Covered

- Create in-place conceptual mass elements.
- Create building elements from massing studies.
- Use rooms and areas for space planning and analysis.
- Create perspectives, sketches, exploded views, and solar studies.
- Render views that include materials, lighting, and enhancements such as people and plants.

Prerequisites

- Access to the 2026.1 version of the software to ensure compatibility with this guide. Future software updates that are released by Autodesk may include changes that are not reflected in this guide. The practices and files included with this guide are not compatible with prior versions (e.g., 2025).
- You should be comfortable with the fundamentals of the Autodesk Revit software, as taught in the *Autodesk Revit: Fundamentals for Architecture* guide. Knowledge of basic techniques is assumed, such as creating walls, roofs, and other objects; copying and moving objects; creating and working with views; etc.
- Collaboration Tools, BIM Management, and Site Planning and Design are taught in additional guides.

Note on Software Setup

This guide assumes a standard installation of the software using the default preferences during installation. Lectures and practices use the standard software templates and default options for the Content Libraries.

Note on Learning Guide Content

ASCENT's learning guides are intended to teach the technical aspects of using the software and do not focus on professional design principles and standards. The practices aim to demonstrate the capabilities and flexibility of the software rather than following specific design codes or standards.

Lead Contributor: Cherisse Biddulph

Cherisse is an Autodesk Certified Professional for Revit as well as an Autodesk Certified Instructor. She brings over 19 years of industry, teaching, and technical support experience to her role as a Learning Content Developer with ASCENT. With a passion for design and architecture, she has worked in the industry assisting firms with their Building Information Modeling (BIM) management and software implementation needs as they modernize to a BIM design environment. Although her main devotion is the Revit design product, she is also proficient in AutoCAD, Autodesk BIM 360, and Autodesk Navisworks. Today, Cherisse continues to expand her knowledge in the ever-evolving AEC industry and the software used to support it.

Cherisse Biddulph has been the Lead Contributor for *Autodesk Revit Architecture: Conceptual Design and Visualization* since 2019.

In This Guide

The following highlights the key features of this guide.

Feature	Description
Practice Files	The Practice Files page includes a link to the practice files and instructions on how to download and install them. The practice files are required to complete the practices in this guide.
Chapters	A chapter consists of the following: Learning Objectives, Instructional Content, Practices, Chapter Review Questions, and Command Summary. • **Learning Objectives** define the skills you can acquire by learning the content provided in the chapter. • **Instructional Content**, which begins right after Learning Objectives, refers to the descriptive and procedural information related to various topics. Each main topic introduces a product feature, discusses various aspects of that feature, and provides step-by-step procedures on how to use that feature. Where relevant, examples, figures, helpful hints, and notes are provided. • **Practice** for a topic follows the instructional content. Practices enable you to use the software to perform a hands-on review of a topic. It is required that you download the practice files (using the link found on the Practice Files page) prior to starting the first practice. • **Chapter Review Questions**, located close to the end of a chapter, enable you to test your knowledge of the key concepts discussed in the chapter. • **Command Summary** concludes a chapter. It contains a list of the software commands that are used throughout the chapter and provides information on where the command can be found in the software.
Appendices	Appendices provide additional information to the main course content. It could be in the form of instructional content, practices, tables, projects, or skills assessment.

Practice Files

To download the practice files for this guide, use the following steps:

1. Type the URL *exactly as shown below* into the address bar of your Internet browser to access the Course File Download page.

   Note: If you are using the ebook, you do not have to type the URL. Instead, you can access the page by clicking the URL below.

   https://www.ascented.com/getfile/id/aquilaPF

2. On the Course File Download page, click the **DOWNLOAD NOW** button, as shown below, to download the .ZIP file that contains the practice files.

3. Once the download is complete, unzip the file and extract its contents.

   The recommended practice files folder location is:
   C:\Revit Conceptual Design and Visualization Practice Files

   Note: It is recommended that you do not change the location of the practice files folder. Doing so may cause errors when completing the practices.

Stay Informed!

To receive information about upcoming events, promotional offers, and complimentary webcasts, visit:

www.ASCENTed.com/updates

Chapter 1

Massing Studies

The Autodesk® Revit® software is a powerful tool for creating accurate building models. When you are just beginning a design, however, you do not need to have that level of accuracy and may only want to model general features, such as the overall shape of a building. The massing tools help with this initial modeling stage by enabling you to create and modify simple and complex forms directly in a project.

Learning Objectives

- Place and modify massing elements using existing mass families.
- Create mass forms (and void forms), including extrusions, revolves, sweeps, blends, swept blends, and lofts.
- Modify mass faces, edges, or vertices using the 3D control feature.
- Edit profiles of mass elements.
- Add edges and profiles to mass elements.
- Divide and pattern the faces of masses.
- Create floors at selected levels in the mass.
- Add walls, roofs, curtain systems, and floors to a mass element using the *Model by Face* tools.

1.1 Overview of Massing Studies

When you start designing a building, you normally do not know its exact size or the locations of doors and windows. You probably do not even know what type of wall system you want to use. In some cases, you need to establish the relationship of the forms of the new building to those of the existing structures around it first, as shown in Figure 1–1. The focus is the overall shape and footprint of the building, which you develop in a massing study.

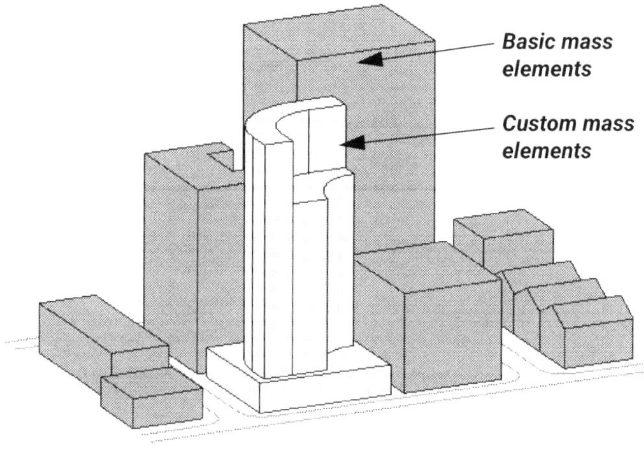

Figure 1–1

- Massing elements are intended for large forms that define the overall shape and size of a building. For smaller elements (e.g., furniture or columns), create or use family elements.
- By default, mass elements do not display in views until the Show Mass mode has been toggled on. In the *Massing & Site* tab>*Conceptual Mass* panel, select either:
    -  (Show Mass by View Settings): The Mass category must be toggled on in the *Visibility/Graphic Overrides* dialog box. Use this if you want to print or export the mass elements.
    -  (Show Mass Form and Floors): Overrides the Visibility/Graphic Overrides and toggles on mass elements and mass floors.
- **Show Mass Surface Types** and **Show Mass Zones and Shades** are connected to the subscription based Mass Analysis tools.

Hint: Other Sketching Programs

There are a variety of standalone sketching programs, like Autodesk's FormIt Pro. These offer intuitive sketching and modeling capabilities. The 3D models can be imported into Revit in a variety of ways.

The advantage of creating the massing directly in Revit is that the massing model resides in the same file (or family) as the entire Revit model and is not dependent on external programs.

Premade Mass Elements

Premade mass elements (families) can be inserted into a project using the **Place Mass** command. Revit includes several basic massing elements that work like building blocks to help you create the conceptual design, some of which are shown in Figure 1–2.

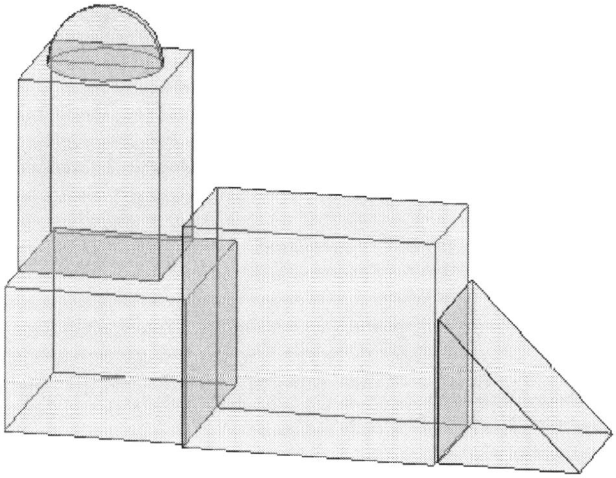

Figure 1–2

Custom Mass Elements

Custom mass elements are created in a project as an **In-Place Mass** or in a separate **Conceptual Mass** family. These families are highly customizable. They are created by drawing profiles, as shown on the left in Figure 1–3, and then applying a form, such as an extrusion (as shown on the right in Figure 1–3) or a loft.

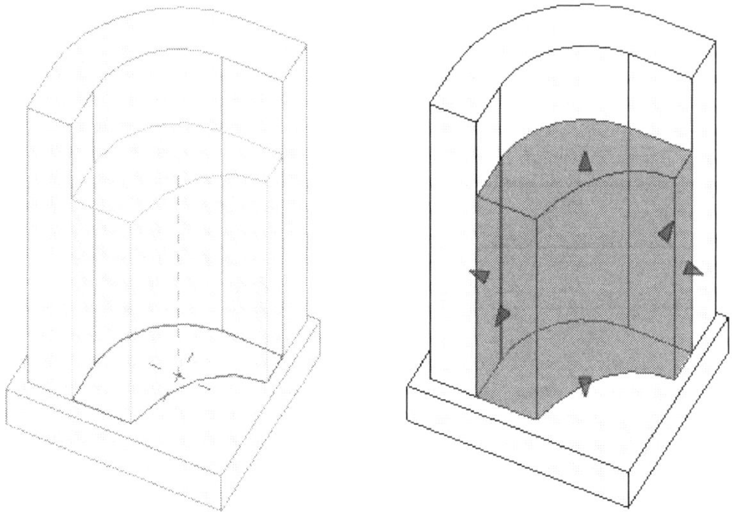

Figure 1–3

Modifying Mass Elements

Premade mass elements can be modified using shape handles in plan, elevation, and section views, as shown in Figure 1–4. Custom mass elements can be modified using shape handles in 3D views and have additional modification options, as shown in Figure 1–5.

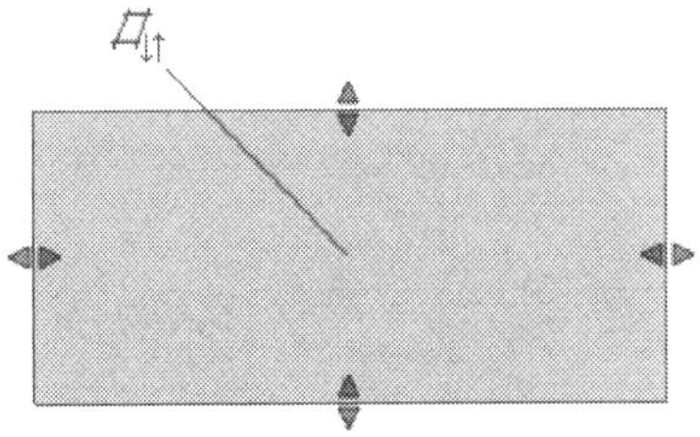

Figure 1–4

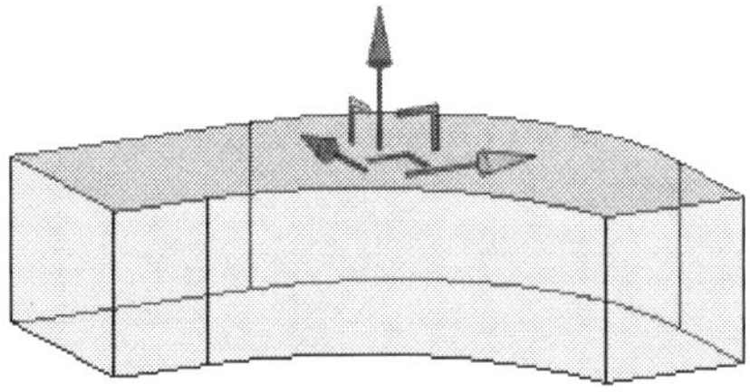

Figure 1–5

Making Buildings from Mass Elements

When you have finished the massing study, you can apply walls, curtain systems, roofs, and floors to the faces of the mass elements (as shown in Figure 1–6), and then proceed to the next step in the design process.

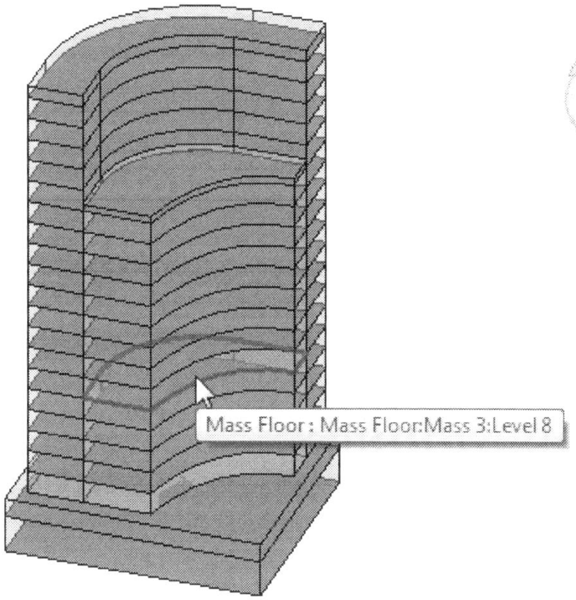

Figure 1–6

1.2 Placing Mass Elements

The most basic building blocks of massing are the mass families included with Revit. These include standard building block shapes, as shown in Figure 1–7, which can be resized using shape handles in plan, elevation, and section views, and in Properties for more precise sizing. These mass families need to be loaded into a project.

> **Note:** *If you know you are going to use these families in your massing studies, you might want to preload them into a template.*

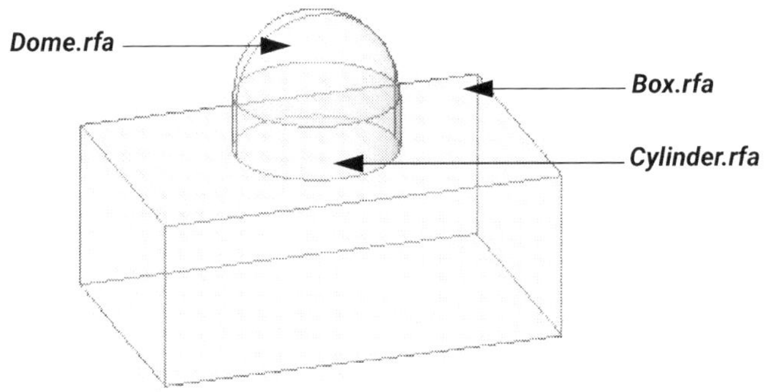

Figure 1–7

- Premade mass families are found in the Revit Library in the *Mass* subfolder.

Hint: Family Library Location

If you do not default to the Revit family folder location, click on the **Imperial Library** folder icon in the *Places* panel, shown in Figure 1–8 within the *Open* or *Load Family* dialog box.

By default, these families do not get downloaded or installed and require a separate installation. For that reason, the families required for the practices in this guide have been included with the practice files.

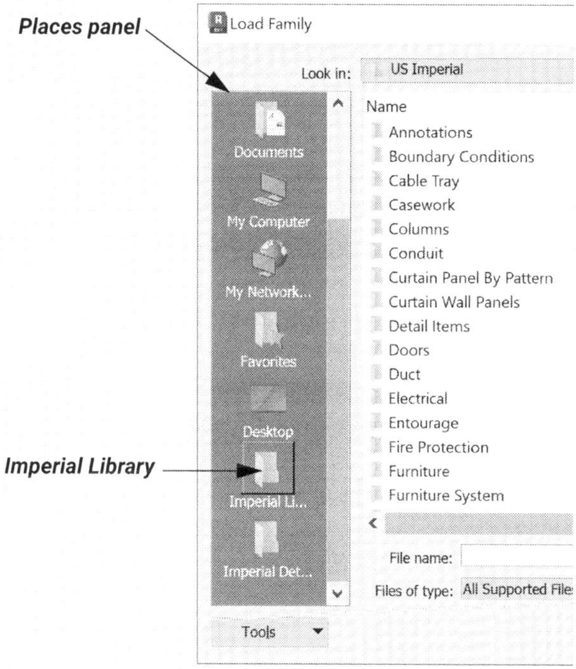

Figure 1–8

How To: Place Massing Elements

1. In the *Massing & Site* tab>*Conceptual Mass panel*, click (Place Mass).

- If you have not already toggled on Show Mass mode from the *Visibility/Graphic Overrides* dialog box, an alert box displays stating the program has toggled it on automatically, as shown in Figure 1–9.

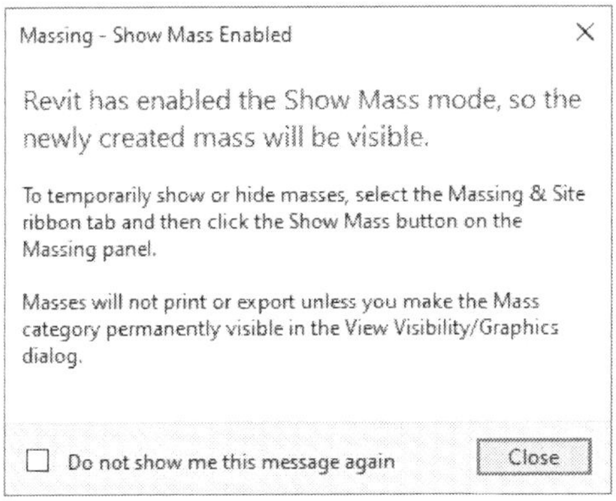

Figure 1–9

- If no mass family is loaded, you are prompted to load a family, as shown in Figure 1–10. Click **Yes** to open up the *Load Family* dialog box.

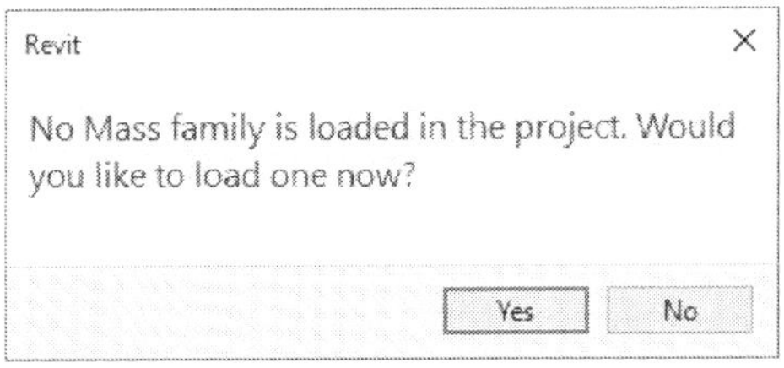

Figure 1–10

2. In the Type Selector, select a mass type, as shown in Figure 1–11.

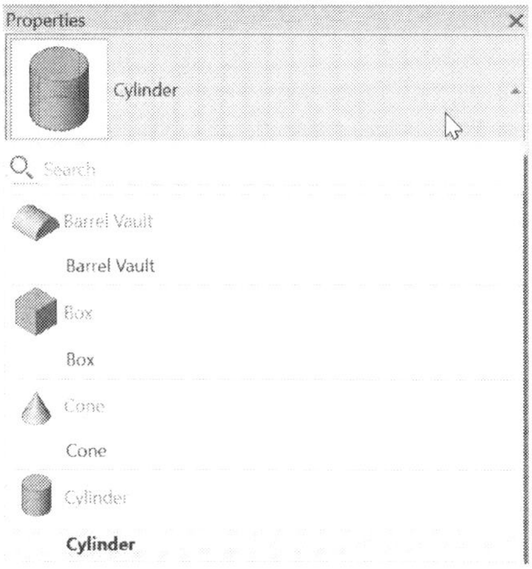

Figure 1–11

3. In the *Modify | Place Mass* tab>*Placement* panel, click either (Place on Face) or (Place on Work Plane). Pick a point on the screen to place the mass.

   Note: *Another element must be in the project for you to be able to use Place on Face.*

   - To rotate the mass before placing it, press <Spacebar> to rotate it in 90 degree increments.
   - To rotate the mass after you place it, select **Rotate after placement** in the Options Bar.

Modifying Basic Mass Elements

You can use Properties to modify an element's shape, material, and offset from host. You can also use shape handles to change the sizes of mass elements in plans or elevations (but not in 3D views), as shown in Figure 1–12. This method is not very precise but might be all that you need to do at this early stage of the conceptual design. The shape handle in the center flips the work plane.

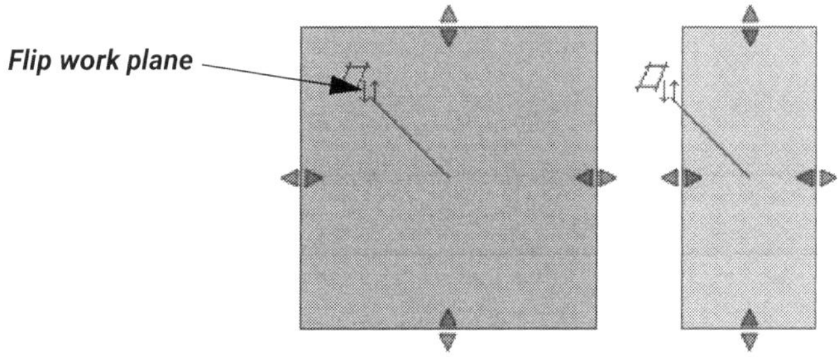

Figure 1–12

- Figure 1–13 shows the Properties for a box mass element. Dimension options vary according to the parameters of the shape.

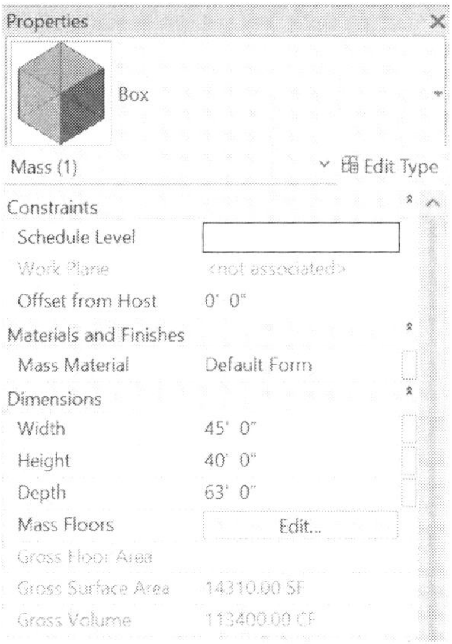

Figure 1–13

- If you want to move an existing mass element to a different work plane, in the *Modify | Mass* tab>*Work Plane* panel, click (Edit Work Plane). Specify the new work plane in the *Work Plane* dialog box.

Applying Materials

The material (Default Form) for mass elements is transparent by default. Therefore, all of the edges of the mass are displayed, as shown using a Rectangle-Blended form in Figure 1–14.

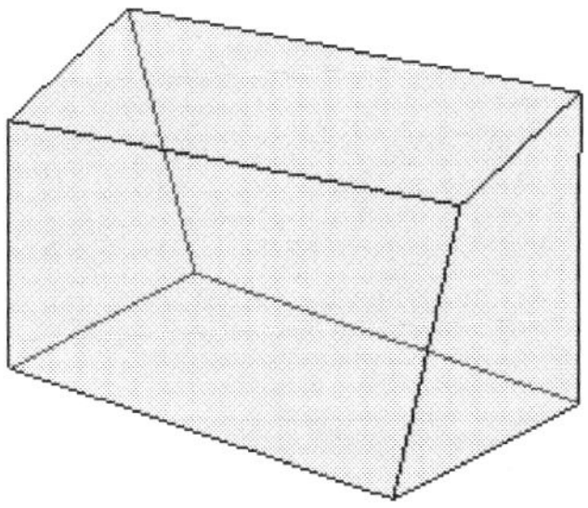

Figure 1–14

- To change the material for the entire mass element, select it and in Properties, change the **Mass Material** parameter (as shown in Figure 1–15) to a different material (as shown in Figure 1–16). This only works for the standard mass elements that are included in the library.

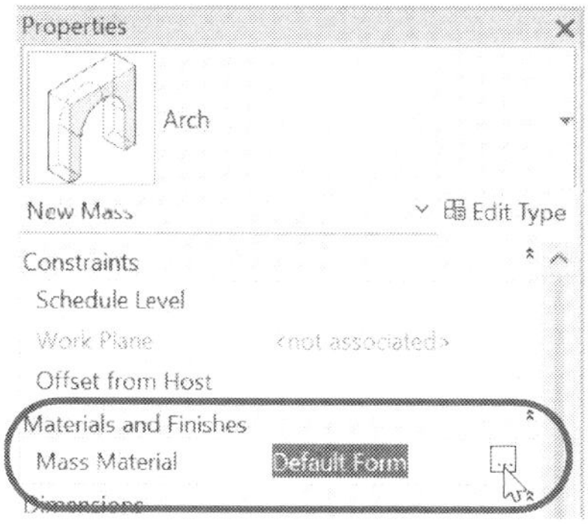

Figure 1–15

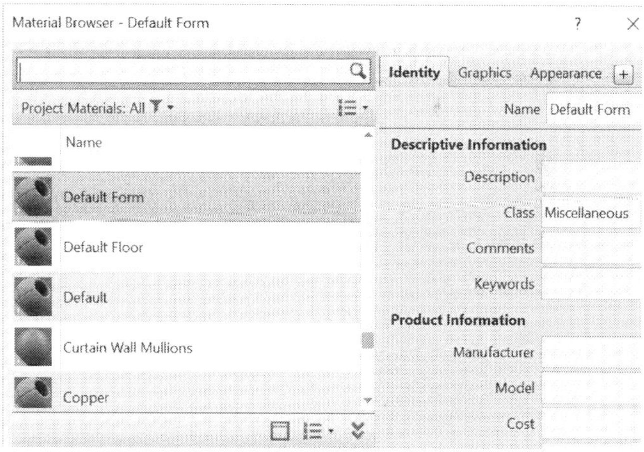

Figure 1–16

Practice 1a
Place Mass Elements

Practice Objective

- Add mass elements using existing mass families.

In this practice, you will use basic shapes from the massing families supplied with the Revit software to model existing buildings around a proposed site, as shown in Figure 1–17. The footprint and height for each mass are included on the toposurface.

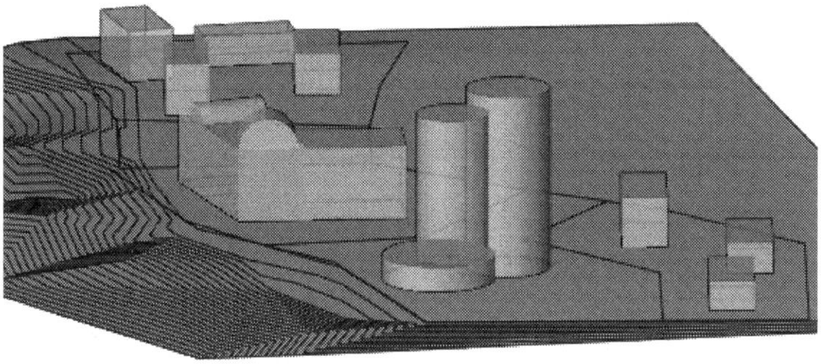

Figure 1–17

Task 1: Add box mass elements.

1. In the practice files folder, open **Edmon-Towers.rvt**.
2. Open the **Floor Plans: Existing Site** view.
3. In the *Massing & Site* tab>*Conceptual Mass* panel, expand (Show Mass by View Settings) and click (Show Mass Form and Floors).
4. In the *Massing & Site* tab>*Conceptual Mass* panel, click (Place Mass). The Box mass element family is already loaded.

In the *Modify | Place Mass* tab>*Placement* panel, click (Place on Work Plane) and select **Level 1** in the *Plane Selection* panel, as shown in Figure 1–18.

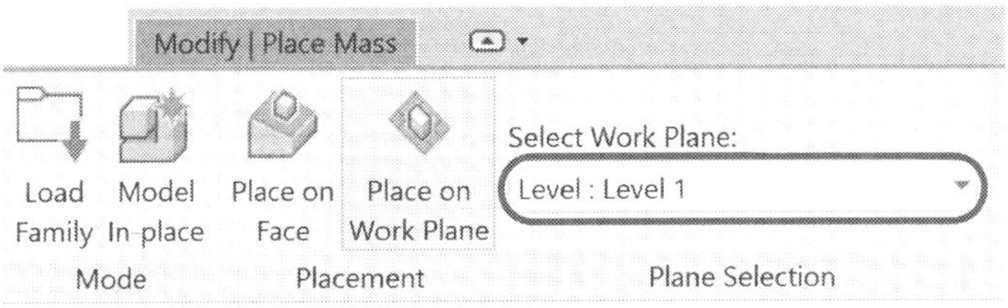

Figure 1–18

5. Zoom in to the top of the site. Hover your cursor over the first leftmost rectangular outline, making sure the line highlights, as shown in Figure 1–19.

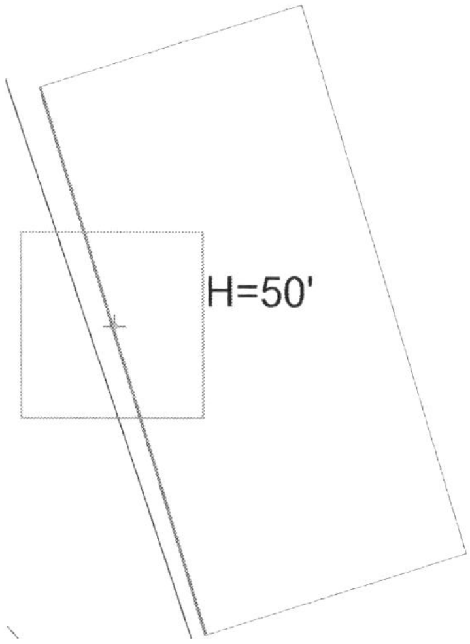

Figure 1–19

6. Press <Spacebar> to rotate your box massing element so it aligns to the rectangular outline, as shown in Figure 1–20. Move the box to the desired area and click to place the box.

Note: *Hovering over any of the lines on the rectangle will work to align your mass.*

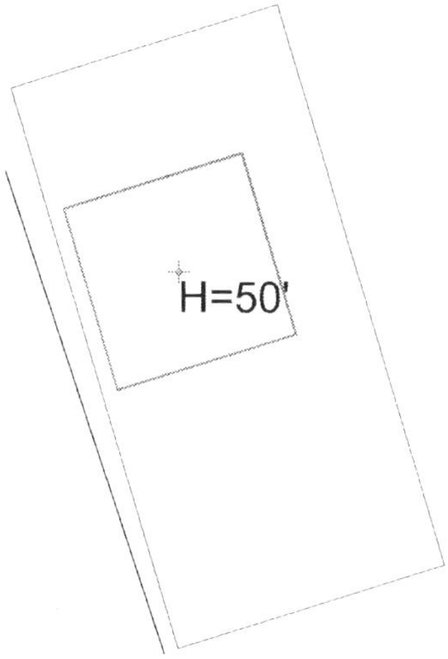

Figure 1–20

7. Continue to place box massing elements on the site plan where you see rectangular outlines and repeat the process of pressing <Spacebar> to rotate the box mass elements and moving them to the desired locations accordingly.
8. For the angled building, use two box masses to create the base building, as shown in Figure 1–21. The two masses need to overlap slightly.

   Note: *If greater accuracy is required, an in-place mass could be created to match the building footprint. For this practice, use two boxes.*

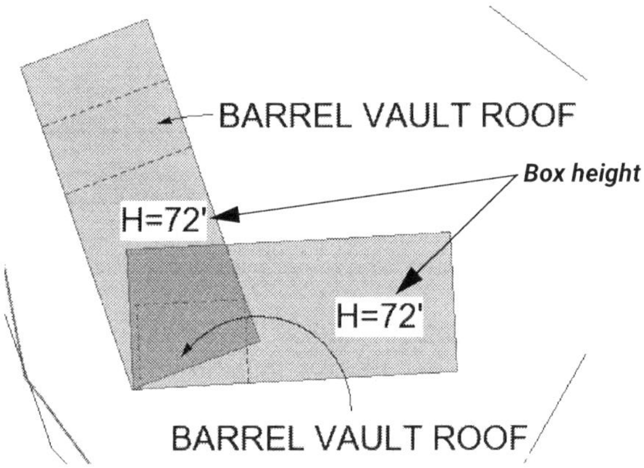

Figure 1–21

9. Click (Modify).
10. Select each box and use shape handles to resize them to fit the outline. When you drag the shape handles, they automatically snap to nearby elements, as shown in Figure 1–22.

11. Use Properties to set the heights as indicated on the existing site plan, as shown in Figure 1–23.

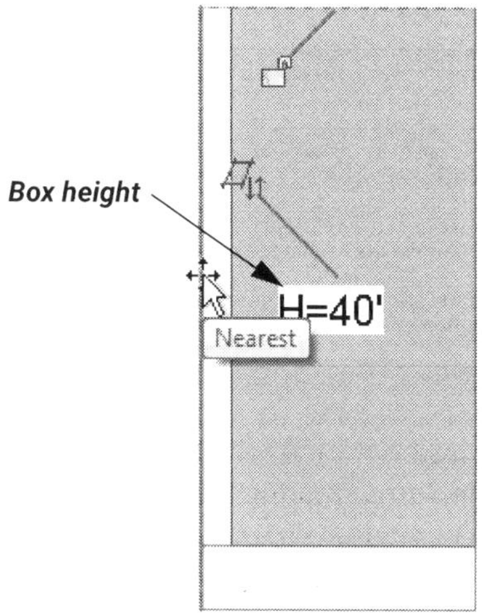

Figure 1–22

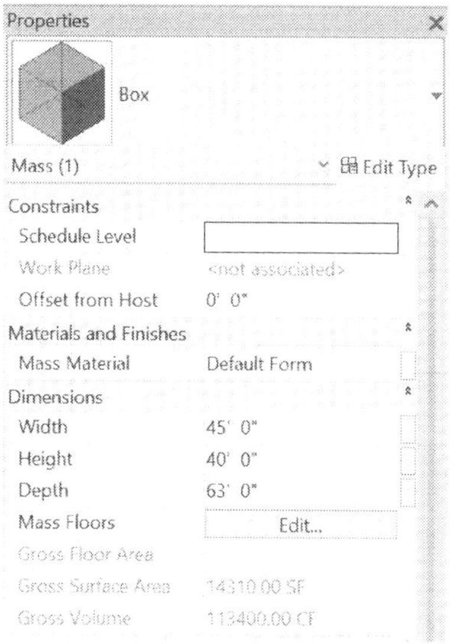

Figure 1–23

12. Switch to the default **{3D}** view and check that the masses are at the correct elevations (as defined by the Work Plane **Level 1**).
13. Click on the **Existing Site** view's tab to make it the active view, then type **WT** to tile the views.
14. Save the project.

Task 2: Load and add other mass elements.

1. Click (Place Mass). In the *Place | Mass* tab>*Mode* panel, click (Load Family).
2. Navigate to the practice files *Families>Mass* folder, select **Barrel Vault.rfa** and **Cylinder.rfa**, and click **Open**.
3. In the Type Selector, select **Cylinder**.
4. Click (Place on Work Plane), then to position the Cylinder masses at the center of the existing circles, type **SC** (Snap Center) and select the edge of the circle to place it. Place the Cylinder mass on the three circles.
5. Click (Modify).

6. Change the radius by stretching the grips and heights to match the plan, as shown in Figure 1–24.

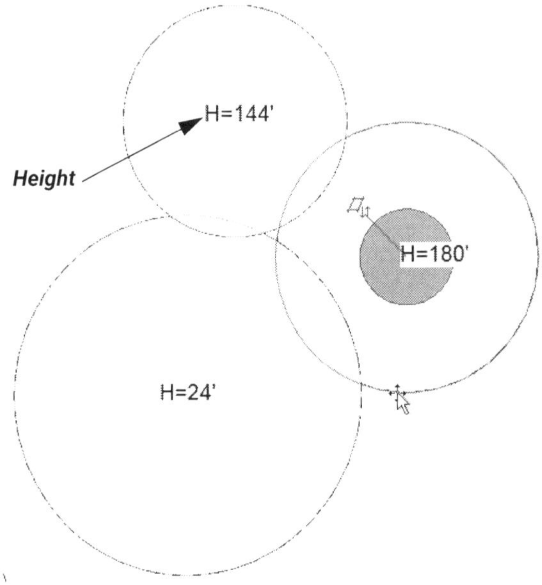

Figure 1–24

7. Switch to the **{3D}** view.

8. Add two barrel vault mass elements using (Place on Face) to place them on the top of the box elements. Remember to hover over the line and press <Spacebar> to rotate and align the massing element.

9. Click (Modify).

10. Select each box and use shape handles to resize them to fit the outline, as shown on the left in Figure 1–25.

11. View the project in 3D, as shown on the right in Figure 1–25.

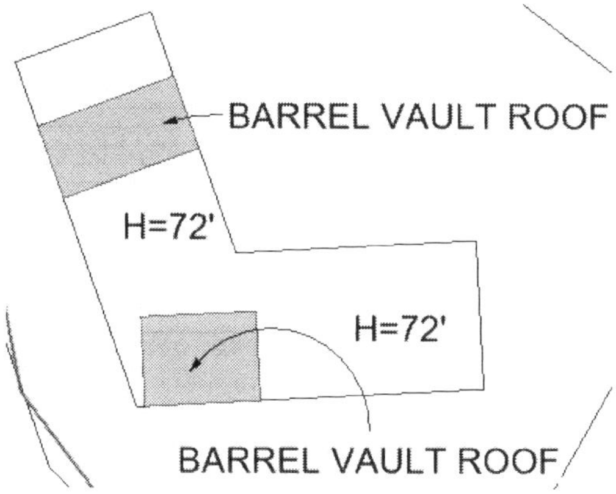

Plan view

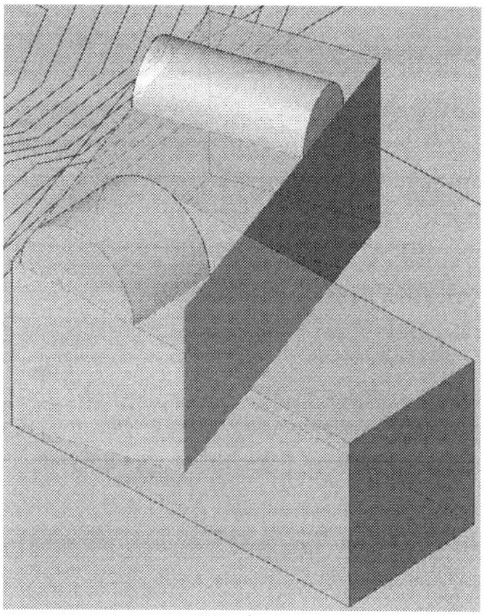

3D view

Figure 1–25

12. Save the project.

End of practice

1.3 Creating Conceptual Massing

To create custom massing elements, you need to start with an in-place mass where you can create a 3D form from 2D sketches. Masses can be made up of solid and void forms, as shown in Figure 1–26.

> ***Note:*** *If you want to use a massing element more than once in a project, you should create a separate mass family.*

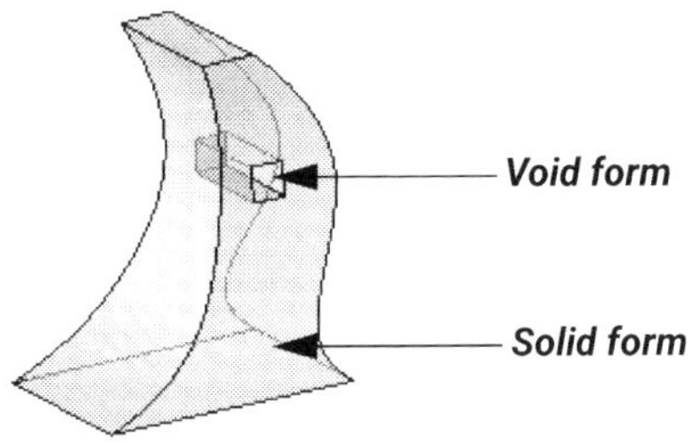

Figure 1–26

Forms are created from a mixture of profiles, paths, and points. For example, one profile becomes an extrusion, as shown in Figure 1–27, while a profile, a point, and a path become a sweep, as shown in Figure 1–28.

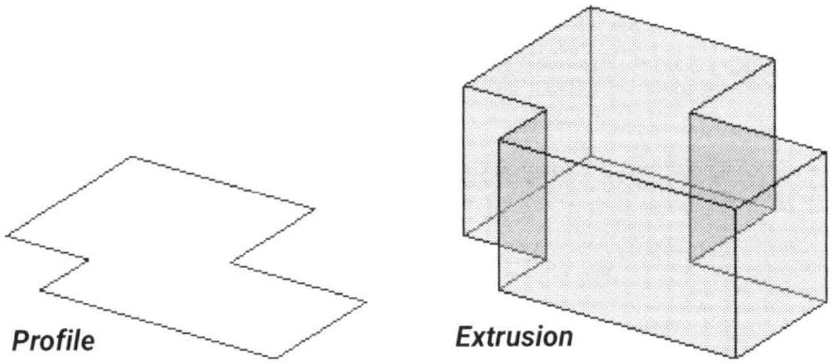

Figure 1–27

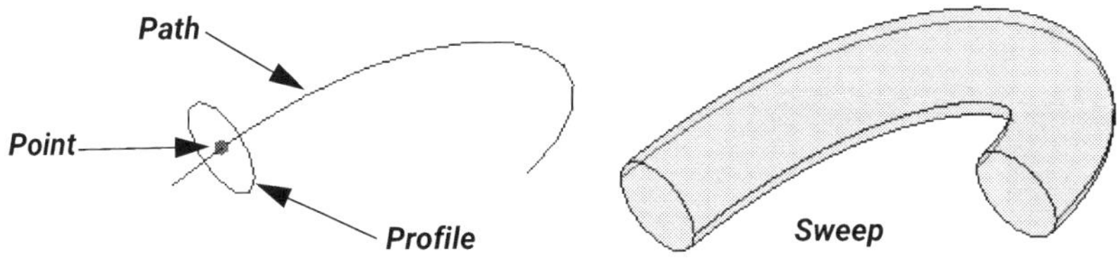

Figure 1–28

How To: Create an In-Place Mass (Overview)

1. In a project, in the *Massing & Site* tab>*Conceptual Mass* panel, click (In-Place Mass).
2. In the *Name* dialog box, set a new name for the mass.
3. In the *Create* tab>*Draw* panel, click (Model) and use the draw tools to sketch the profiles, paths, and points that make up the form.
   - Use (Reference Line) or (Reference Plane) as guidelines to help you draw the sketches.
4. Select the profile as well as any related path or points.
   - For the profile, ensure that you select the chain of lines, as shown in Figure 1–29, instead of individual sketch lines, as shown in Figure 1–30.

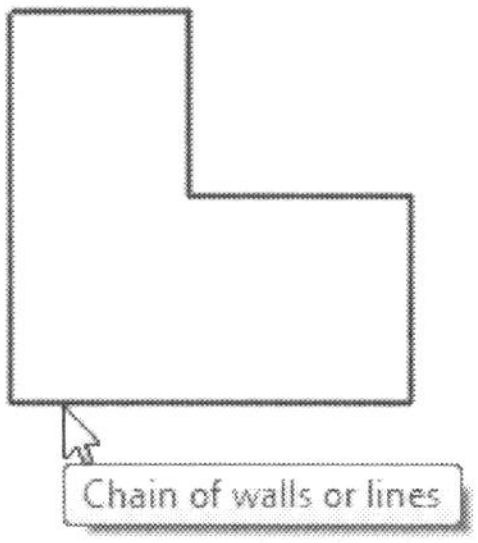

Figure 1–29

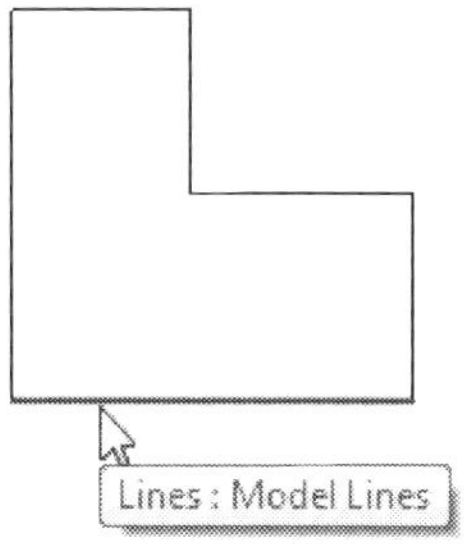

Figure 1–30

5. In the *Modify | Lines* tab>*Form* panel, expand (Create Form) and select (Solid Form) or (Void Form).
   - A closed profile becomes a solid and an open profile becomes a surface, as shown in Figure 1–31.

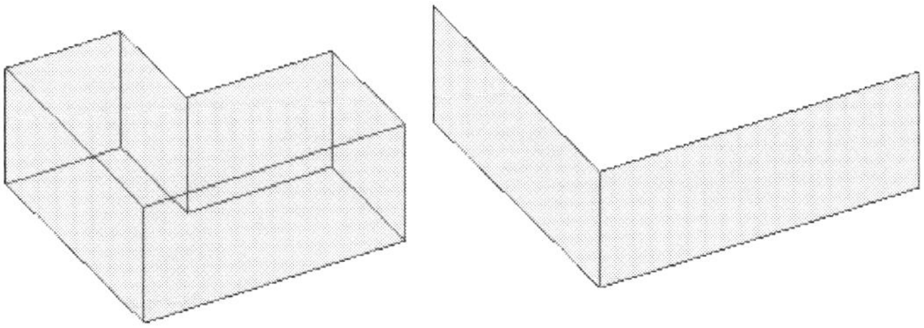

Figure 1–31

6. Click (Finish Mass).

Types of Forms

Six different types of forms can be created, as shown in Figure 1–32.

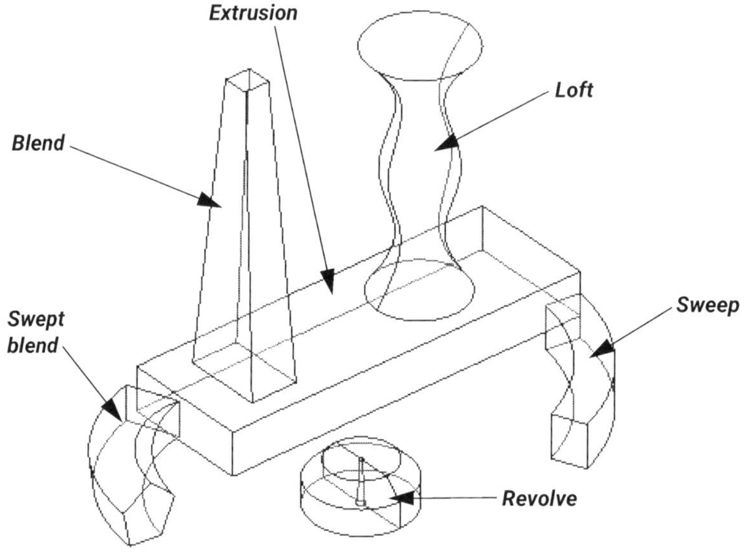

Figure 1–32

Extrusions

An extrusion pushes a single profile in one direction. Although the default extrusion height is preset, you can modify it using the 3D control or temporary dimensions in a 3D view, as shown in Figure 1–33.

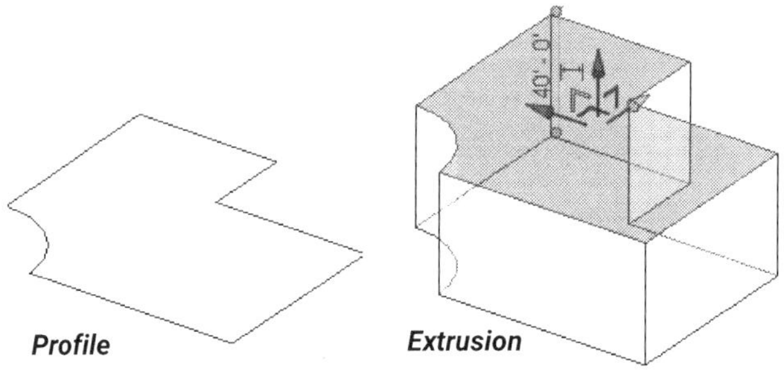

Figure 1–33

- Some profile shapes, such as a circle, have options for the shape of the form. After the profile is drawn and you click **Create Form**, at the bottom of the interface will be images showing the different forms that you can select from. You can select the image or press <Spacebar> to view the different forms, as shown in Figure 1–34. If you click anywhere in the view, you will not see the form options. As soon as you click **Finish Mass**, you will not be able to change the form or retrieve the different form options again.

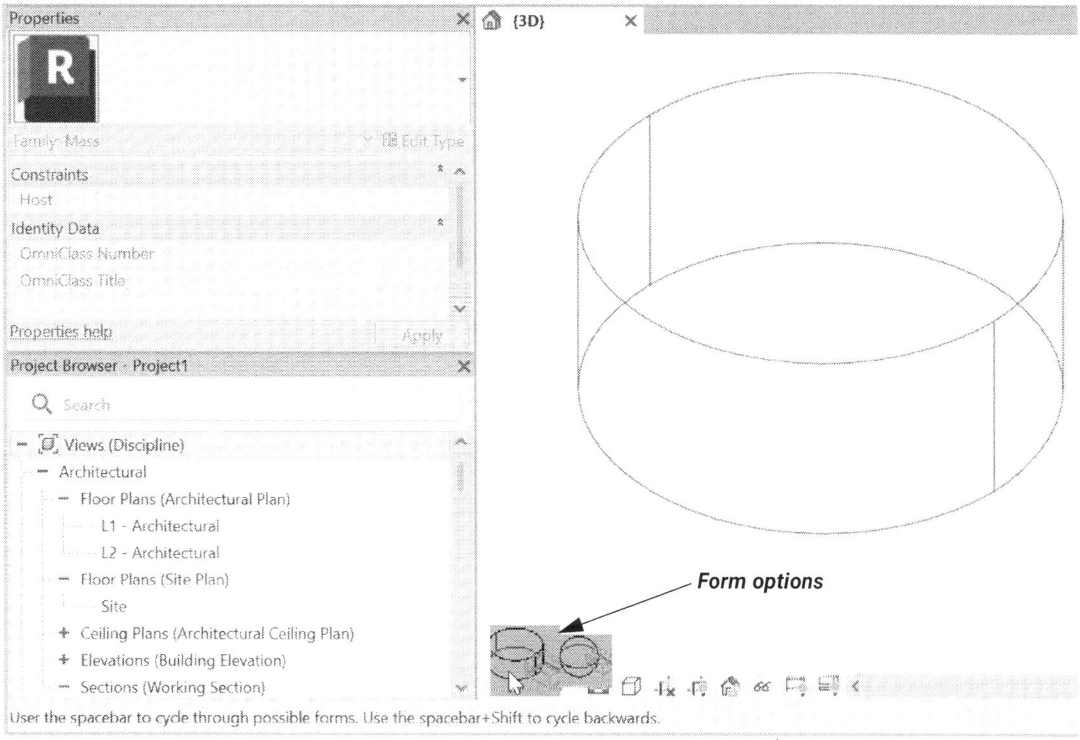

Figure 1–34

Blends

A blend links two profiles together. It is similar to an extrusion but is created when you select two profiles in different planes, as shown in Figure 1–35.

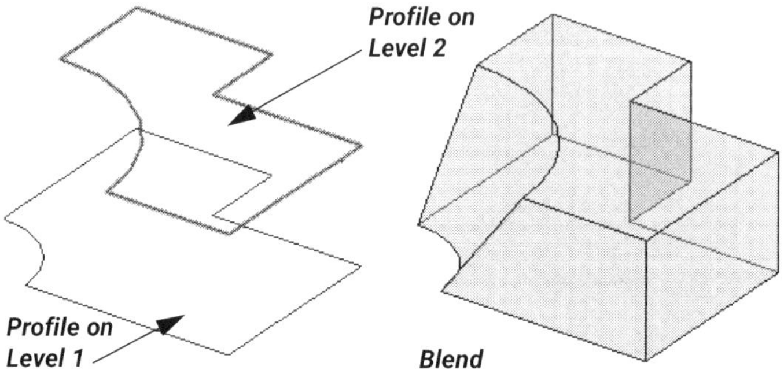

Figure 1–35

Lofts

A loft connects multiple profiles that do not need to be on parallel planes.It is created when you select more than two profiles in different planes, as shown in Figure 1–36.

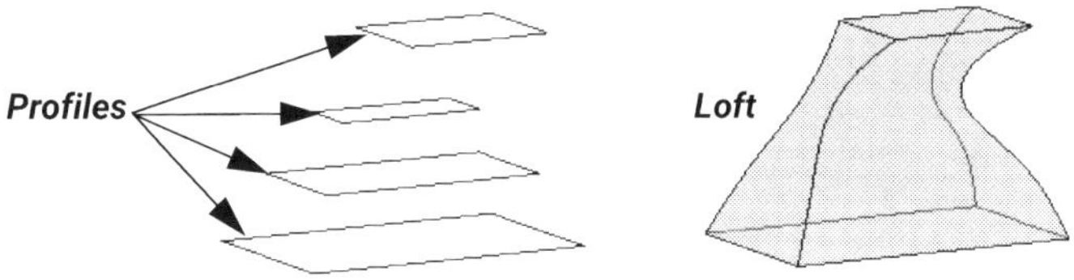

Figure 1–36

Revolves

A revolve rotates a profile about an axis. It is created when you select an axis and a profile that are both in the same plane, as shown in Figure 1–37.

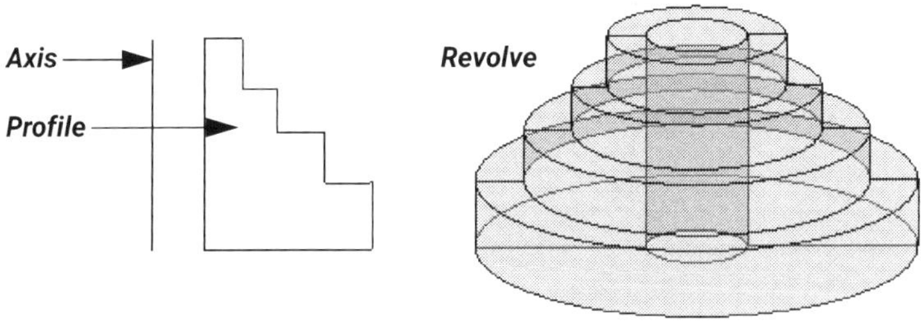

Figure 1–37

- When the axis is away from the profile, a hole is generated in the center of the revolve. To create an entirely closed shape, use a reference line for the axis, as shown in Figure 1–38.
- By default, a full circle form is created. To change this, you can select the start edge of the profile, as shown in Figure 1–38, and use the gold arrows to open it, as shown in Figure 1–39.

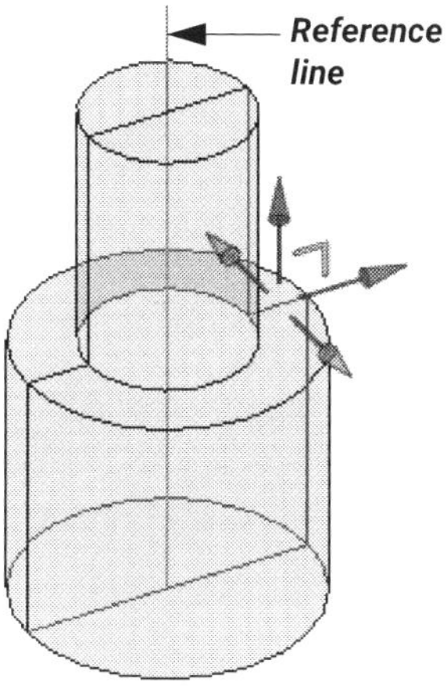

Figure 1–38

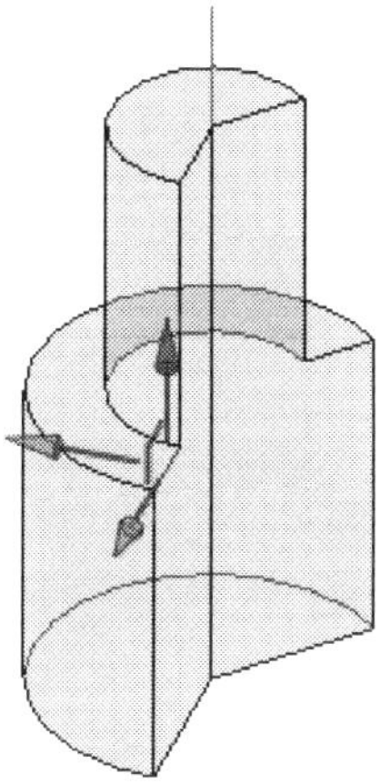

Figure 1–39

- You can also modify the *Start Angle* and *End Angle* in Properties, as shown in Figure 1–40.

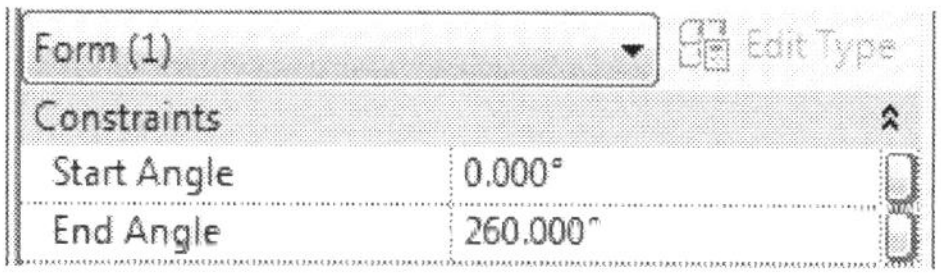

Figure 1–40

Sweeps and Swept Blends

A sweep extends a profile along a path. It is created when you select a path and a profile, as shown in Figure 1–41. The point element defines the location of the profile on the path.

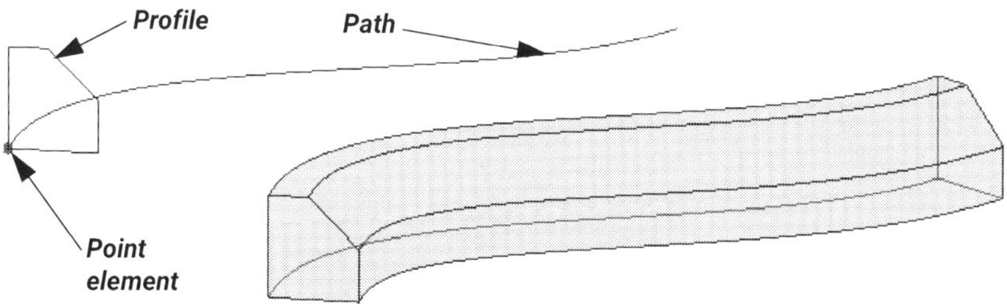

Figure 1–41

A swept blend connects two profiles along a path. It is created when you select a path connecting two profiles in different planes, as shown in Figure 1–42.

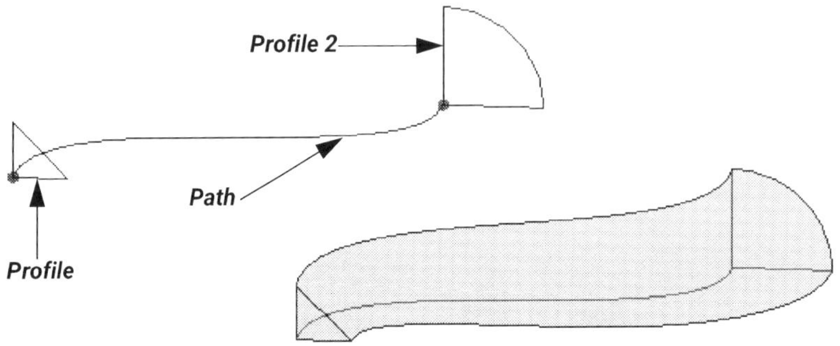

Figure 1–42

How To: Create Sweeps and Swept Blends

1. In the *Modify | Place Lines* tab>*Draw* panel, click (Model).
2. Use the drawing tools to sketch a path for the sweep to follow.
   - A single-segment path can be used with an open or closed profile. A multi-segment path requires a closed profile.
   - A swept blend can only be made from a single-segment path but you can use arcs and splines to create it.
3. In the *Draw* panel, click (Point Element) and click on the path.
   - For a sweep, place a point at one end of the path.
   - For a swept blend, place a point at each end of the path.
4. Open a 3D view if you are not already in one.
5. Click (Modify) and select the point element. A reference plane perpendicular to the path is displayed. It becomes the work plane on which you can draw the profile for a sweep, as shown in Figure 1–43.

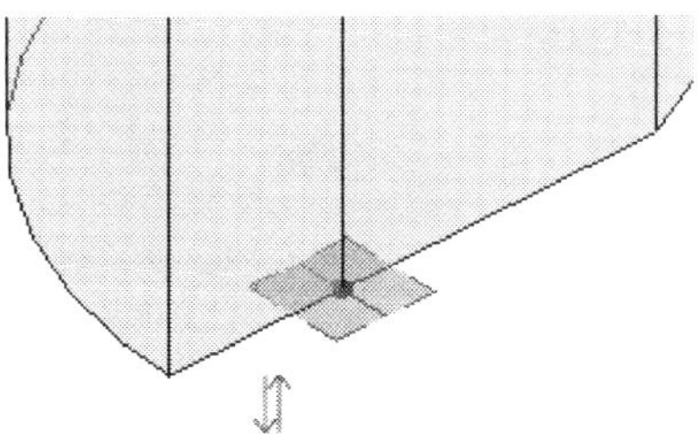

Figure 1–43

6. Use the drawing tools to sketch a profile on the new reference plane.
7. For a swept blend, repeat the process of drawing a profile on the other end of the path.
8. Click (Modify) and select both the path and the profile(s).
9. In the *Modify | Multi-select* or *Lines* tab>*Form* panel, click (Create Form).

Void Forms

The process of creating void forms is essentially the same as the one for creating solid forms. The only difference is that void forms are designed to be inside a solid form so that it has a solid element to cut out, as shown in Figure 1–44.

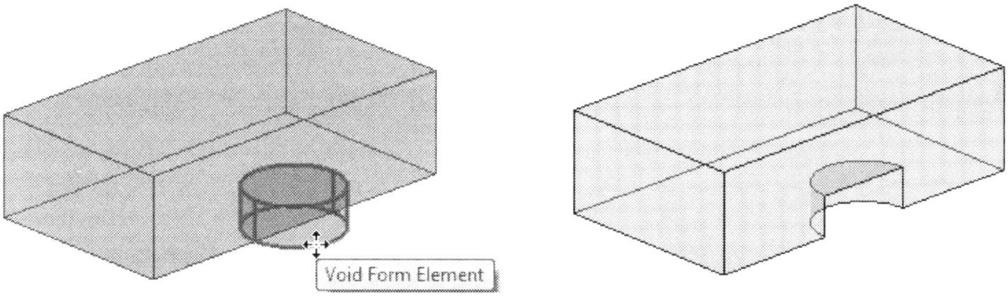

Figure 1–44

You can change a form from solid to void. Select the solid form and in Properties in the *Identity Data* area, change the *Solid/Void* parameter, as shown in Figure 1–45.

> ***Note:*** *This change can only be done to in-place mass forms.*

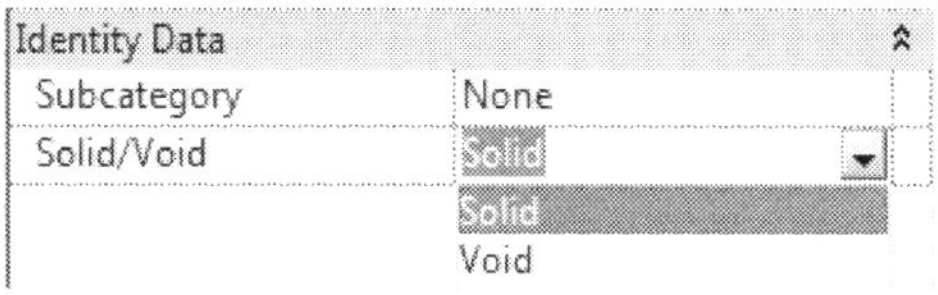

Figure 1–45

Hint: Cutting Solid Forms with Other Solid Forms

If you have two solid forms that overlap, you can use (Cut Geometry) to cut out one of the forms, as shown in Figure 1–46.

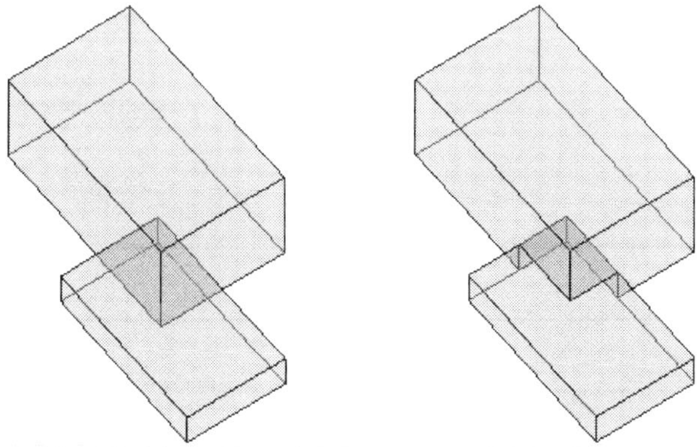

Before cut ***After cut***

Figure 1–46

- The first form selected is cut and the second form selected remains as is.

1.4 Setting the Work Plane

Profiles and paths are the building blocks of the mass form elements. They are sketched on the current work plane which can be a face, as shown in Figure 1–47, or a specified work plane, as shown in Figure 1–48.

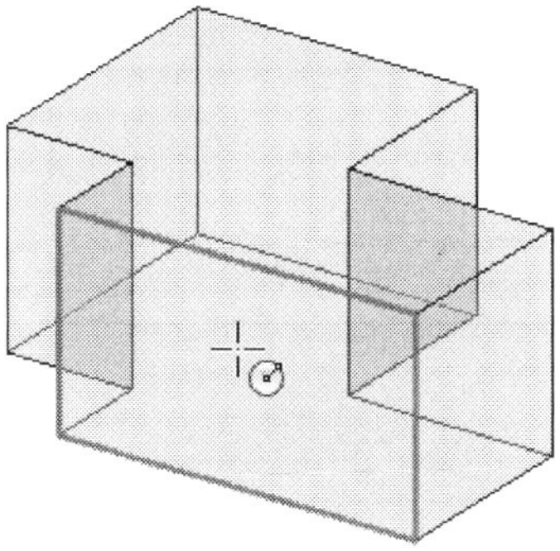

Figure 1–47

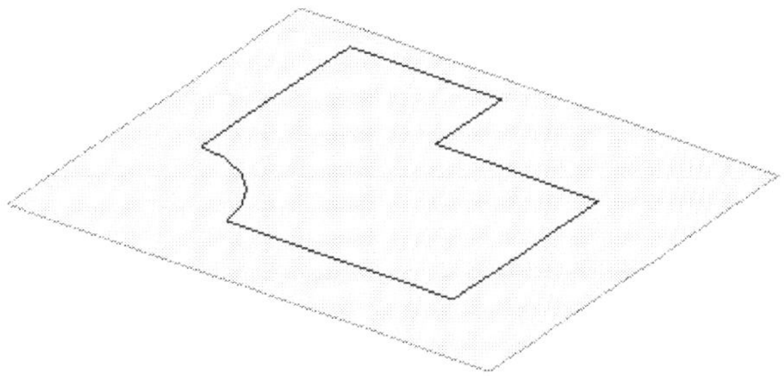

Figure 1–48

- If you are in a plan view, the related level is the active work plane by default.

How To: Establish a Work Plane by Face

1. In the *Create* tab>*Draw* panel, select a sketching tool.
2. In the *Modify | Place Lines* tab>*Draw* panel, click  (Draw on Face). This is typically selected by default.
3. Hover the cursor over the face of an existing element. It highlights and you can then draw the sketch, as shown in Figure 1–49.

   Note: *Sketches can be locked to faces. Press <Tab> to cycle through nearby faces.*

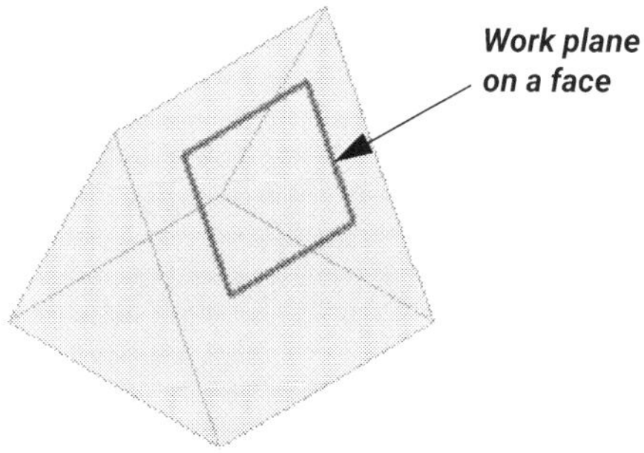

Figure 1–49

4. You can move directly to another face and continue drawing sketches.

How To: Establish a Work Plane by Placement Plane

1. In the *Create* tab>*Draw* panel, select a sketching tool. The active work plane displays with a heavy outline.
2. In the *Modify | Place Lines* tab>*Draw* panel, click (Draw on Work Plane).

   Note: *To display the work plane in a view, in the Work Plane panel, click (Show).*

3. In the *Properties* panel, *Constraints* section, in the *Placement Plane:* drop-down list, select a *Level* or named reference plane, as shown in Figure 1–50.

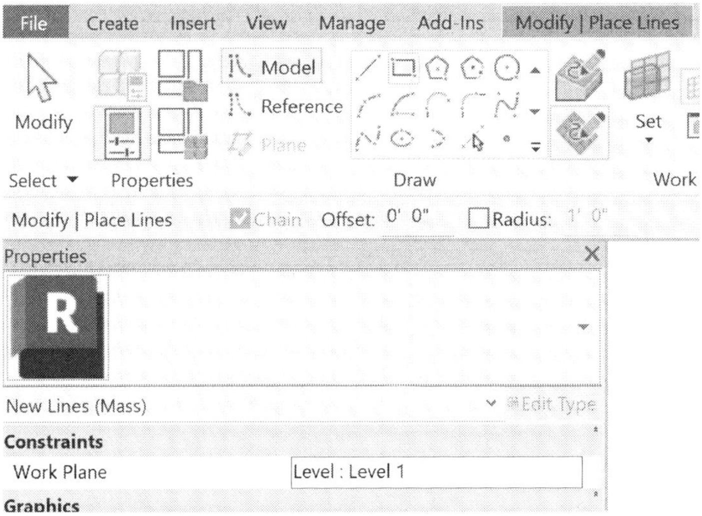

Figure 1–50

- This list varies according to the elements contained in the massing study.

4. Draw the sketch on the plane, as shown in Figure 1–51.

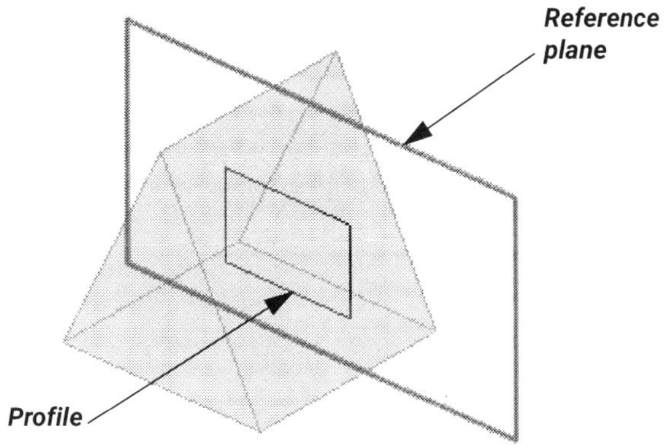

Figure 1–51

- If you have used the **Pick...** option, the selected face becomes the active work plane.

Hint: Naming Reference Planes

You can name reference planes so that they can be specified as a work plane. Select the reference plane and <*Click to name*> or in Properties, set a *Name*, as shown in Figure 1–52.

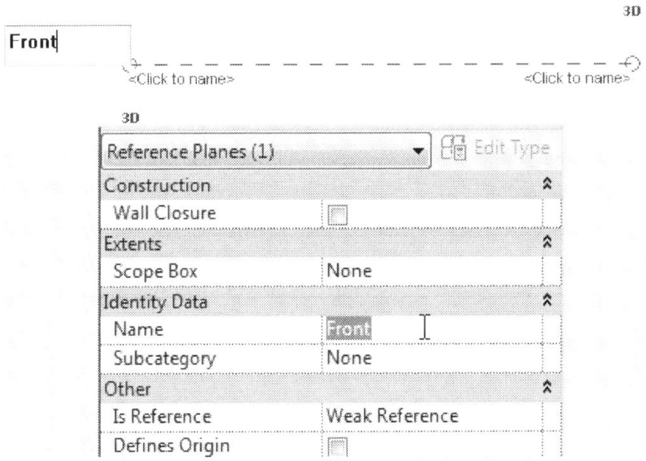

Figure 1–52

How To: Change the Work Plane of a Sketch or Form

1. Select the sketch or form.
2. In the *Positioning* panel, click **Show Host**. The host work plane highlights, as shown in Figure 1–53.
3. In the *Host:* drop-down list, as shown in Figure 1–53, select a new host for the sketch. The sketch moves to the selected plane.

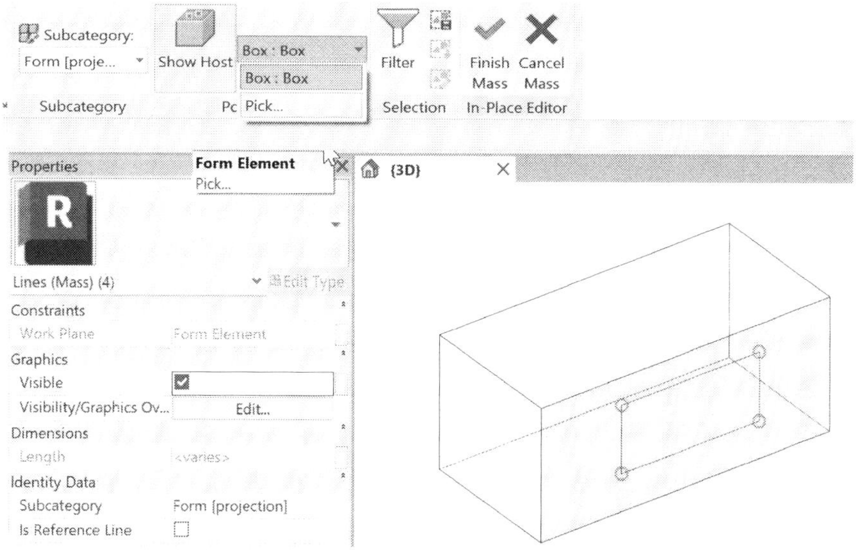
Subcategory:
Form [proje...
Show Host
Box : Box
Box : Box
Pick...
Filter
Finish Mass
Cancel Mass
Subcategory
Selection
In-Place Editor
Properties
Form Element
Pick...
{3D}
Lines (Mass) (4)
Edit Type
Constraints
Work Plane
Form Element
Graphics
Visible
Visibility/Graphics Ov...
Edit...
Dimensions
Length
<varies>
Identity Data
Subcategory
Form [projection]
Is Reference Line

Figure 1–53

Practice 1b
Create Mass Forms

Practice Objectives

- Create an extruded mass form.
- Create a lofted mass form.
- Add a swept void form.

In this practice, you will create two towers in a massing study. For one building, you will extrude a mass form using a simple profile. For the other building, you will create a lofted form using a variety of profiles at different levels and then add a void form using a swept profile, as shown in Figure 1–54.

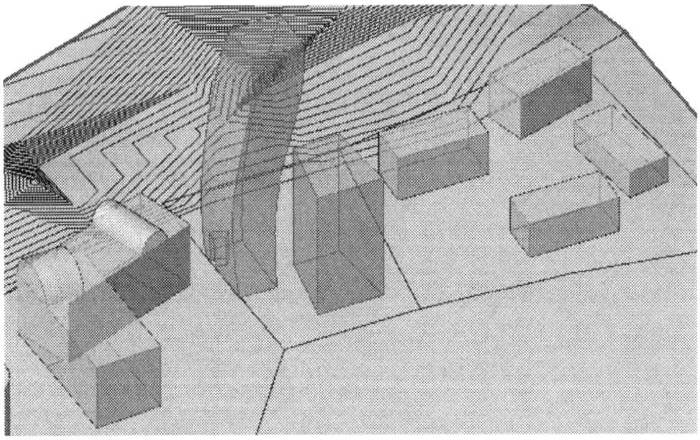

Figure 1–54

Task 1: Create an extruded in-place mass.

1. In the practice files folder, open **Edmon-Towers-New.rvt**.
2. Open the **Floor Plans: New Site** view. This view displays the new site area with a property line around the area.
3. In the *Massing & Site* tab>*Conceptual Mass* panel, click (In-Place Mass).

4. The *Massing - Show Mass Enabled* dialog box, shown in Figure 1–55, displays. Read it and click **Close** to continue with creating a mass.

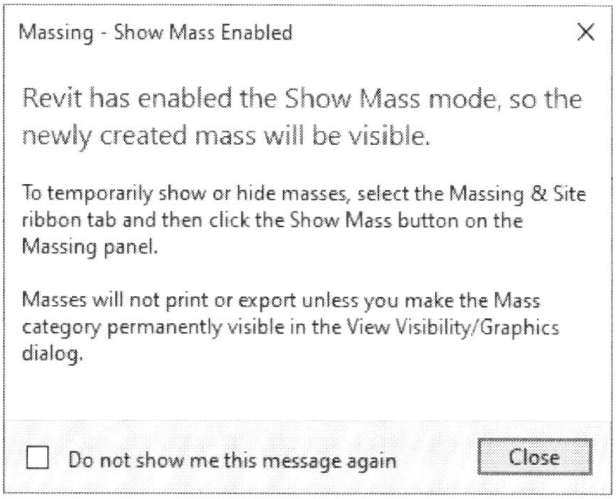

Figure 1–55

5. In the *Name* dialog box, enter **Tower-1** and click **OK**.

6. In the *Create* tab>*Draw* panel, click (Model) and then click (Line).

   Note: *Add reference planes first, if needed.*

7. In the northwest quadrant of the new site, draw a trapezoid shape that has a base that is roughly **59'-4"** wide, a top that is **36'** wide, and a distance between the parallel sides of **80'**, as shown in Figure 1–56.

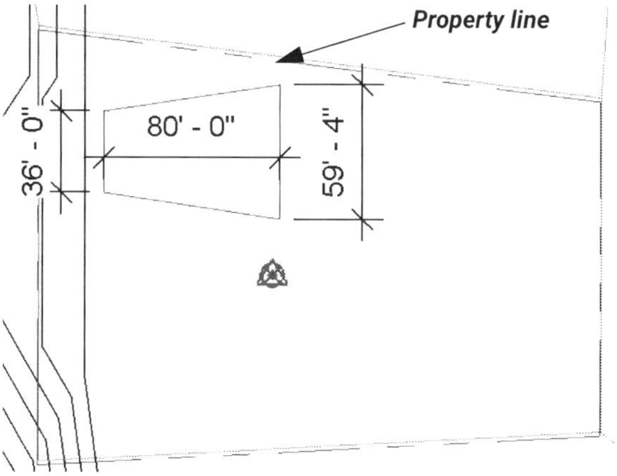

Figure 1–56

8. Open the default 3D view.

9. Select the lines. In the *Modify | Lines* tab>*Form* panel, click (Create Form). Revit extrudes the profile to create a solid form.
10. Switch to the 3D view.
11. Select the blue temporary dimension and change it to **140'**.
12. In the *Modify* tab>*In-Place Editor* panel, click (Finish Mass).

Task 2: Create levels.

1. Open the **Elevations (Building Elevation): East** view and zoom in towards the newly created mass to see the level markers.
2. Set the *elevation* of **Level 2** to **18'**.
3. Set the *name* of the existing **Roof** level to **Level 3**, and its *elevation* to **30'**. Click **Yes** when prompted to rename any corresponding views.

   Note: *If you are having issues selecting the elevation height, you can select the level and change this information in Properties.*

4. Select the newly named **Level 3**.
5. In the *Modify | Levels* tab>*Modify* panel, click (Array). In the *Modify | Array\Array* panel, set the following, as shown in Figure 1–57:
   - Clear the **Group and Associate** option (no blue sheen under icon)
   - *Number*: **30**
   - *Move To*: **2nd**

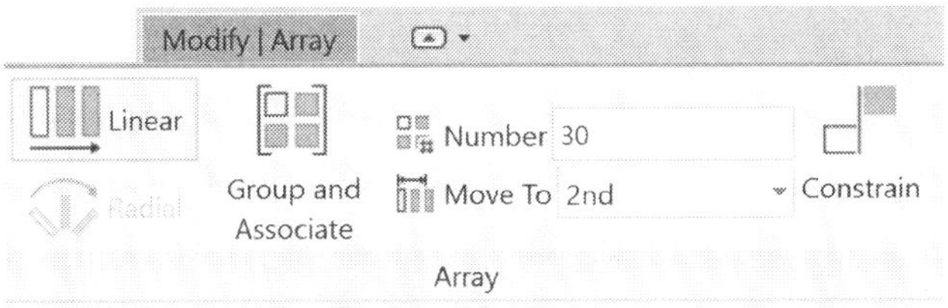

Figure 1–57

6. Create the array of 30 levels by picking two points, **12'-0"** apart heading upwards.
7. Click (Modify) and type **ZE** to zoom out to the extents of the view.

Task 3: Create a lofted in-place mass.

1. Return to the default 3D view.
2. Create a new in-place mass named **Tower-2**.

3. In the *Create* tab>*Draw* panel, click (Model) and then click (Rectangle).
4. In the *Draw* panel, click (Draw on Work Plane).
5. In the *Properties* panel, *Constraints* section, verify that *Work Plane* is set to **Level: Level 1**, as shown in Figure 1–58.

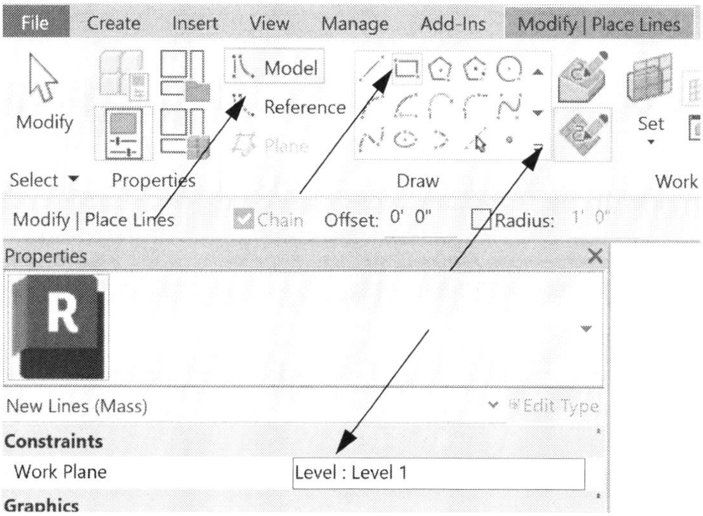

Figure 1–58

6. Draw a **40' x 80'** rectangle south of the **Tower-1**.
7. In the *Properties* panel, *Constraints* section, change *Work Plane* to **Level: Level 10**.
8. Draw another rectangular shape using the **Pick Line** draw tool to line up at least one of the sides with the rectangle that was drawn at Level 1. Note that when you hover the cursor over the lines on the active work plane, they highlight.

- Figure 1–59 shows an example of the Level 1 edge highlight when you hover over the rectangle. You will also see an alignment line indicating you are aligned with the edge of the Level 1 rectangle.

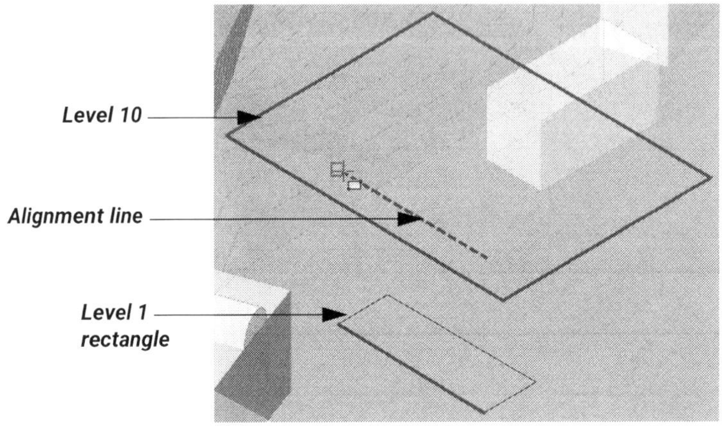

Figure 1–59

9. Repeat the process at **Level 20** and **Level 30**, varying the size at each level.
10. Click (Modify) and select the four rectangles.
11. In the *Modify | Lines* tab>*Form* panel, click (Create Form). The new tower displays as shown in Figure 1–60. Your design will vary according to the profiles you drew.

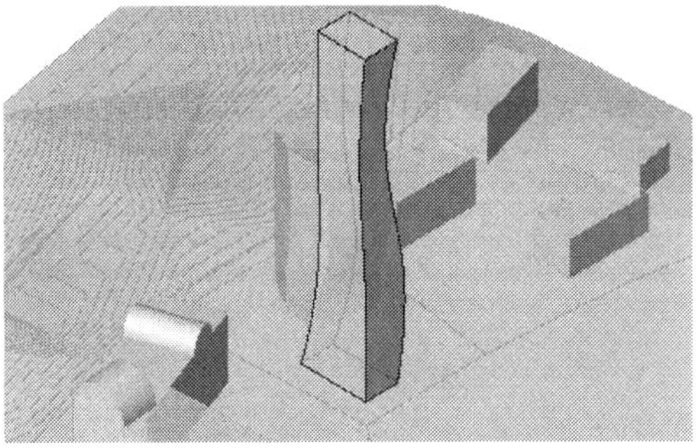

Figure 1–60

12. In a plan view, move the new massing form so it does not overlap the trapezoid, if needed.
13. Do not click **Finish Mass** or save the project yet because you want to remain in the same in-place mass element.

Task 4: Add a void form.

1. In a 3D view, zoom in to the base of the new tower.

2. Click (Model) and then select one of the arc drawing tools. In the *Properties* panel, set the *Work Plane* to **Level: Level 1**.

3. Draw an arc, as shown in Figure 1–61. This is the path for a sweep. It needs to start outside the existing mass to create the expected void form.

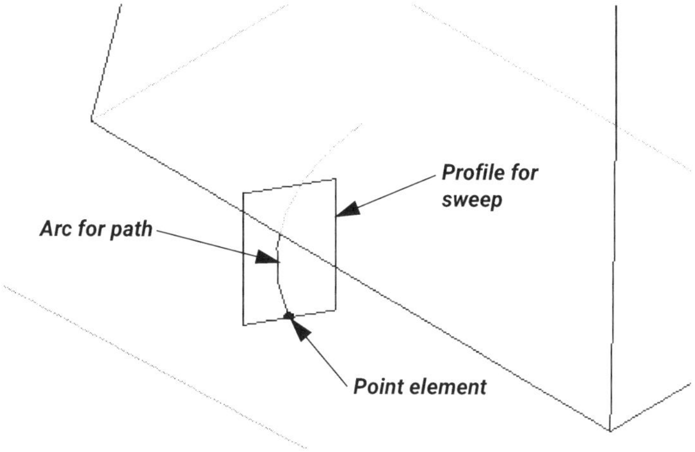

Figure 1–61

4. In the *Draw* panel, click (Point Element).

5. Add a point at the end of the arc, as shown above in Figure 1–61.

6. Click (Modify). Select the point element and draw a profile for the desired shape of the sweep.

7. Click (Modify) and select the path and profile(s).

8. In the *Form* panel, expand (Create Form) and click (Void Form). The new void form is cut out of the existing solid form, as shown in Figure 1–62.

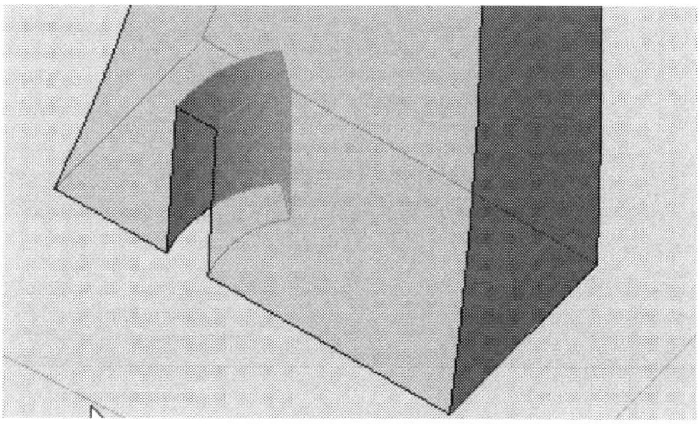

Figure 1–62

9. Click ✔ (Finish Mass).
10. Zoom out to see the entire site with the new towers.
11. Save and close the project.

End of practice

1.5 Dynamic Editing for Conceptual Massing

When a completed in-place mass element is selected, you can modify the length of its faces by dragging the controls, as shown in Figure 1–63. However, for more precise modification, you can edit the mass in-place, as shown in Figure 1–64.

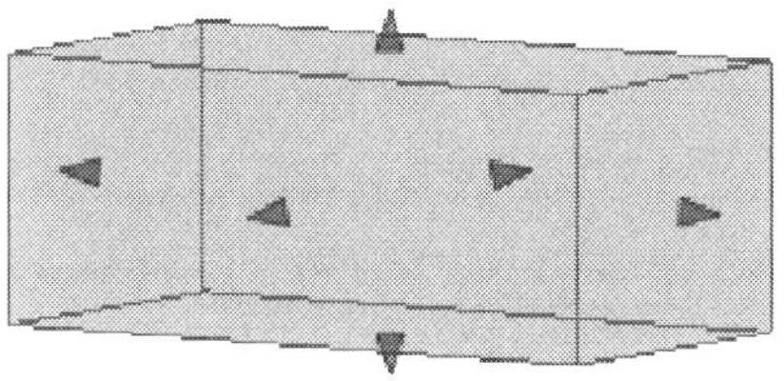

Figure 1–63

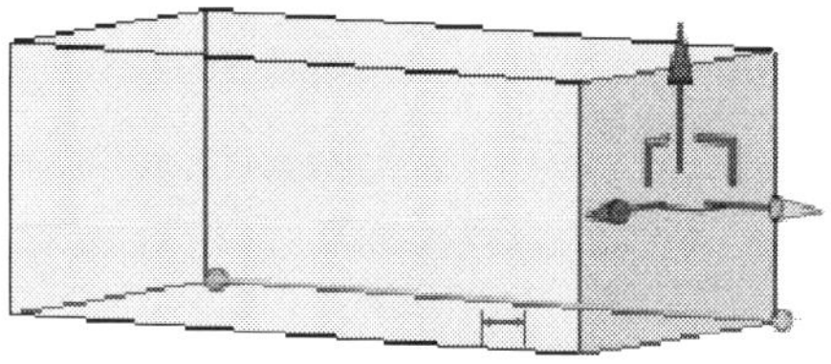

Figure 1–64

Double-click on an in-place mass, or select it and in the *Modify | Mass* tab>*Model* panel, click (Edit In-Place). In the Edit In-Place mode, you have direct access to the surface, edges, and vertices of a solid or void form, as shown in Figure 1–65. You can quickly and easily manipulate these sub-elements and create new edges and profiles.

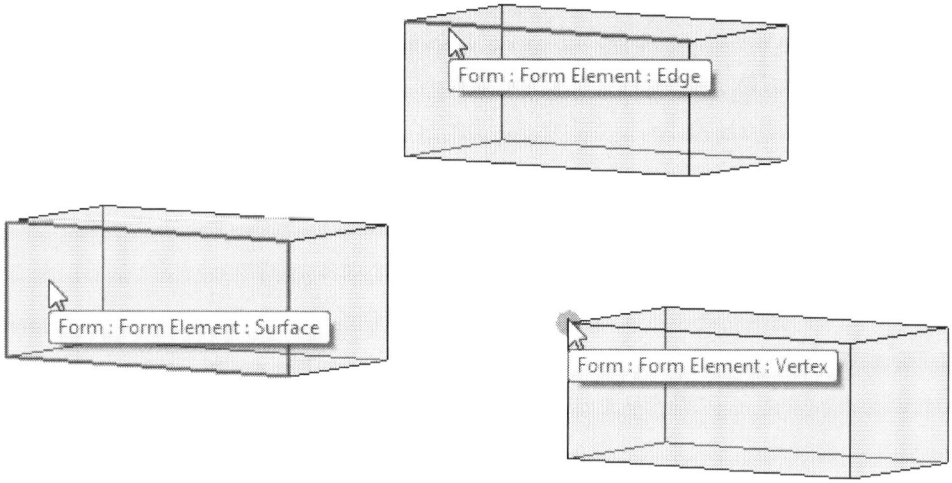

Figure 1–65

- Press <Tab> to cycle between sub-elements to select the right one.
- Predefined masses that you load from the Revit library do not have dynamic editing capabilities.

Using the 3D Control

When a face, edge, or vertex is selected, the 3D control is displayed.

- To move a selected sub-element directly along an axis, select one of the arrows and drag it in the appropriate direction, as shown in Figure 1–66.
- To move a selected sub-element along a plane (as shown in Figure 1–67), click and drag the plane indicator.

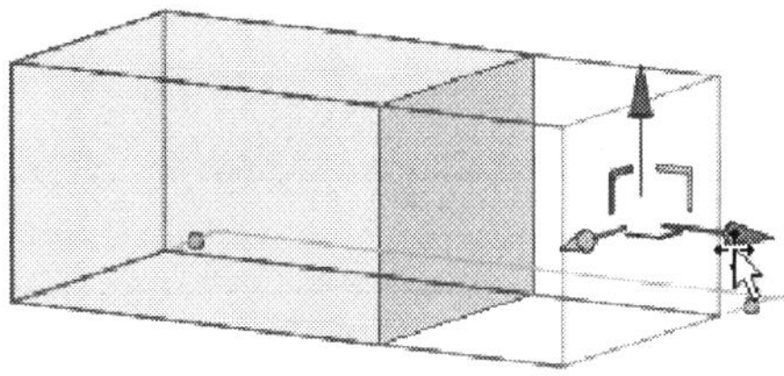

Figure 1–66

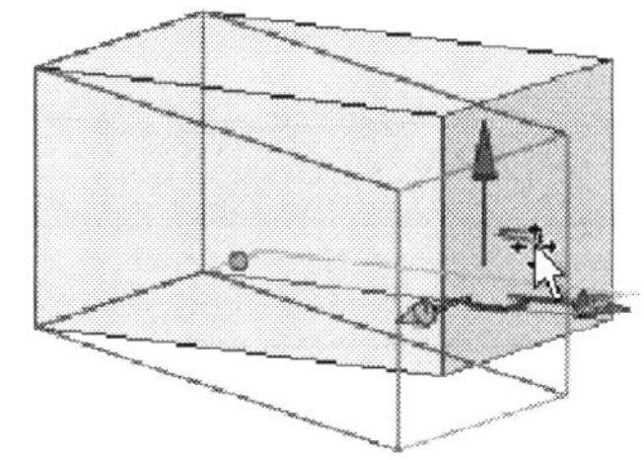

Figure 1–67

Other Modification Options

- You can use (Move) and (Rotate) when you select a face, an edge, or a vertex. In the example shown in Figure 1–68, the face has been rotated.

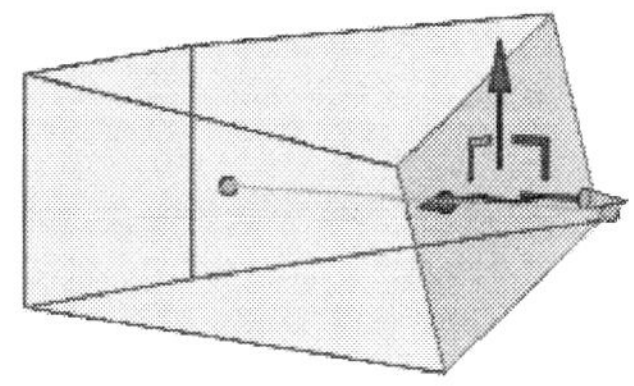

Figure 1–68

- To remove a face, an edge, or a vertex, select it and click (Delete), or press <Delete>. In the example shown in Figure 1–69, a vertex has been selected and deleted.

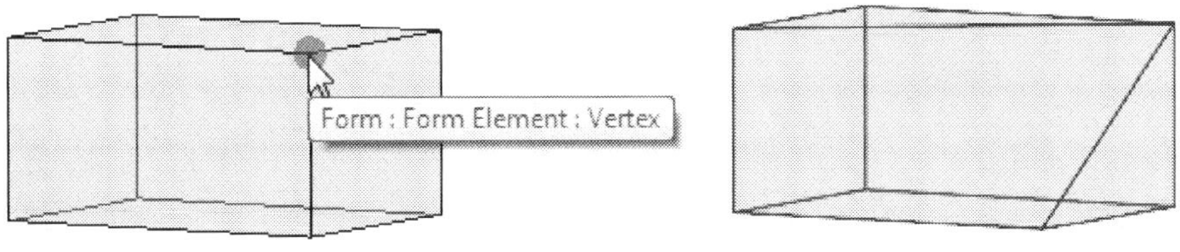

Figure 1–69

- You can lock a mass element so that the profiles in a form work together rather than separately. Select at least one part of the form and, in the *Modify | Form* tab>*Form Element* panel, click (Lock Profiles).
- When you select an edge and the form is not locked, only the selected edge moves, as shown in Figure 1–70. If you lock the form and move the same edge, the entire form based on that profile moves, as shown in Figure 1–71.

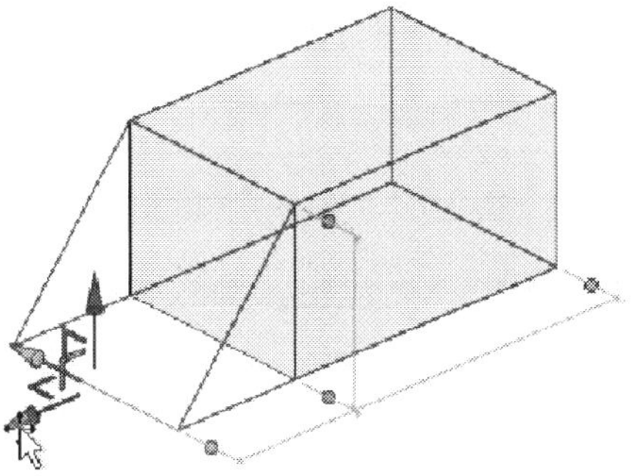

Figure 1–70

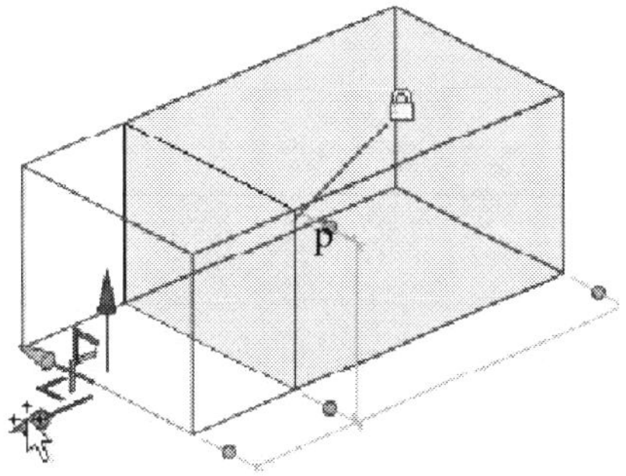

Figure 1–71

- To return the form to its component parts, select the mass element, and in the *Modify | Form* tab>*Form Element* panel, click (Dissolve). Once you have done this, remake the entire form again.

Hint: Use X-Ray to Display a Form's Geometric Framework

Vertices, profiles, and paths do not automatically display while editing forms. In X-Ray mode, the surfaces of a form are transparent and all of the key geometric datums display, as shown in Figure 1–72.

- To enable X-Ray mode, first select a form. Note that you might need to hover the cursor over the edge and press <Tab> until a form has been highlighted. With the form selected, in the *Modify | Form* tab>*Form Element* panel, click (X-Ray).

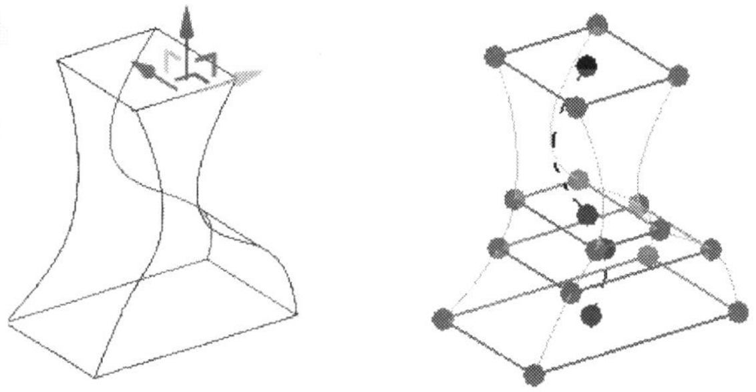

Figure 1–72

- To toggle off X-Ray mode, select the form again and click (X-Ray).
- Only one form can have X-Ray mode on at a time.

1.6 Working with Profiles and Edges

While a lot can be done to manipulate mass elements using the dynamic editing tools, there are some additional commands where you can do more precise and complex editing, as shown in Figure 1–73. These include editing and adding a profile, adding edges, dividing surfaces, and splitting faces.

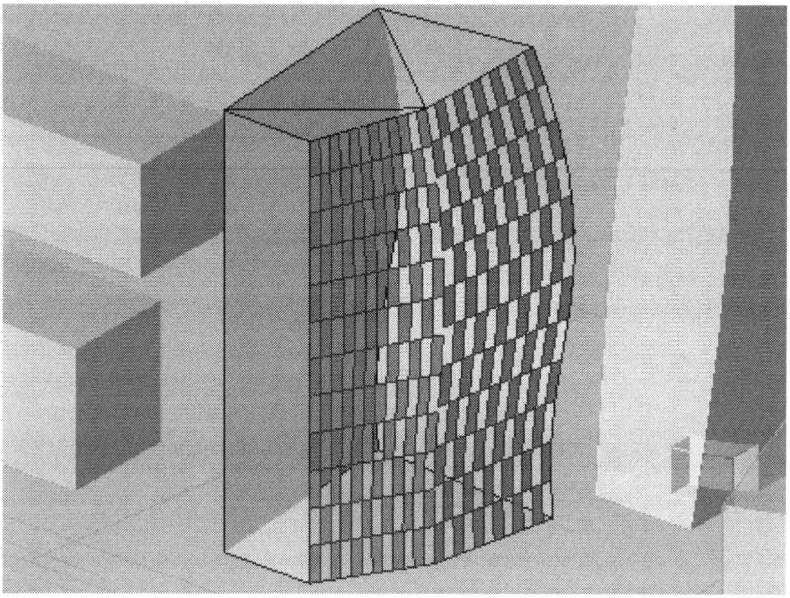

Figure 1–73

Editing Profiles

Form profiles are the basic shape that make up a form's geometry. While in Edit mode, you can edit the profile or path of a swept form, depending on which edge you selected before starting the editing process. For example, you can edit the profile of the bottom outline of an extruded form, as shown in Figure 1–74.

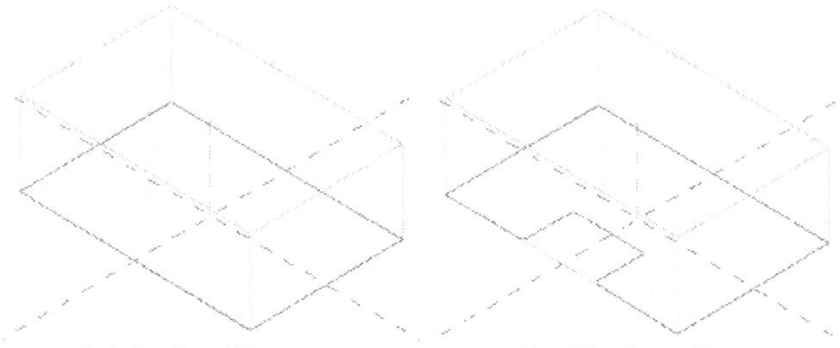

Figure 1–74

How To: Edit Profiles

1. Double-click on the form to enter Edit mode or select the form and in the *Modify | Mass* tab>*Model* panel, click (Edit In-Place).
2. Select the form or any part of the form and in the *Modify | Form* tab>*Mode* panel, click (Edit Profile).
3. Pick any profile or path to edit.
4. Sketch mode opens with the profile or path highlighted in magenta. Using the **Draw** and **Modify** tools, make changes.
5. Click (Finish Edit Mode).
6. The selected profile or path is modified.
7. Click (Finish Mass).

Adding Edges and Profiles

You can also add edges and profiles to existing forms and then modify the resulting edges, faces, and vertices. An edge can be added to the sides of a form, while a profile can be added along the path of the profile, as shown in Figure 1–75.

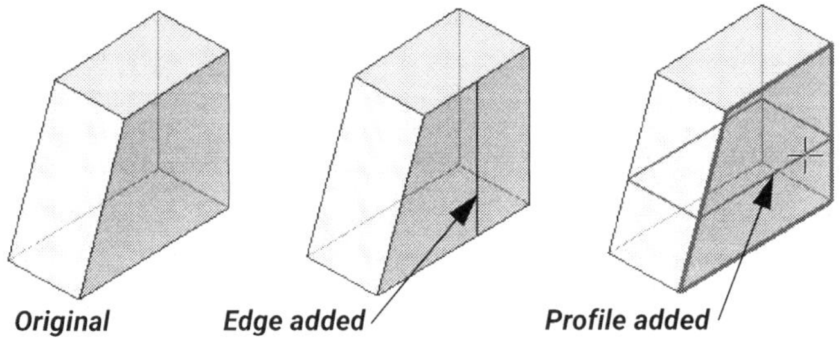

Figure 1–75

Once the edge or profile is placed, you can use the 3D control to create new shapes, as shown in Figure 1–76. You cannot add an edge to the face that is parallel to the sweep path.

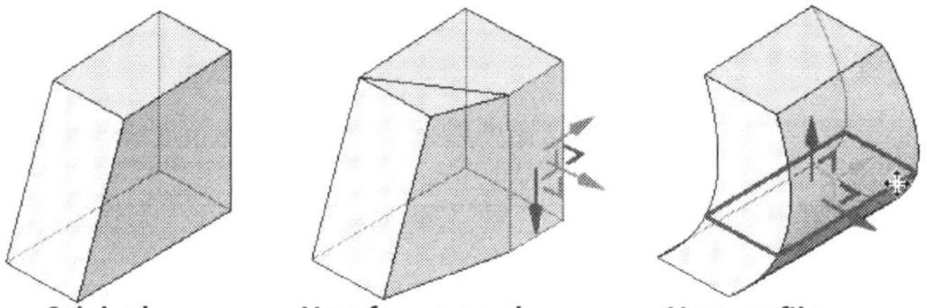

Figure 1–76

- If you cannot add an edge to a face,  displays, as shown in Figure 1–77.

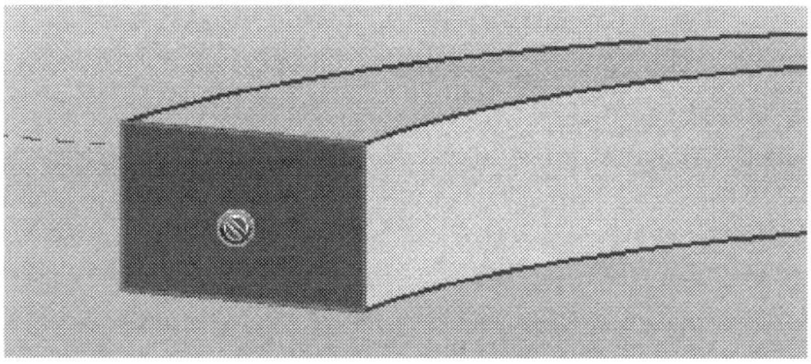

Figure 1–77

How To: Add an Edge

1. While in Edit mode, select anywhere on the form.
2. In the *Modify | Form* tab>*Form Element* panel, click  (Add Edge) or right-click and select **Add Edge**.
3. Hover the cursor over a face. A new edge that reflects the geometry displays, as shown in Figure 1–78. Alternately, pick two points at the vertices or edges of a face, as shown in Figure 1–79.

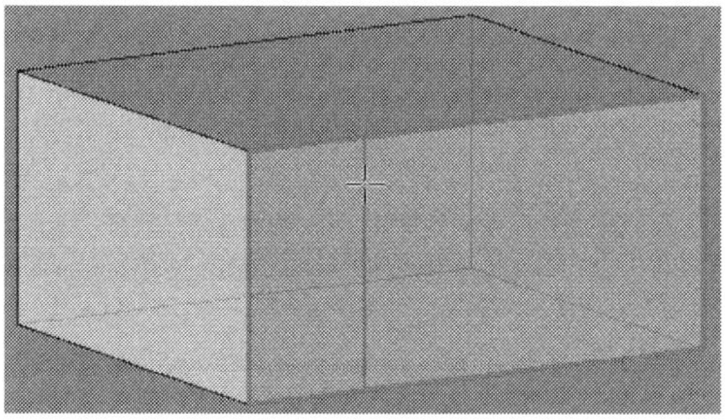

Figure 1–78

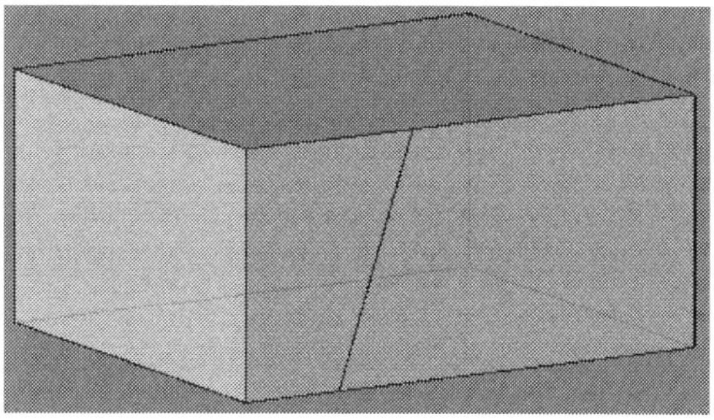

Figure 1–79

How To: Add a Profile

1. While in Edit mode, select anywhere on the form.
2. In the *Modify | Form* tab>*Form Element* panel, click (Add Profile) or right-click and select **Add Profile**.
3. A new profile displays on the selected form when the cursor is moved onto and follows it.
   - The profile automatically adjusts its shape to match the exterior of the form wherever the cursor is located, as shown in Figure 1–80.

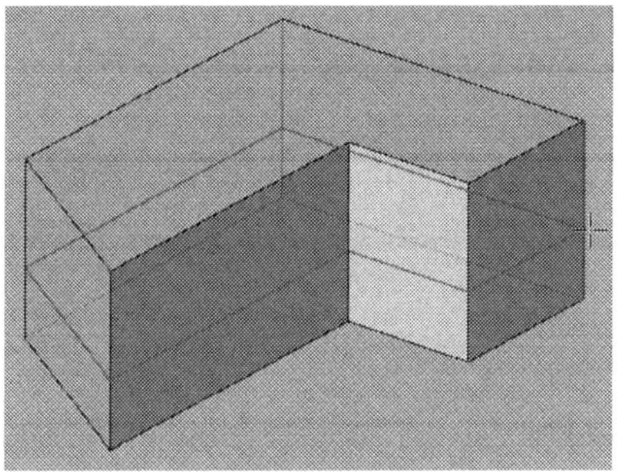

Figure 1–80

4. Click to place the new profile.

Modifying the Faces of Mass Elements

Mass faces can be modified to show patterns and materials. You can apply a pattern similar to creating a curtain wall layout using the **Divide Surface** option, as shown on the top of the mass element in Figure 1–81. You can also split a face into separate surfaces so you can apply different materials to each part, as shown on the base of the mass element in Figure 1–81.

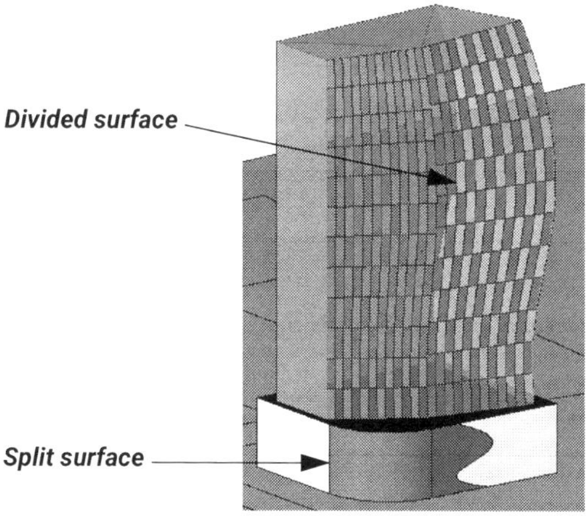

Figure 1–81

How To: Divide and Pattern a Mass Face

1. Double-click on the form to enter Edit mode or select the form and in the *Modify | Mass* tab>*Model* panel, click (Edit In-Place).
2. Select the face of a mass element.
3. In the *Modify | Form* tab>*Divide* panel, click (Divide Surface).
4. The surface is divided using a basic U-V Grid, as shown in Figure 1–82.

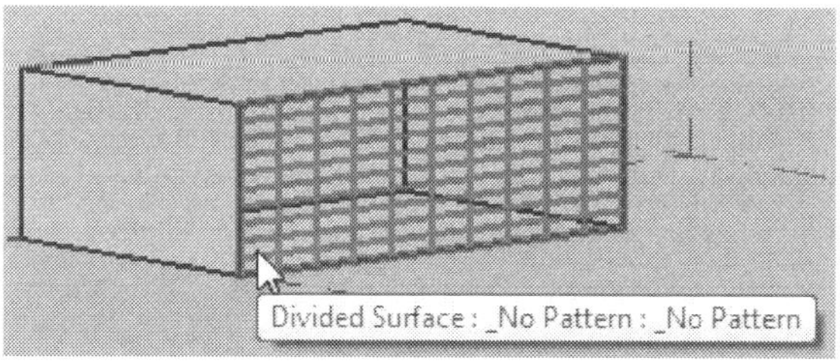

Figure 1–82

5. In the Type Selector, select a pattern from the patterns available, as shown in Figure 1–83.
6. In the *Properties* panel (as shown in Figure 1–84), modify the U-V Grid layout.

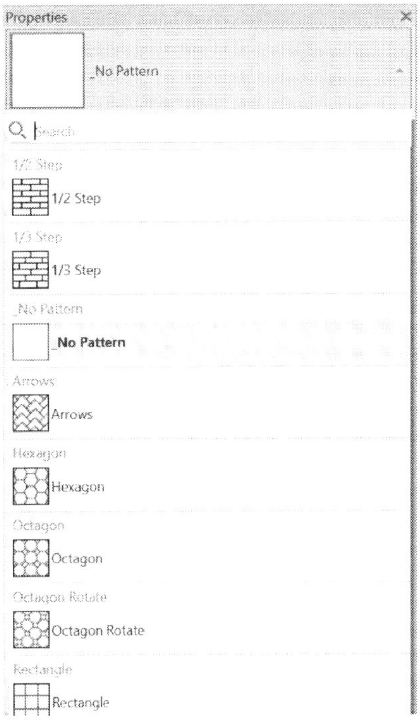

Figure 1–83

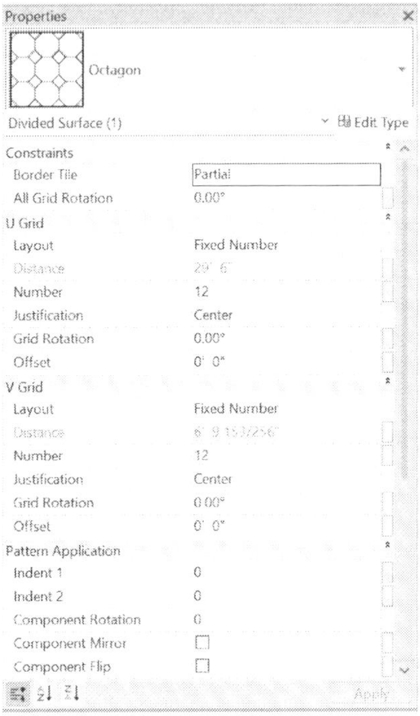

Figure 1–84

7. In the *Modify | Divide Surface* tab's contextual panels (shown in Figure 1–85), you can further modify and display the patterns.

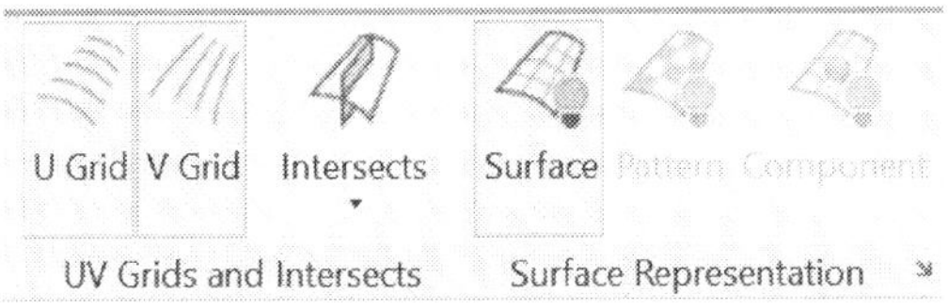

Figure 1–85

How To: Split Mass Faces

1. In the *Modify* tab>*Geometry* panel, click (Split Face).
2. Select the face of the mass element you want to modify.
3. In the *Modify* tab>*Draw* panel, use the sketch tools to create a sketch as required, to define the split (as shown in Figure 1–86).

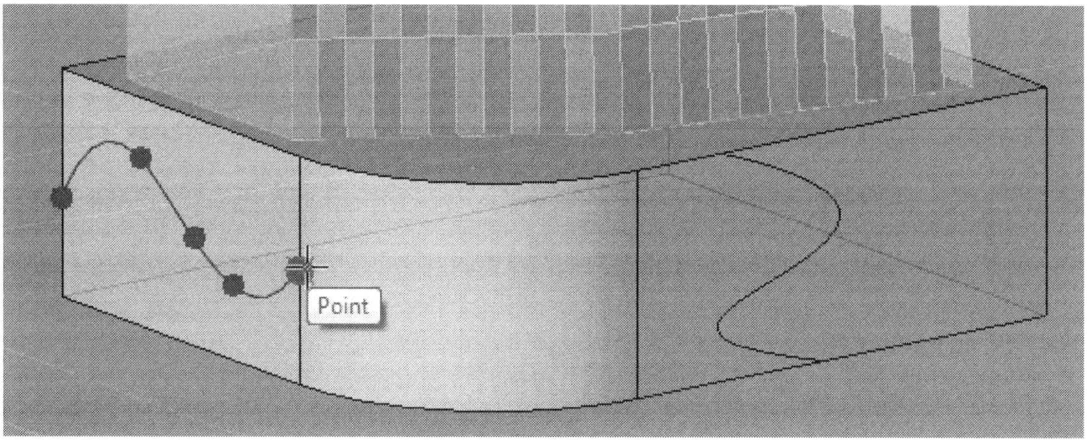

Figure 1–86

- Splitting faces does not create an additional face but you can modify the material in each area.
- The sketch that defines the split must be a closed shape completely inside the face or an open shape that touches the face edges.
- You can split the face of an in-place mass either directly on the face (without entering the mass) or in the In-Place Edit mode.

How To: Add Materials to Individual Mass Faces

1. In the *Modify* tab>*Geometry* panel, click (Paint).
2. Select a material in the Material Browser, as shown on the left in Figure 1–87.
   - Use the search at the top of the dialog box to narrow down your search for materials.
3. Select the face(s) of the mass that you want to paint, as shown on the right in Figure 1–87.

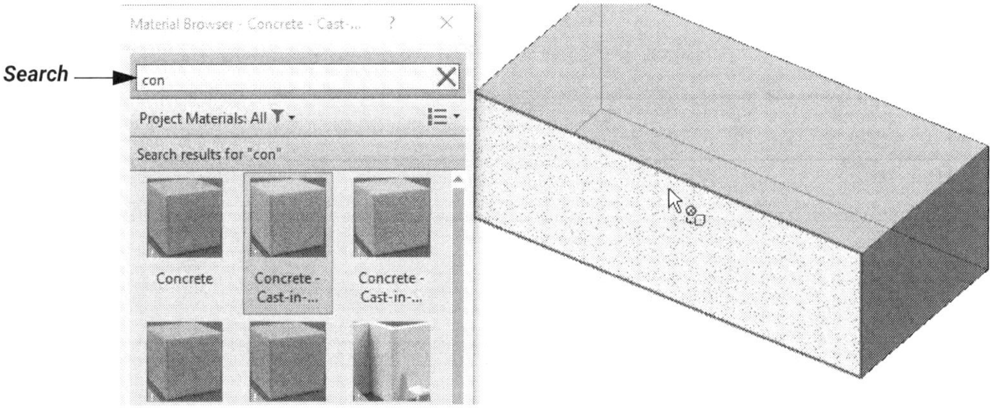

Figure 1–87

- Some material patterns display as shaded when you zoom out. Zoom in to display the pattern. Other material patterns only display when you are in the (Realistic) visual styles.
- To change the material applied to a face, in the *Modify* tab>*Geometry* panel, expand (Paint) and click (Remove Paint). Select the face(s) from which you want to remove the material.
- Older versions of materials may need to be updated with appearance assets. All legacy materials still work but they may not be as complex and nuanced when rendering.

Practice 1c
Modify In-Place Masses

Practice Objectives

- Modify mass elements.
- Add new profiles and edges.
- Modify faces by dividing or splitting them.

In this practice, you will manipulate the vertices, faces, and edges of an extruded in-place mass element using the 3D control. You will also add profiles and an edge. An example of a possible outcome is shown in Figure 1–88. Additionally, you will divide a face, apply a pattern, split another face, and then paint them with a material.

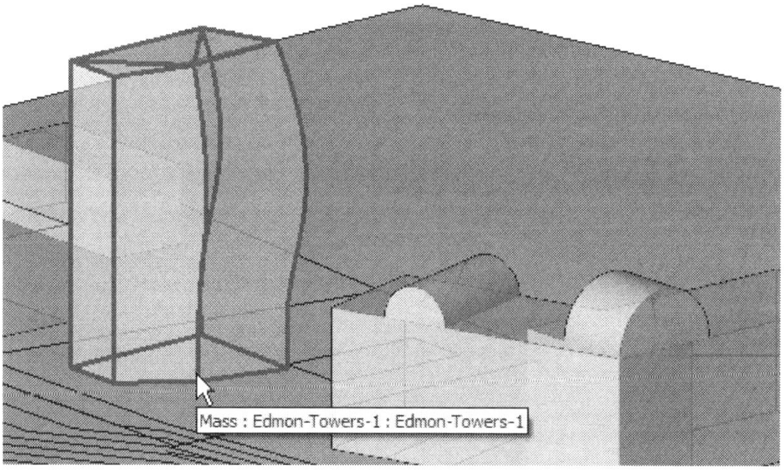

Figure 1–88

Task 1: Modify an in-place mass.

1. In the practice files folder, open **Edmon-Towers-Modify.rvt**.
2. Select the tall mass **Tower-2** and, from the *View Control Bar,* temporarily hide the element.
3. Orient the 3D view so you can see the **Tower-1** extruded mass element.

4. Click on the mass element and modify it slightly using the controls, as shown in Figure 1–89. You can make minor modifications to an in-place mass without editing the entire mass form.

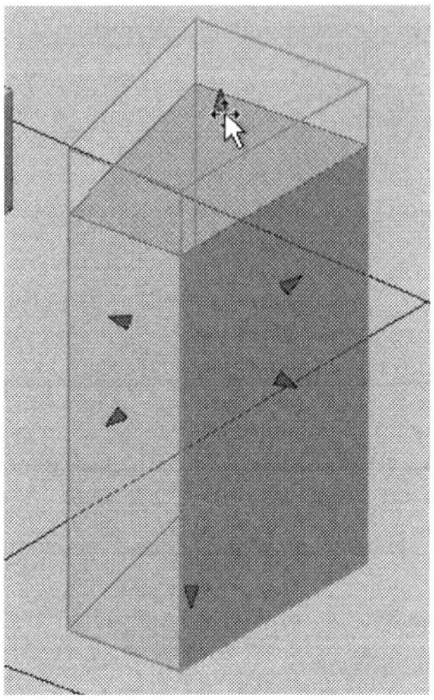

Figure 1–89

5. With the mass still selected, in the *Modify | Mass* tab>*Model* panel, click (Edit In-Place).
6. Select one of the edges and modify it slightly using the 3D control, similar to that shown in Figure 1–90.

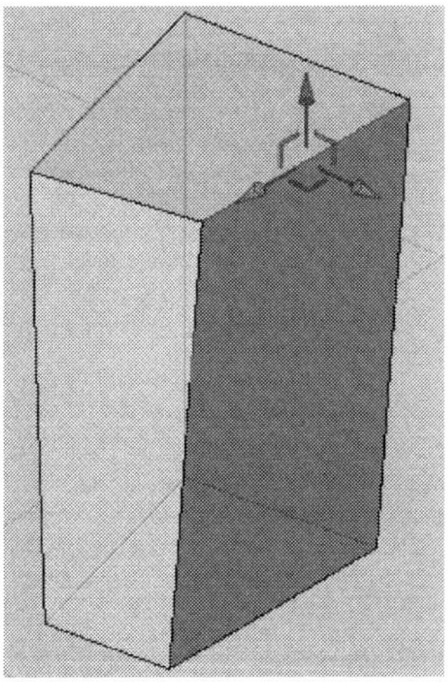

Figure 1–90

Task 2: Add and modify profiles and an edge.

1. Select an edge in the form. (It does not matter which edge.)
2. In the *Modify | Form* tab>*Form Element* panel, click (X-Ray).
3. In the *Form Element* panel, click (Add Profile).
4. Add a profile about one quarter of the way up the form.
5. Repeat this process to add two more profiles, so that the form is divided into four sections, as shown in Figure 1–91. Hint: Press <Enter> to restart the **Add Profile** command again.

   Note: *Do not worry about placing the profiles exactly. Their locations can be adjusted later.*

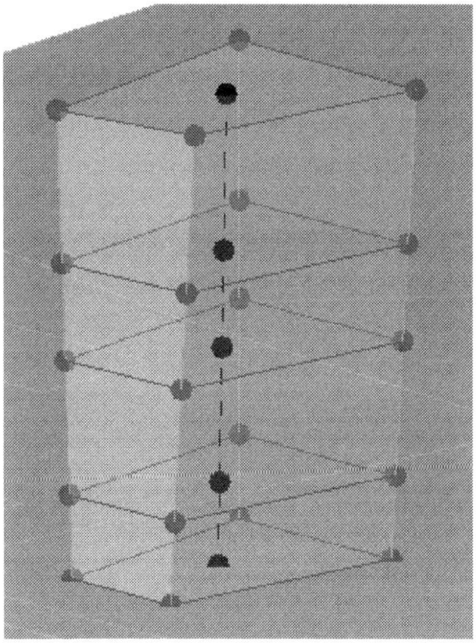

Figure 1–91

6. Use (Add Edge) to add an edge to one side of the building.
7. Click (Modify) to exit the **Add Edge** command.
8. Select the new face and move it out sightly using the 3D control. Make sure you have **Select Elements by Face** enabled.
9. Manipulate the various vertices and edges to reshape the mass.
10. Toggle off X-ray mode.

Task 3: Divide and pattern surfaces.

1. Select one of the mass faces.

   Note: *Use <Tab> to select the face.*

2. In the *Modify | Form* tab>*Divide* panel, click (Divide Surface).
3. In *Properties*, in the *Type Selector*, select a pattern.
4. Modify the pattern properties using tools in the *Properties* panel.
5. (Optional) Select a different face and in the *Modify | Form* tab>*Geometry* panel, use (Split Face) and (Paint) to apply materials.
6. Click (Finish Mass).
7. Save and close the project.

End of practice

1.7 Moving from Massing to Building

When you have established a massing study, you can start the design development with walls, etc., you do not have to start over. Instead, you can use tools in Revit to create walls, floors, roofs, and curtain systems from the faces of the masses in the project as shown in Figure 1–92.

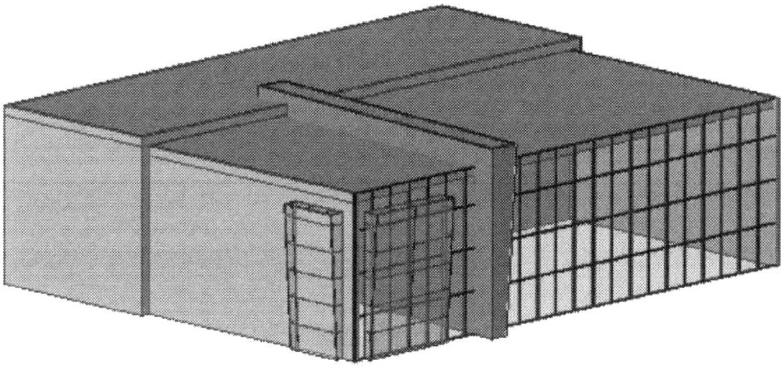

Figure 1–92

- You can add a slope to a wall style from the wall's Properties, but you can also do this with mass elements by creating the shape you want and applying the material or wall style to the mass.
- You can add walls, floors, roofs, and curtain systems to the faces of mass elements using the **Wall**, **Roof**, and **Floor** commands in the *Architecture* tab>*Build* panel. For example, when you start the **Wall** command, you can click (Pick Faces) as the drawing method, as shown in Figure 1–93.

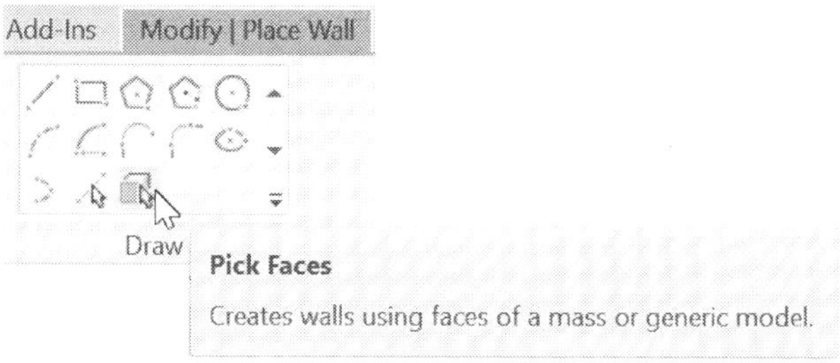

Figure 1–93

- You can also use the specific commands found in the *Massing & Site* tab>*Model by Face* panel, as shown in Figure 1–94.

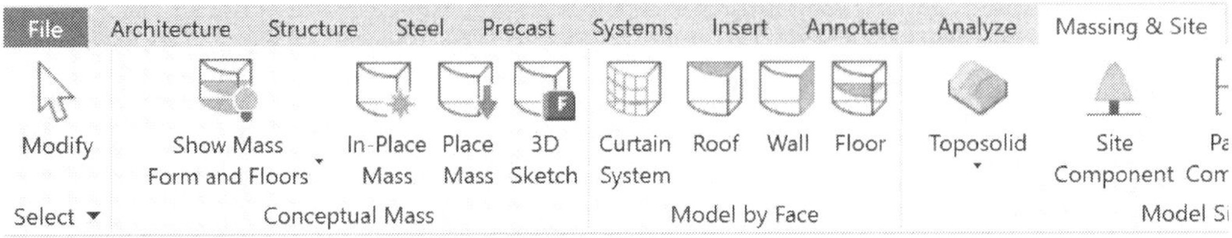

Figure 1–94

How To: Use the Model by Face Tools

1. Open a view where the mass faces display and where you want to apply the building elements. This can be done in either a 3D or elevation view.
2. In the *Massing & Site* tab>*Model by Face* panel, click (Curtain System), (Roof), (Wall), or (Floor).
3. In the Type Selector, select an element type.
4. Select the faces you want to turn into elements.
5. In the contextual tab>*Multiple Selection* panel, click the related **Create** command.

Wall by Face Options

- Ensure that the *Location Line value* is set to **Finished Face: Exterior**. This keeps the walls on the inside of the mass.

  Note: *Location Line is grayed out if a curtain wall style is selected.*

- You can create walls on sloped faces using this tool.

Curtain Systems Options

Note: *A Curtain System is a type of curtain wall made up of mullions, panels, and curtain grids. You can apply curtain systems to irregular shapes such as curved or angled face shapes.*

- In the *Modify | Place Curtain System by Face* tab>*Multiple Selection* panel, verify that (Select Multiple) is highlighted if you are planning to select more than one face for a curtain system at a time.

Roof by Face Options

- In the *Modify | Place Roof by* Face tab, hover over the surface so the entire face highlights, then click to place.
- In Properties, in the *Constraints* section, set *Picked Faces Location* to **Faces at Bottom of the Roof**.
- From the *Modify | Place Roof by Face* tab>*Multiple Selection* panel, click (Create Roof) to place your roof.
- After you have created a roof by face, you can use shape handles to modify the overhang of the roof, as shown in Figure 1–95.

Note: *The overhang distance is remembered if you change the mass.*

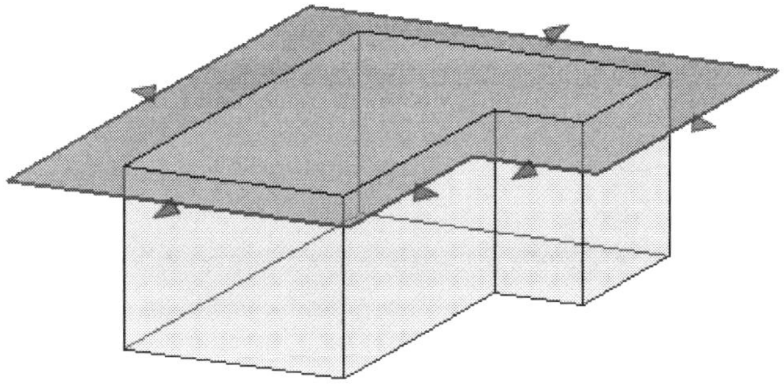

Figure 1–95

Creating Floors from Mass Elements

To create floors in a massing study, you must first create mass floors. These are the basis for creating floors and also help track the floor area of the building. Once you have the mass floors in a project, you can click (Floor by Face) to add the floor elements on the faces.

How To: Create Mass Floors

1. Select a mass.
2. In the *Modify | Mass* tab>*Model* panel, click  (Mass Floors).
3. In the *Mass Floors* dialog box, select the levels where you want floor area faces to be located, as shown in Figure 1–96, and click **OK**.

   Note: *If you have a lot of levels to select, hold <Ctrl> or <Shift> to select multiple levels.*

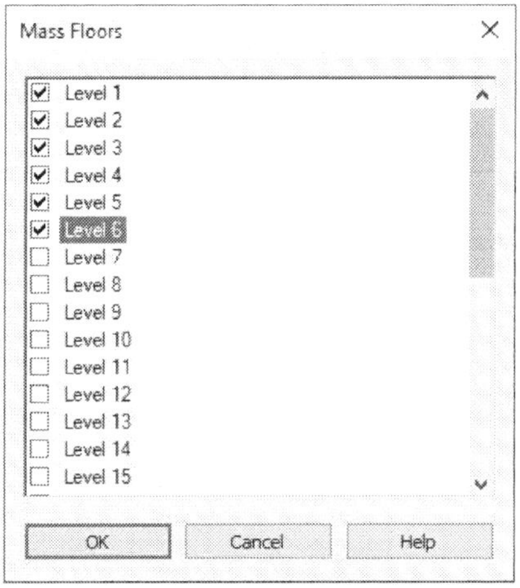

Figure 1–96

The mass floors display in the massing study, as shown in Figure 1–97.

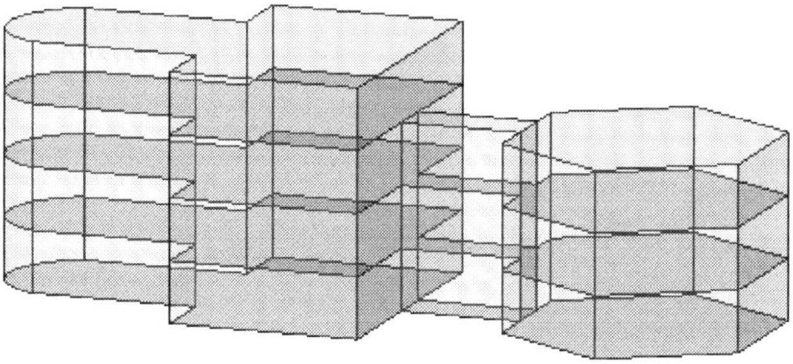

Figure 1–97

- Mass floors keep track of the area, exterior surface area, volume, and perimeter of each floor. This information can be used in schedules and tags.

Hint: Updating Elements Connected to Mass Elements

Elements applied to mass elements, such as walls, floors, roofs, and curtain systems do not automatically update when the massing element changes as shown on the left in Figure 1–98. Select the mass element and in the *Modify | Mass* tab>*Model* panel, click (Related Hosts). Then in the *Modify | Multi-Select* tab>*Model by Face* panel, click (Update to Face). The elements update, as shown on the right in Figure 1–98.

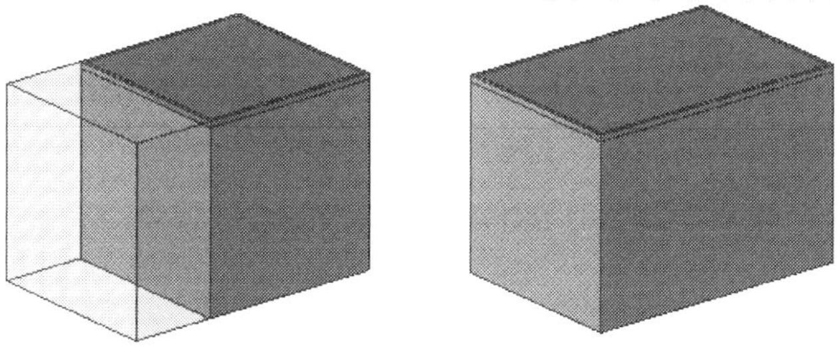

Mass modified ***Walls and roof remade***

Figure 1–98

- If you only want to update one element (such as a roof), select the element that is hosted by the mass and in the *Modify | <element type>* tab>*Model by Face* panel, click (Update to Face). Note that the icon varies according to the element type selected.

Practice 1d
Move from Massing to Building

Practice Objectives

- Add mass floors.
- Use existing schedules to track the coverage of the site and the gross area of the mass, while making changes to one of the towers.
- Add walls, floors, roofs, and curtain systems to the finished mass towers.

In this practice, you will add mass floors to specified levels and investigate the site coverage and building volume, as shown in Figure 1–99. You will also add walls, floors, curtain systems, and roofs to the faces of the conceptual mass elements.

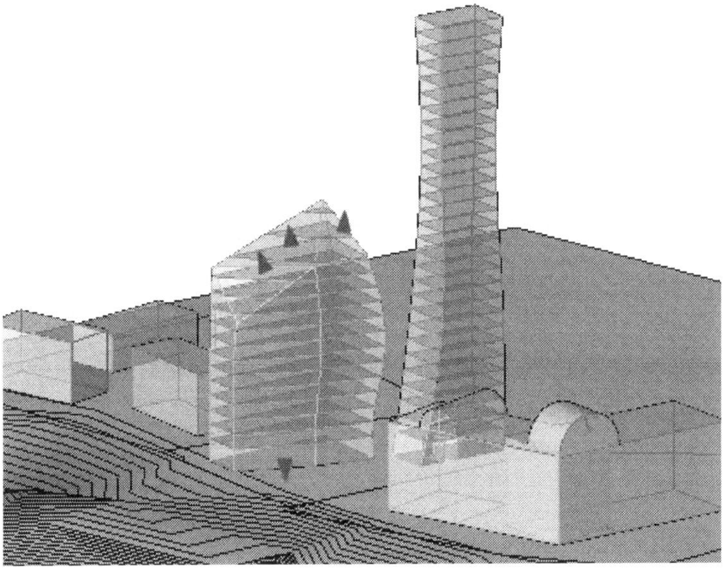

Figure 1–99

Task 1: Add massing floors.

1. In the practice files folder, open **Edmon-Towers-Building.rvt**.
2. Select the two curved tower masses included in the project.
3. In the *Modify | Mass* tab>*Model* panel, click  (Mass Floors).

4. Select all of the levels in the *Mass Floors* dialog box and click **OK**. The new mass floors display as shown in Figure 1–100. Hint: Use <Shift> to select all the levels, then check one check box to check them all.

   Note: *Some levels are higher than the current height of the masses. By selecting them now, they will automatically be applied when the height of the masses is changed.*

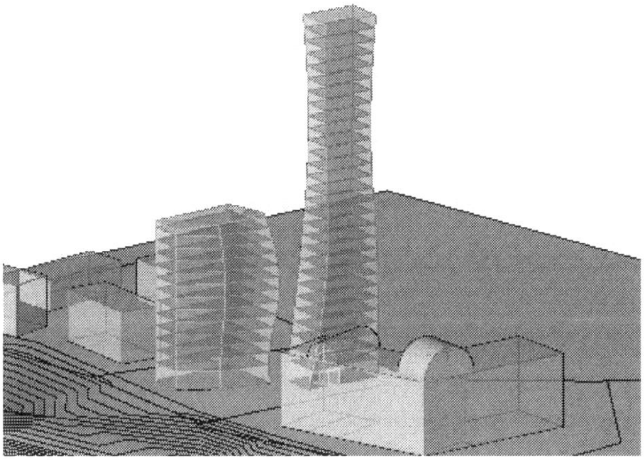

Figure 1–100

Task 2: Track site coverage and gross area using schedules.

1. If necessary, close any other projects and in the Quick Access Toolbar, click (Close Inactive Views) to close any windows that do no need to be open.
2. Open the following four views on your screen:
   - *3D Views:* **Site View** (currently opened)
   - *Floor Plans:* **New Site**
   - *Schedules/Quantities:* **Building Volume Schedule**
   - *Schedules/Quantities:* **Coverage of Site**

- The **Coverage of Site** schedule enables you to track how much of the site the proposed building covers. It lists the actual and maximum footprints in both square feet and percentage. You can enter the actual site area in the *Parcel* column, and the amount of the site that the building is permitted to cover in the *Max Footprint (%)* column. The Revit software does the rest.
- **Building Volume Schedule** displays the Total Floor Area and Total Floor Volume at the bottom of the schedule. If the zoning restrictions or program requirements limit the overall floor area of the building, the schedule tracks this for you.

3. Return to the 3D Site View and type **WT** (Window Tile) so that all four views display.
4. Type **ZA** (Zoom All) to display the entire 3D view and the New Site plan.

5. Click in the **New Site** view and select the property line.
6. In Properties, the *Area* is **43,298.77 SF**. This is the size you use for the *Parcel* column.
7. In the **Coverage of Site** schedule, enter **43299** in the *Parcel* cell and **20** in the *Max Footprint (%)* cell. Click in another column to calculate the *Max Footprint*, as shown in Figure 1–101.

<Coverage of Site>

A	B	C	D	E
Parcel	Actual Footprint	Max Footprint	Current Footprint (%)	Max Footprint (%)
43,299 SF	8,263 SF	8,660	19.1	20

Figure 1–101

8. Based on initial numbers in the **Coverage of Site** schedule, both towers are within the *Max Footprint*.
9. In the 3D Site View, select one of the tower masses. Use the shape handles to change the height and shape of the mass. Watch the schedules to ensure that the *Current Footprint* value remains below 20% and the **Building Volume schedule** *Floor Area* total remains below **160,000 SF**.
10. Save the project.

Task 3: Add walls, floors, roofs, and curtain systems.

1. Return to a tab view by selecting the **3D Site View** and typing **TW**.
2. Zoom in on one of the mass elements.
3. In the *Massing & Site* tab>*Model by Face* panel, click (Floor).
4. Select the floors and click (Create Floor).
5. Repeat the process with walls, roofs, and curtain systems. Hint: hide the mass to make this process easier.
6. Save and close the project.

End of practice

Chapter Review Questions

1. Mass elements display by default in a view.

   a. True

   b. False

2. Which of the following elements was NOT created using the basic family types that come with the Revit software?

   a. 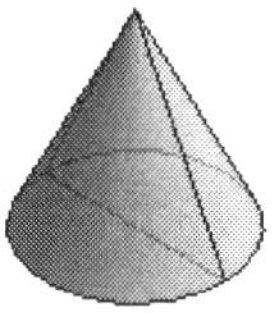

   b. 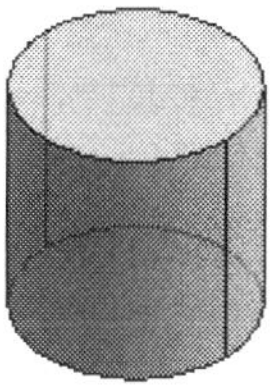

   c. 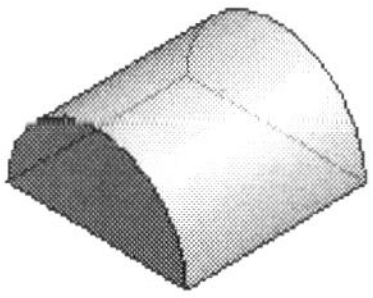

   d. 

3. What element(s) need to be placed first to create a blended sweep form?
    a. Two profiles on different work planes.
    b. A profile on an extrusion.
    c. More than two profiles on different levels.
    d. Two or more existing forms.

4. How do you cut a portion out of a conceptual mass element, as shown in Figure 1–102?

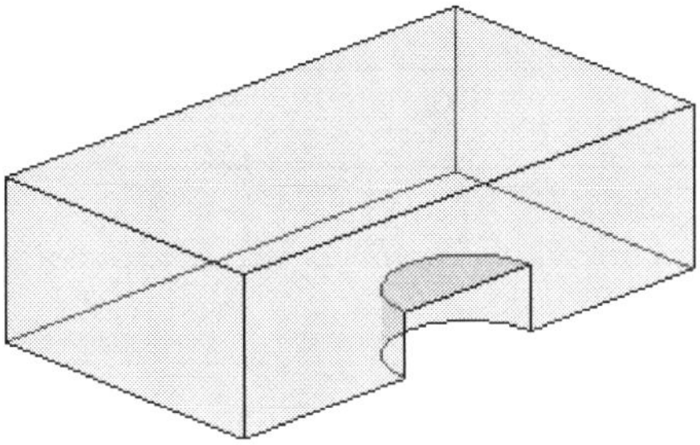

Figure 1–102

    a. Select the form and click  (Edit Profile).
    b. Create a void form in the mass element.
    c. Create another mass element and use  (Cut Geometry).
    d. Edit the form and add another profile to it.

5. Which of the mass form types is created from three or more profiles?
    a. Sweep
    b. Swept Blend
    c. Loft
    d. Extrusion

6. The start of a mass form is a sketch. How do you place a sketch on another form, as shown in Figure 1–103?

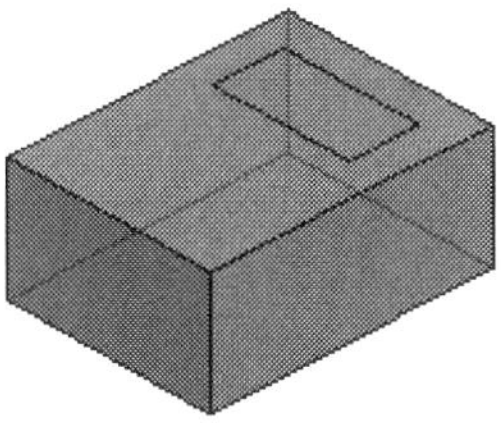

Figure 1–103

   a. Select the Draw tool that you want to use, then use the Draw on Face tool.
   b. Select the Draw tool that you want to use, then use the Draw on Work Plane tool.
   c. Select the Draw tool that you want to use, then set the Placement Plane to a Level.

7. How do you move a sketch from one plane to another plane, as shown in Figure 1–104?

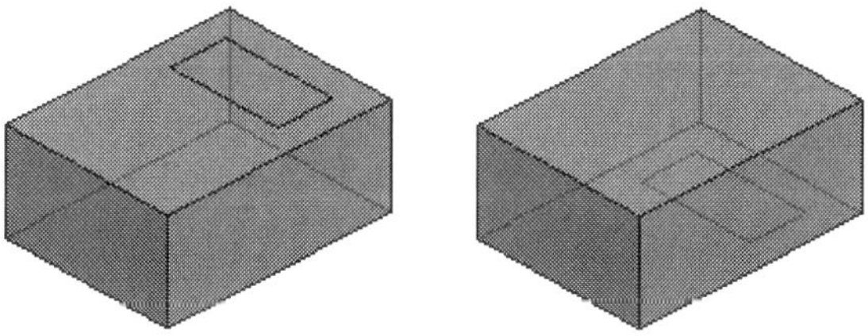

Figure 1–104

   a. Change the *Placement Plane*.
   b. Use the Move command.
   c. Change the Host.
   d. Use the Align command.

8. What must be in place before you can add a floor to a mass element, as shown in Figure 1–105?

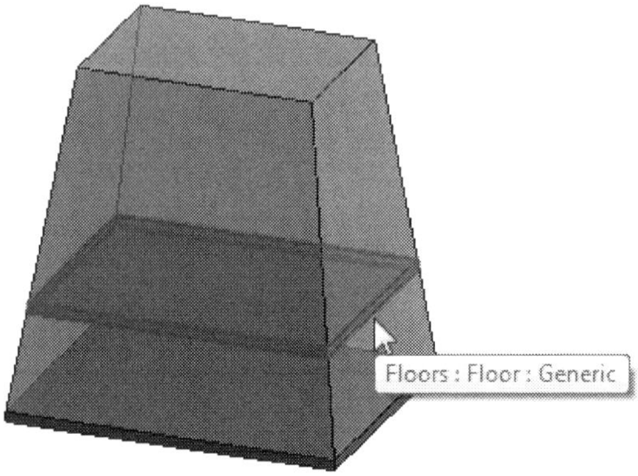

Figure 1–105

a. Additional mass elements at each floor.
b. Sketches for each floor.
c. An additional floor parameter in Properties.
d. Mass floor elements at each floor.

Command Summary

Button	Command	Location
	**Cut Geometry**	• **Ribbon:** *Modify* tab>*Geometry* panel
	**Edit In-Place**	• **Ribbon:** *Modify | Mass* tab>*Model* panel
	**Edit Work Plane**	• **Ribbon:** *Modify | Mass* tab>*Work Plane* panel
	**In-Place Mass**	• **Ribbon:** *Massing & Site* tab>*Conceptual Mass* panel
	**Load Family**	• **Ribbon:** *Modify | Place Mass* tab>*Mode* panel
	**Paint**	• **Ribbon:** *Modify* tab>*Geometry* panel
	**Place Mass**	• **Ribbon:** *Massing & Site* tab>*Conceptual Mass* panel
	**Place on Face**	• **Ribbon:** *Modify | Place Mass* tab>*Placement* panel
	**Place on Work Plane**	• **Ribbon:** *Modify | Place Mass* tab>*Placement* panel
	**Show Mass by Form and Floors**	• **Ribbon:** *Massing & Site* tab>*Conceptual Mass* panel, expand Show Mass
	**Show Mass by View Settings**	• **Ribbon:** *Massing & Site* tab>*Conceptual Mass* panel, expand Show Mass
Conceptual Mass Environment		
	**Add Edge**	• **Ribbon:** *Modify | Form* tab>*Form Element* panel • **Right-click:** Add Edge
	**Add Profile**	• **Ribbon:** *Modify | Form* tab>*Form Element* panel • **Right-click:** Add Profile
	**Create Form**	• **Ribbon:** *Modify | Place Lines* tab>*Form* panel
	**Divide Surface**	• **Ribbon:** *Modify | Form* tab>*Divide* panel
	**Draw on Face**	• **Ribbon:** *Modify | Place Lines* tab>*Draw* panel
	**Draw on Work Plane**	• **Ribbon:** *Modify | Place Lines* tab>*Draw* panel

Button	Command	Location
	Point Element	• **Ribbon:** *Modify | Place Lines* tab>*Draw* panel
	**Model Line**	• **Ribbon:** *Modify | Form* tab>*Draw* panel
	**Reference Line**	• **Ribbon:** *Modify | Form* tab>*Draw* panel
	**Reference Plane**	• **Ribbon:** *Modify | Form* tab>*Draw* panel
	**X-Ray**	• **Ribbon:** *Modify | Form* tab>*Form Element* panel • **Right-click:** X-Ray
	**Void Form**	• **Ribbon:** *Modify | Lines* tab>*Form* panel, expand Create Form
From Massing to Building		
	**Create Roof**	• **Ribbon:** *Modify* | *Place Roof by Face* tab>*Multiple Selection* panel
	**Curtain System (by Face)**	• **Ribbon:** *Massing & Site* tab>*Model by Face* panel
	**Floor (by Face)**	• **Ribbon:** *Massing & Site* tab>*Model by Face* panel
	**Mass Floors**	• **Ribbon:** *Modify | Mass* tab>*Model* panel
	**Related Hosts**	• **Ribbon:** *Modify | Mass* tab>*Model* panel
	**Roof (by Face)**	• **Ribbon:** *Massing & Site* tab>*Model by Face* panel
	**Wall (by Face)**	• **Ribbon:** *Massing & Site* tab>*Model by Face* panel
	**Update to Face**	• **Ribbon:** *Modify | Multi-Select* tab>*Model by Face* panel

Chapter 2

Adding Rooms and Areas

Rooms and areas can be used in conceptual design and as part of the Building Information Model. These tools in Revit® are very powerful and enable you to place room elements in a view and track room information through all of the phases of a project. If you are working with rentable spaces, you can also add similar elements that keep track of the areas in a project. Both rooms and areas can have customized views that use color schemes that show the information graphically.

Learning Objectives

- Add rooms, room boundaries, and room tags to a project.
- Create area plans.
- Place area boundaries and areas.
- Set up a color scheme in a view.
- Define new color schemes by value and by range.

2.1 Room Elements

The room element is a powerful tool in Revit. With this element, you can set up information to use in schedules and color diagrams to help present data or do take-offs. They also contain area, perimeter, and volume information about each room as well as the room name and number, as shown in Figure 2–1.

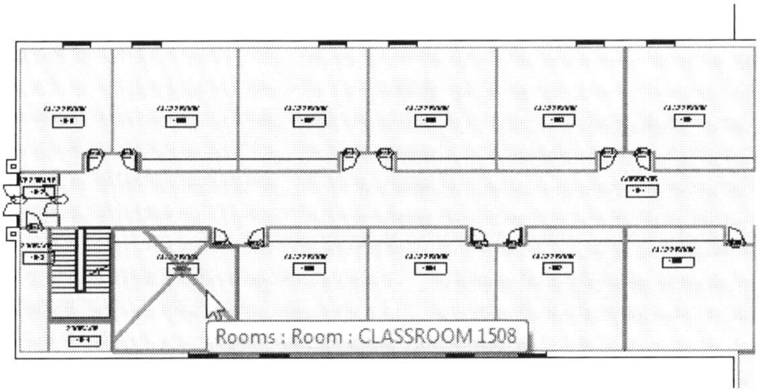

Figure 2–1

- Most walls, roofs, floors, ceilings, columns, and curtain systems are *Room Bounding* elements. One exception is the retaining wall type, which typically does not enclose rooms.
- You can add room separation lines to create rooms that are not bounded by walls.
- You can place room elements without any original bounding elements. They expand to fit any boundary that later encloses them.

How To: Create Rooms in a Plan

1. Draw the walls and other bounding elements that you want to have in your building.
2. In the *Architecture* tab>*Room & Area* panel, click  (Room), or type **RM**.
3. In the *Modify | Place Room* tab>*Tag* panel, click  (Tag on Placement) if you want to include a tag as you place the room.
4. Use the Options Bar (shown in Figure 2–2) to:
   - Set the *Upper Limit* and *Offset.*
   - Set the *Orientation* of the tag and the *Leader*.
   - Select a *Room* name from the drop-down list (if room names have been previously created in a schedule).

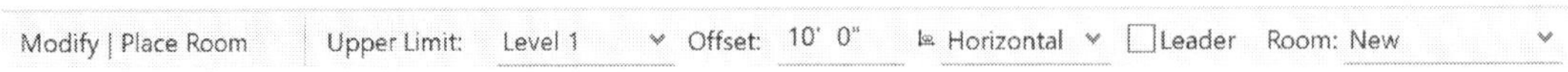

Figure 2–2

5. Move the cursor into a boundary area and click to place the room, as shown in Figure 2–3.

   Or, in the *Modify | Place Room* tab>*Room* panel, click (Place Rooms Automatically) to add rooms to every bounding area.

   - Select one room and set the first number before placing rooms automatically so they will increment as expected.

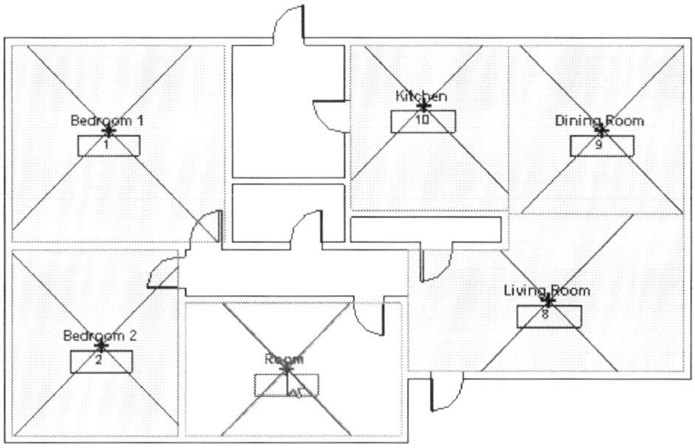

Figure 2–3

6. Continue adding rooms.

- In the *Modify | Place Room* tab>*Room* panel, click (Highlight Boundaries) to display all of the bounding objects in the project in orange. An alert box displays a warning that the room bounding elements are highlighted. When you close the alert box, it toggles off the highlighting of the bounding objects.

Hint: Setting Up Views to Show Rooms

Rooms do not display in views by default, so it can help to create views specifically for rooms. To do this, duplicate an existing plan or elevation view. Then, in the *Visibility/Graphic Overrides* dialog box, in the *Model Categories* tab, toggle on **Rooms**, then expand **Rooms** to toggle on **Interior Fill** and/or **Reference** to show the crossing lines.

Room Separation Boundaries

Boundaries for rooms can also be defined by room separation lines. Use these where you might not have a wall to separate the areas, but still want to specify them as different rooms. For example, in a house you can have a kitchen, dining area, and living area in a larger room that is not separated by walls, as shown in Figure 2–4.

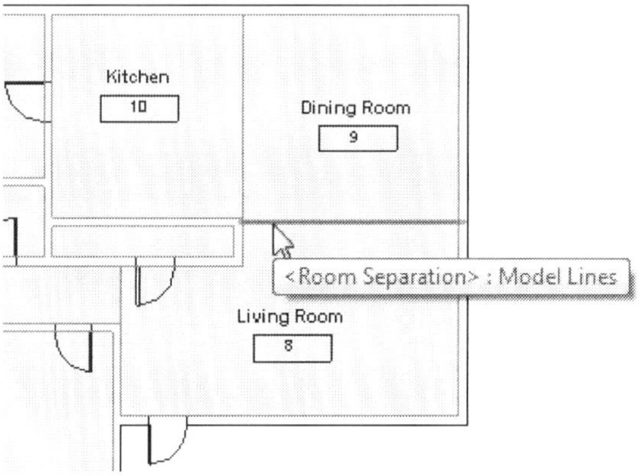

Figure 2–4

How To: Create Room Separation Boundaries

1. In the *Architecture* tab>*Room & Area* panel, click (Room Separator).
2. In the *Modify | Place Room Separation* tab>*Draw* panel, use the sketch tools to draw the edges of the boundary. Click (Modify) to end the command.
3. Use (Room) to add rooms in the areas bounded by the separation lines.

- You can edit room separation lines by splitting, trimming, etc.

Modifying Rooms

To select a room, hover the cursor over it until you see the reference lines (crossing lines) highlight, as shown in Figure 2–5. Then, select one of the reference lines to select the room.

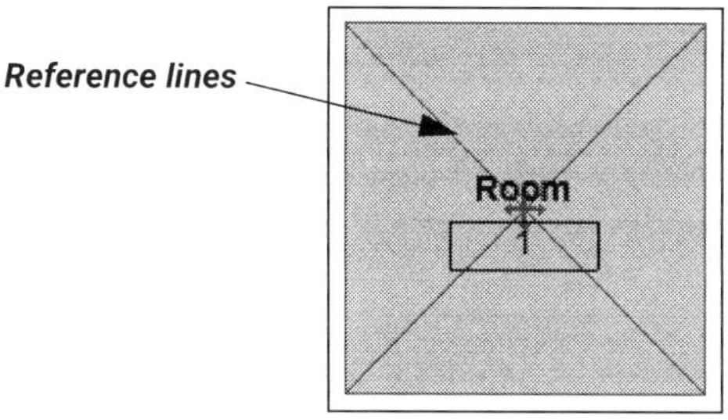

Figure 2–5

- When a room is selected, you can modify its Properties, as shown in Figure 2–6.

  Note: *You can select several rooms at once to add the same information to all of them. <Ctrl> lets you add to your selection and <Shift> removes items from your selection group.*

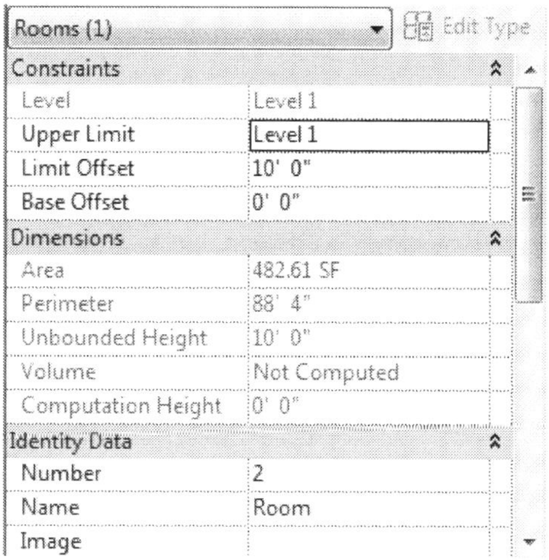

Figure 2–6

- You can also modify the vertical height of rooms in sections by using controls, as shown in Figure 2–7, or temporary dimensions.

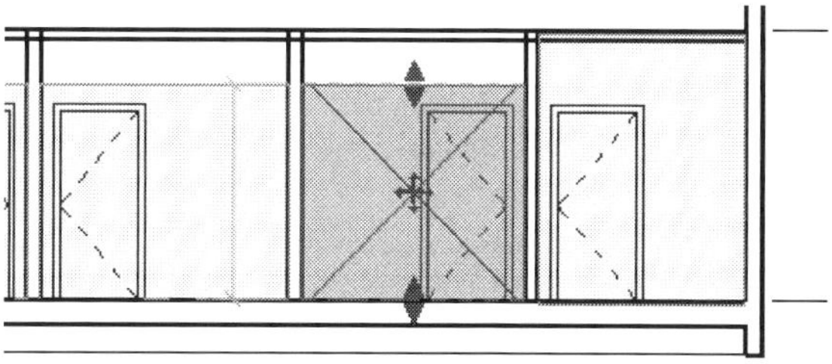

Figure 2–7

Adding Room Tags

Room tags can be added during or after rooms are added to a project. There are three room tag types: **Room Tag**, **Room Tag With Area**, and **Room Tag With Volume**, as shown in Figure 2–8.

> **Note:** *The Room Tag command is separate from other tag commands.*

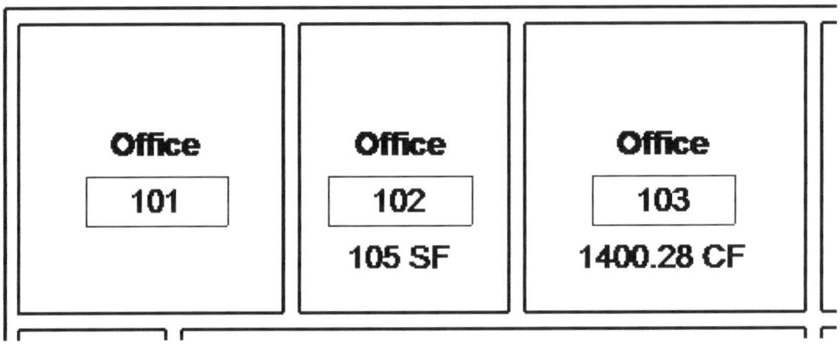

Figure 2–8

How To: Place a Room Tag

1. Place rooms without tags in the project.
2. In the *Architecture* tab>*Room & Area* panel, click (Tag Room) or in the *Annotate* tab>*Tag* panel, click (Room Tag), or type **RT**.
3. In Properties, select the tag type.
4. Click in the room you want to tag and repeat to tag as many rooms as needed.

- Rooms can be tagged in plan or section views.
- Rooms can be tagged using (Tag All Not Tagged).
- To change the room name or number, select the tag and click on the name or number to modify it, as shown in Figure 2–9.

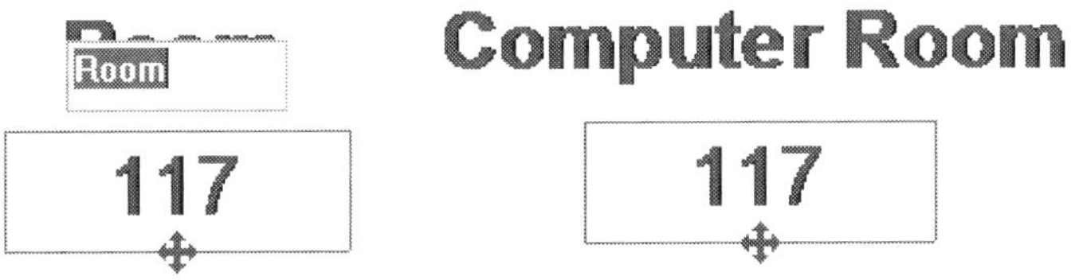

Figure 2–9

- If you delete a room tag, the room is not deleted.

- If you delete a room, the tag is deleted as well.
- If you select a tag, you can add or remove a *Leader Line* and set the *Orientation*, *Angle*, and *Leader Type* in Properties, as shown in Figure 2–10.

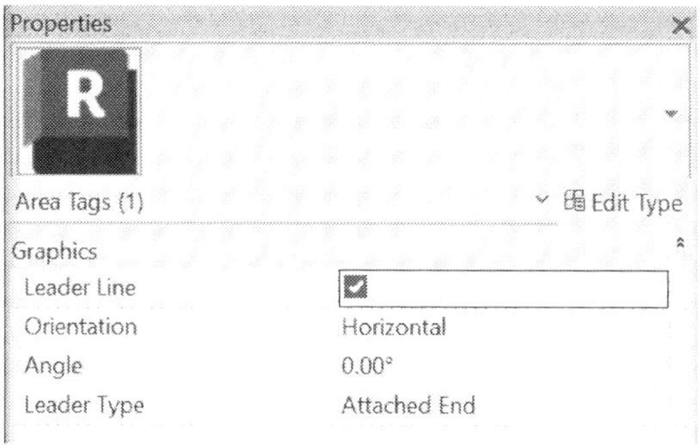

Figure 2–10

- If needed, you can drag the room tag outside of the room boundary and a leader will automatically be added. Figure 2–11 shows the before and after of placing a room with a tag and then dragging it outside of the room boundary.

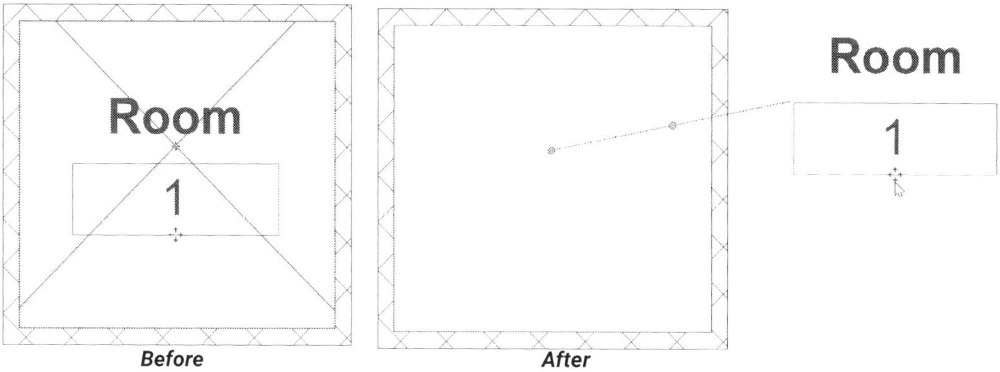

Figure 2–11

Room Schedules

Room schedules are used to keep track of data included in a room, such as the name, number (shown in Figure 2–12), occupancy, area, and finishes. In the schedule, you can select multiple rooms and apply the same information to them all.

<Room Schedule>

A	B	C	D
Number	Name	Department	Room Style
101	Office	Sales	Office-Standard
102	Office	Sales	Office-Standard
103	Workroom	Sales	Workroom
104	Office	Accounting	Office-Standard
105	Office	Accounting	Office-Standard
106	Office	Accounting	Office-Standard
107	Reception	Accounting	Reception
108	Office	Accounting	Office-Executive

Typical room schedule

Figure 2–12

Key Schedules are useful when you have a large number of elements that need to have the same finish information, as shown in Figure 2–13. Fields in key styles are typically controlled by instance rather than by type. Grouping styles together makes it easier to apply this information to large numbers of instances.

<Room Style Schedule>

A	B	C	D	E	F
Key Name	Wall Finish	Floor Finish	Base Finish	Ceiling Finish	Comments
Corridor	Painted	Carpet	Vinyl	Painted	
Executive Office	Wall Paper	Wood	Wood	ACT	
Standard Office	Painted	Carpet	Vinyl	ACT	
Utility	Painted	Vinyl	Vinyl	ACT	

Figure 2–13

Room Settings

You can set the way Revit calculates volumes and boundary locations. In the *Architecture* tab> *Room & Area* panel, expand the panel title and click (Area and Volume Computations) to open the dialog box, as shown in Figure 2–14.

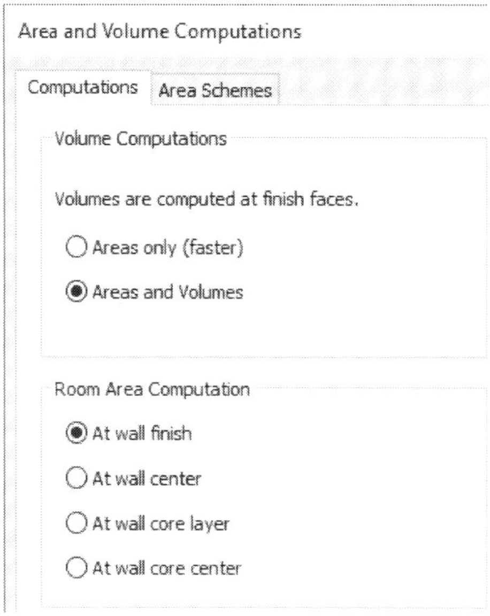

Figure 2–14

- Calculating volumes slows down the speed of working in a project. You might only want to toggle it on only before you do an evaluation.

Practice 2a
Add Room Elements to a Plan View

Practice Objectives

- Set up a view that displays rooms.
- Add rooms and room separation lines to a project.
- Review a room schedule.

In this practice, you will set up a view that displays rooms, add rooms, room separation lines, and room tags to an existing project. You will modify the room tags and give each room a name, as shown in Figure 2–15. Finally, you will review a room schedule and modify some of the contents.

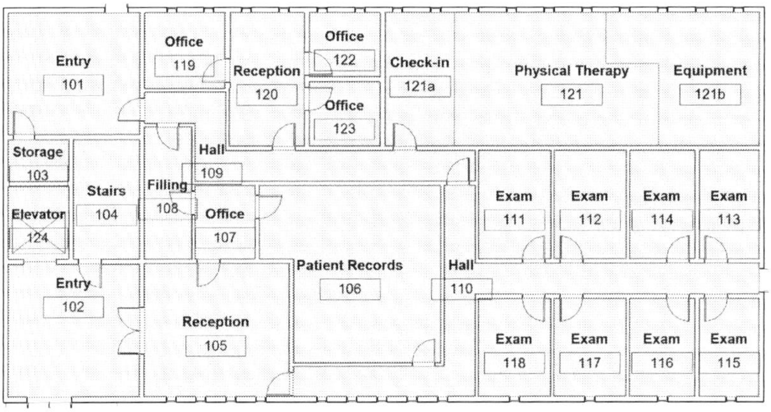

Figure 2–15

Task 1: Create a view and add rooms.

1. In the practice files folder, open **Medical-Office-Rooms.rvt**.
2. Duplicate the **Floor Plans: Level 1** view and rename it **Level 1 - Rooms**.
3. Open the *Visibility/Graphic Overrides* dialog box.
4. In the *Model Categories* tab, expand *Rooms* and select **Interior Fill**. Click **OK**.
5. In the *Architecture* tab>*Room & Area* panel, click (Room), or type **RM**. Verify that (Tag on Placement) is on.
6. Place the first room in the upper left corner of the building and click (Modify).

7. Zoom in on the room and select the tag, then select the number in the room tag. Change the tag's room number to **101**. Press <Enter> and click anywhere outside of the room tag to finish. This will cause subsequent tags to automatically increment from this number, but it does not affect any existing tags.

8. Start the **Room** command again.
   - To control the order of the room numbers, click in each room.
   - If the room number order does not matter, click  (Place Rooms Automatically) in the *Modify | Place Rooms* tab, *Room* panel.

   Note: *There is no way to mass change the order it places the tags in.*

   - Do not change the room names as you place them.

9. After you have placed all of the rooms, click  (Modify). Zoom in and start naming them, as shown in Figure 2–16.

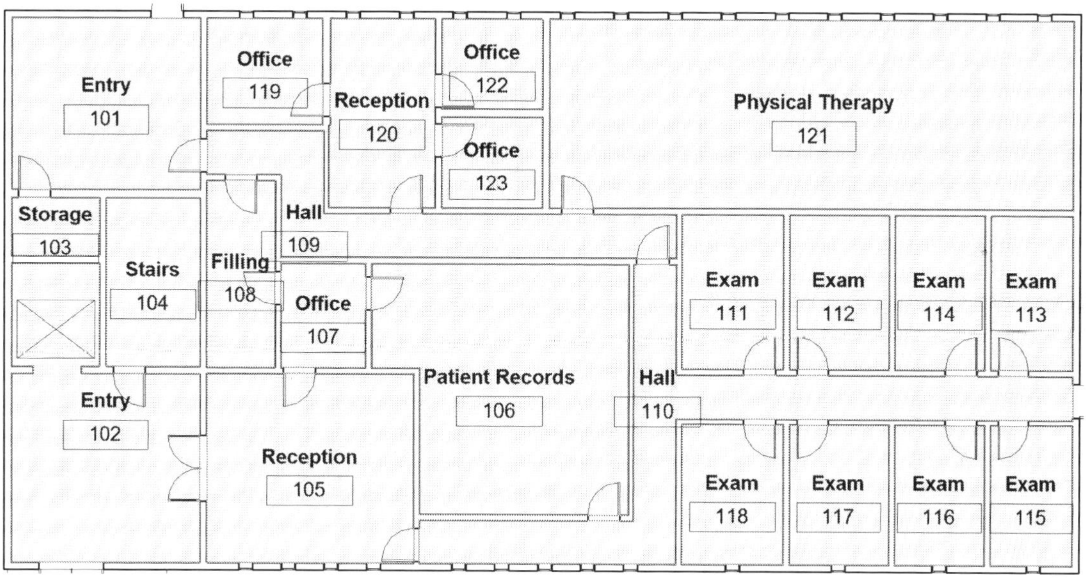

Figure 2–16

   - To modify one room name at a time, click on the room tag and type a new name.

   Note: *You can also rename and renumber rooms in a room schedule.*

   - To modify several rooms that need the same name, select the room elements (not the tags) and, in *Properties,* enter the name for the selected set of rooms.

10. Save the project.

Task 2: Add room separation lines.

1. In the *Architecture* tab>*Room & Area* panel, click (Room Separator).
2. Draw a line across the opening at the elevator. The Entry room remains, but the elevator area does not have a room, as shown in Figure 2–17. Click (Modify) to end the command.

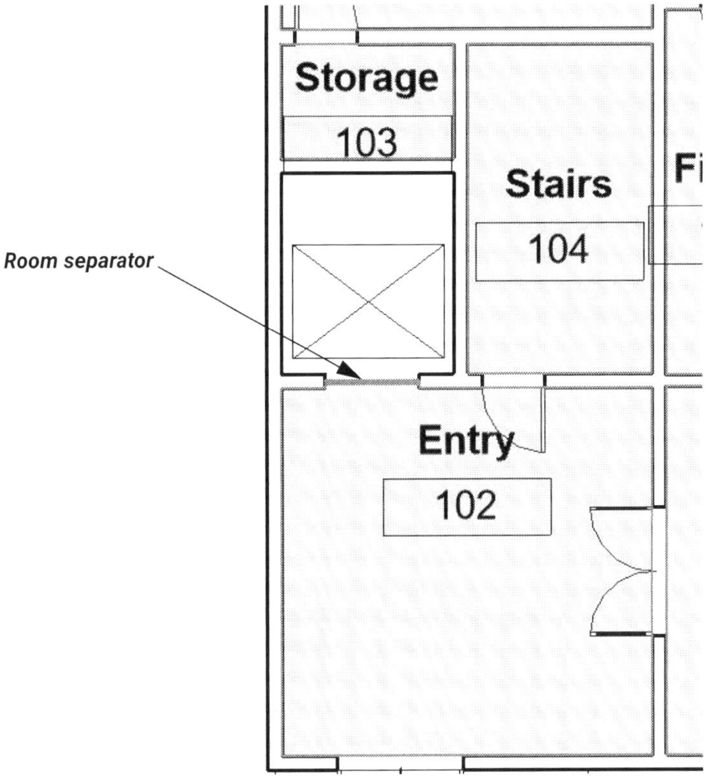

Figure 2–17

3. Add a room and name it **Elevator**.

   Note: *If you have trouble selecting the tag, press <Tab> to cycle through the elements your cursor is hovering over.*

4. In the large room in the upper-right corner, use room separation lines to divide the area, as shown in Figure 2–18. (Room sizes do not have to be exact.) Add rooms to the new spaces and modify the room tag names and numbers.

   Note: *The room number might be different in your drawing.*

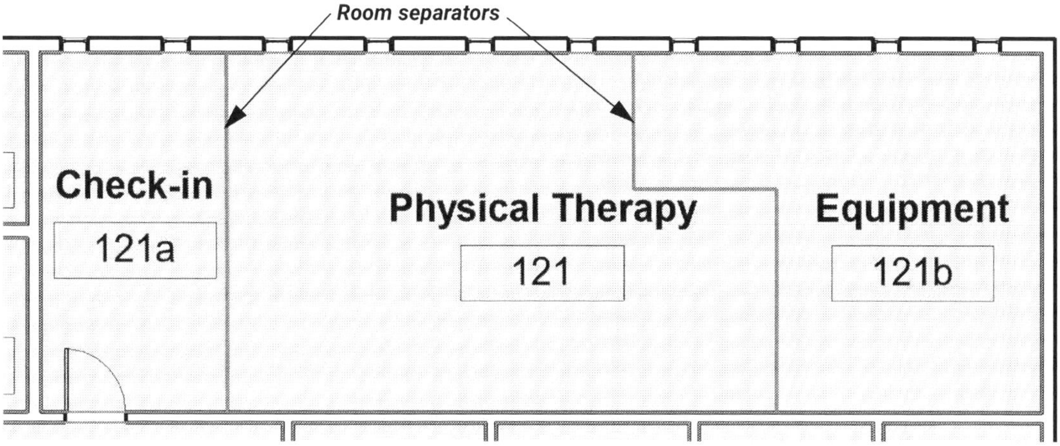

Figure 2–18

5. Save the project.

Task 3: Review a room schedule.

1. In the Project Browser, expand the **Schedule/Quantities** node and select **Room Schedule**. The list of rooms displays.
2. Add information to the *Department* and *Occupancy* columns for individual rooms or groups of rooms. This can be done in plan view by selecting on the room(s) and adding the information in properties or within the schedule.
3. Change the *Number* of some rooms.
4. Change the *Name* of some rooms by using the drop-down menu within the *Name* cell of the room.
5. Save and close the project.

End of practice

2.2 Area Analysis

Rooms calculate areas based on walls and other room bounding elements. However, you might need to define areas that extend across a variety of rooms. In addition, if you are working in a leasing situation, you might need to work with standard building rentable area definitions, as shown in Figure 2–19.

The Area Analysis tools in Revit can accomplish these and related tasks. Many of the processes for area analysis are similar to those for rooms, such as defining boundaries, adding tags, and creating schedules.

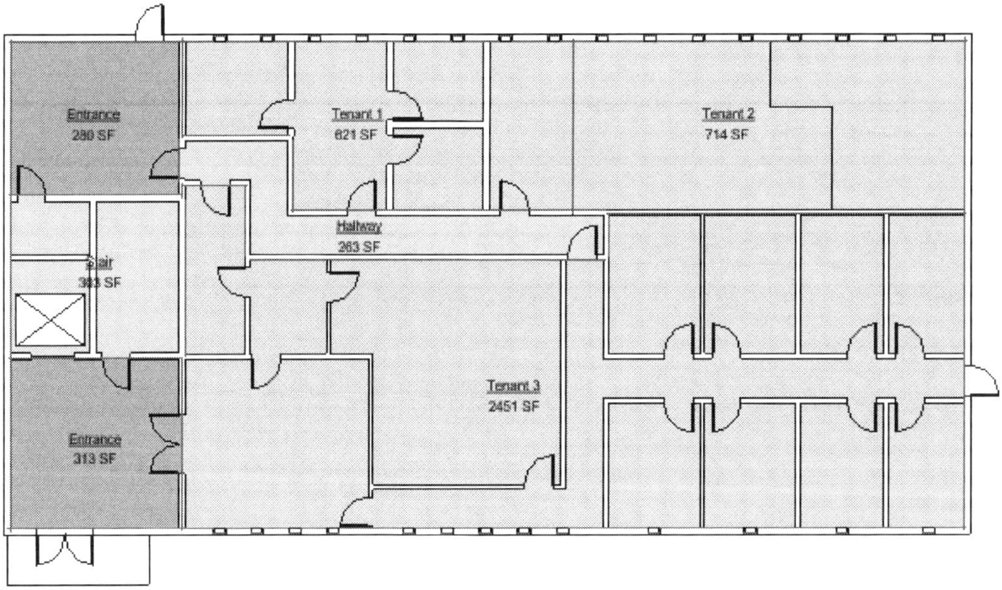

Figure 2–19

Creating Area Plans

You must create an area plan before you can use the Area tools. The plan can provide the overall area of the building footprint, as shown in Figure 2–20, or it can be subdivided into additional areas.

> ***Note:*** *Automatic boundary lines for Rentable space are on the inside of the exterior walls. For Gross Building area plans, the boundary lines are on the outside of the exterior walls.*

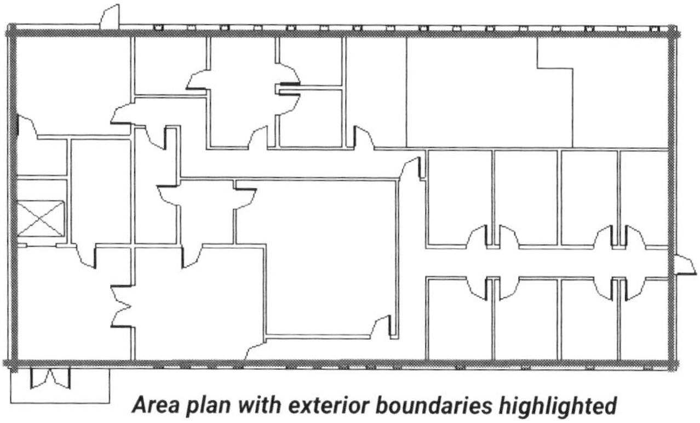

Area plan with exterior boundaries highlighted

Figure 2–20

How To: Create an Area Plan

1. In the *Architecture* tab>*Room & Area* panel, expand (Area) and click (Area Plan).
2. In the *New Area Plan* dialog box, in the *Type* drop-down list, select the type of area plan that you want to create, as shown in Figure 2–21. The standard templates include two types: **Rentable** and **Gross Building**.

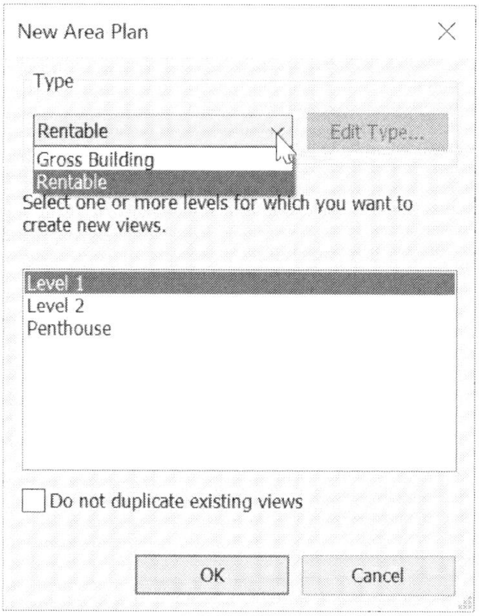

Figure 2–21

*Note: If the **Do not duplicate existing views** option is selected, you will only see views that have not been used to create an area plan.*

3. Select the level you want to create the area plan view for. You can select more than one if needed.
4. Click **OK**.
5. An alert box opens, as shown in Figure 2–22. Click **Yes**.

   Note: *If you do not automatically create boundary lines around the external walls, you need to add them later.*

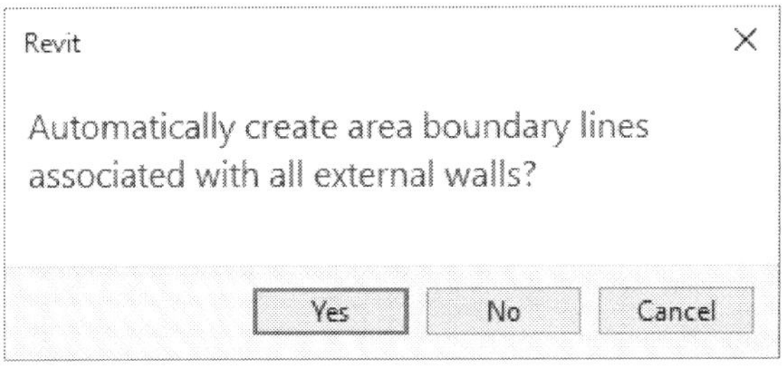

Figure 2–22

- Area plans are created for the selected levels. Each area plan is a separate view. They are listed in the Project Browser in the *Area Plans* area and divided by type, as shown in Figure 2–23.

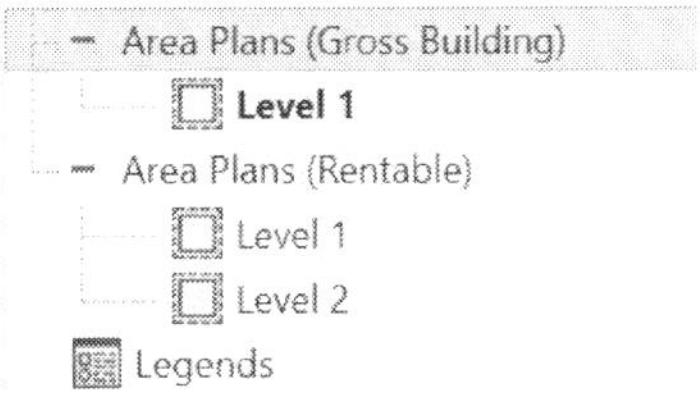

Figure 2–23

Placing Area Boundaries

The next step in creating an area analysis is to add *area boundary* lines in the area plan to define sections of the building, such as offices, stores, and common areas, as shown in Figure 2–24.

> ***Note:*** *The area's type controls the precise location of boundary lines with respect to the walls. For a description of the area measurement rules for each area type, see the Revit Help files.*

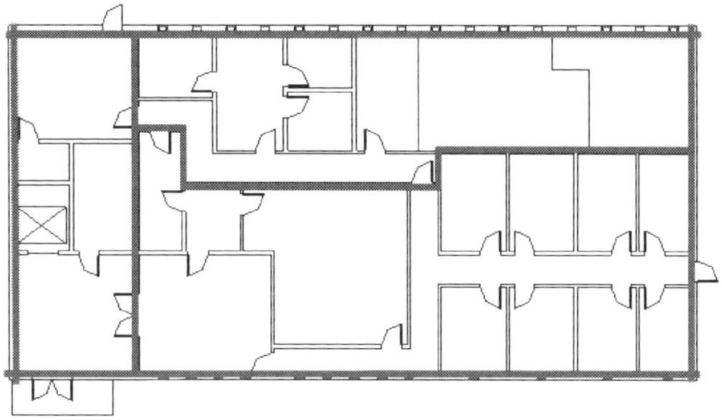

Area boundaries displayed in heavy lines

Figure 2–24

- Area boundaries display in a blue/purple line color.
- Gross Building area plans automatically include the area element.

How To: Create an Area Boundary

1. Open the Area Plan you want to work in.
2. In the *Architecture* tab>*Room & Area* panel, click (Area Boundary).
3. In the *Modify | Place Area Boundary* tab>*Area Boundary* panel, select **Apply Area Rules** so that the boundary lines will move to the face or center of the walls according to the type of area you specify later.
4. In the *Modify | Place Area Boundary* tab>*Draw* panel, use the sketch tools to draw the boundaries or select walls to specify them. Use the modify tools, such as **Trim/Extend to Corner**, as needed.

Adding Areas

Once you have created the area plan and added boundaries to separate areas, you are ready to add area elements, as shown in Figure 2–25. These elements are similar to rooms in that they include much more than just a name for the area.

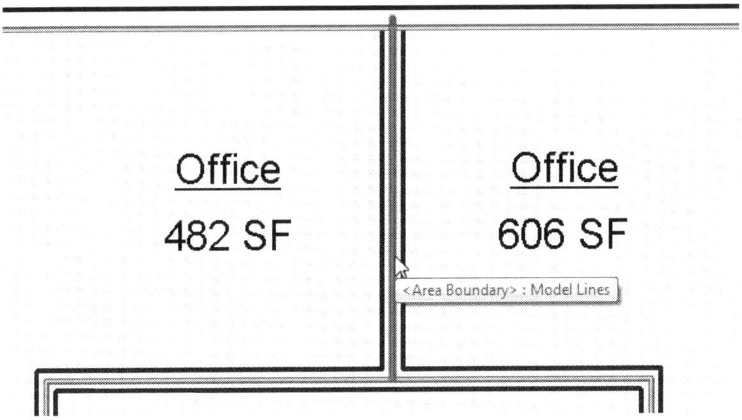

Figure 2–25

- To have the area background display, in the *Visibility/Graphic Overrides* dialog box, expand *Areas* and select **Color Fill**.
- Area information can be displayed in Gross Area or Rentable Area schedules that include the area, name, type, and other options.

How To: Add Areas

1. In the *Architecture* tab>*Room & Area* panel, expand (Area) and click (Area).
2. Move the cursor over the closed area boundaries on the area plan to highlight the area. Click to place the area within the boundary. You can specify tags for the areas as you go.
3. Continue placing areas as needed.

- When you select one or more area elements, you can set the *Area Type* in Properties, as shown in Figure 2–26. Items that are grayed out (such as the *Area* and *Perimeter*) are automatically updated.

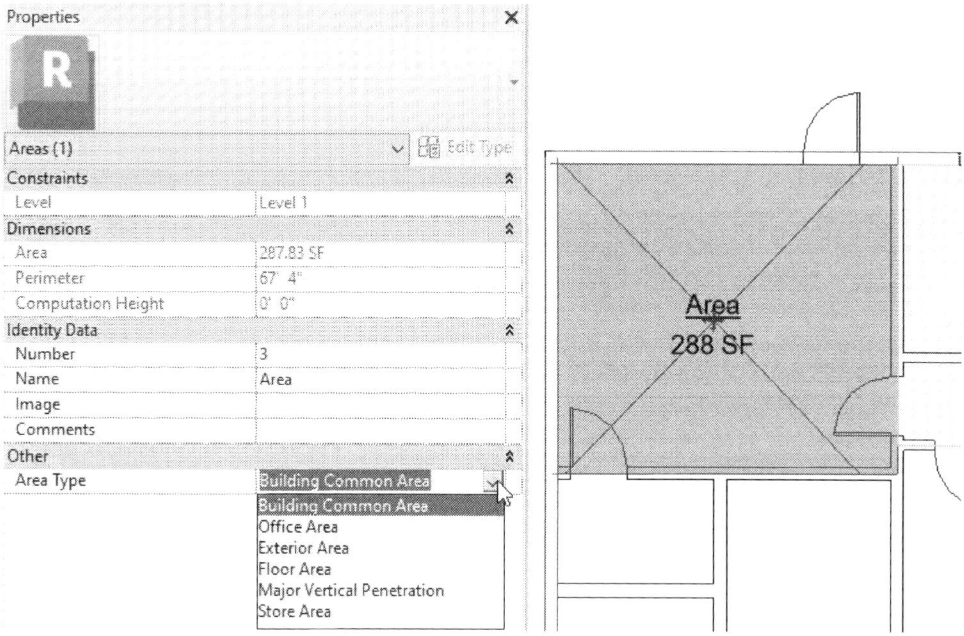

Figure 2–26

- Area types include **Building Common Area**, **Office Area**, **Exterior Area** (such as a patio or balcony), **Floor Area** (utility rooms and corridors), **Major Vertical Penetration**, and **Store Area** (retail), as shown above in Figure 2–26.
- Modifying the area boundaries or associated walls changes the calculated area in the tag.
- In the *Architecture* tab>*Room & Area* panel, click (Tag Area) if you need to add area tags later.
- You can also use (Tag All Not Tagged).

How To: Create Area Schemes

1. In the *Architecture* tab>*Room & Area* panel, expand the panel title and click (Area and Volume Computations).
2. In the dialog box, select the *Area Schemes* tab.

3. Click **New** to add a new scheme, as shown in Figure 2–27.

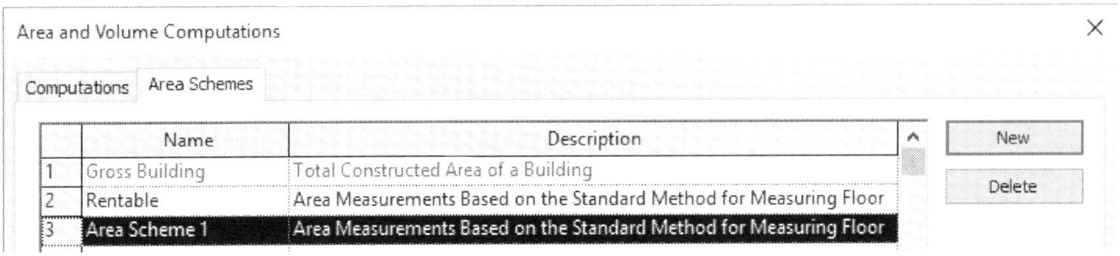

Figure 2–27

4. Rename the scheme and add a description.

- New schemes use the same area types as the rentable scheme and include settings for area calculations and various area boundary locations. These are used in the color schemes.
- To apply the newly created area scheme, create a new area plan.

Practice 2b
Area Analysis

Practice Objectives

- Create a gross area plan and a rentable area plan.
- Modify area types in a schedule.
- Place plans and schedules on a sheet.

In this practice, you will use the Area Analysis tools to create a gross area plan and a rentable area plan. You will then add area boundary lines and areas, as shown in Figure 2–28, and modify the area types using an area schedule.

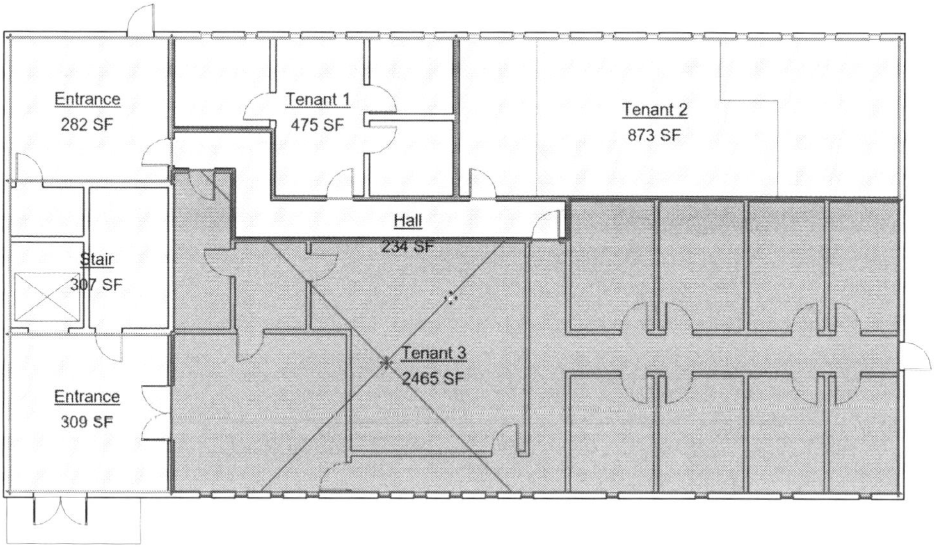

Figure 2–28

- The scale has been changed for clarity.

Task 1: Create a gross area plan.

1. In the practice files folder, open **Medical-Office-Areas.rvt**.
2. In the *Architecture* tab>*Room & Area* panel, expand (Area) and click (Area Plan).
3. In the *New Area Plan* dialog box, set the *Type* to **Gross Building** and select **Level 1**. Ensure that **Do not duplicate existing views** is checked.
4. Click **OK**.

5. In the alert box, click **Yes** (as shown in Figure 2–29) to create area boundary lines at exterior walls and to create an Area Plans (Gross Building) view in the Project Browser, as shown in Figure 2–30.

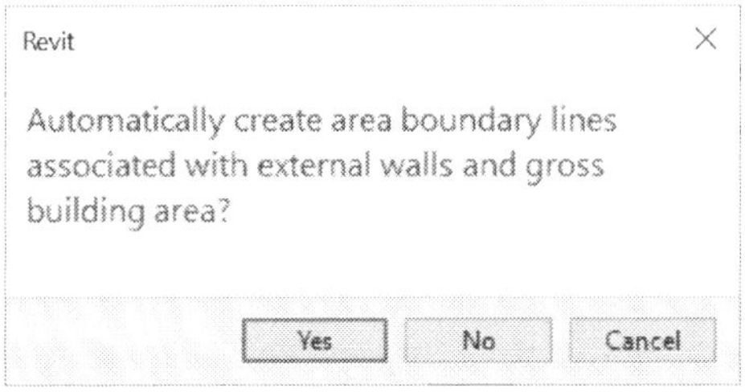

Figure 2–29

6. In the Project Browser, open the **Area Plans (Gross Building) Level 1** view.
7. To see the area, open the *Visibility/Graphic Overrides* dialog box, expand *Areas*, and select **Interior Fill** and **Reference**.
8. Click **OK** and the area displays as shown in Figure 2–30.

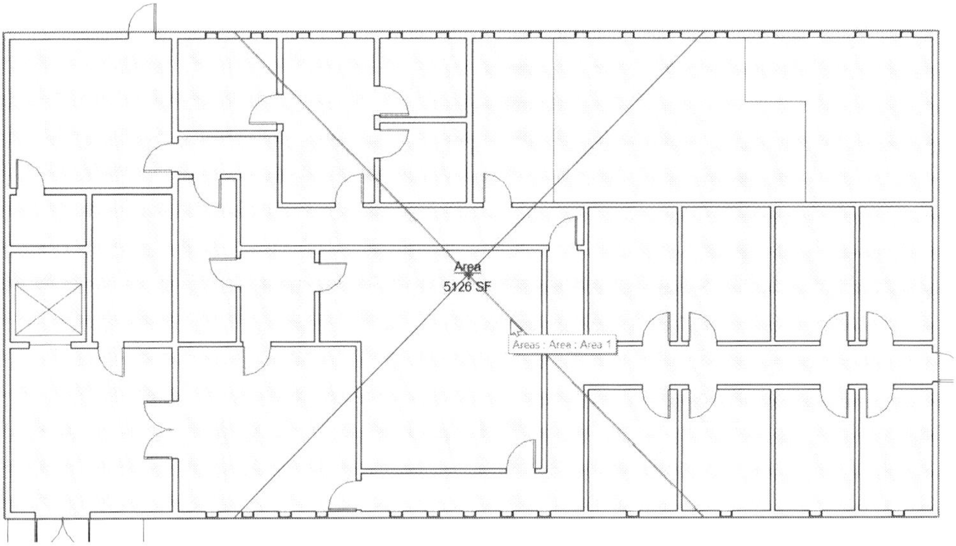

Figure 2–30

9. Save the project.

Task 2: Create a rentable area plan.

1. In the *Architecture* tab>*Room & Area* panel, expand  (Area) and click  (Area Plan).
2. In the *New Area Plan* dialog box, set the *Type* to **Rentable** and select **Level 1**. Click **OK**.

3. In the alert box, click **Yes** to create boundary lines at external walls. The area boundary is on the inside wall of the building, as shown in Figure 2–31. No areas are created automatically.

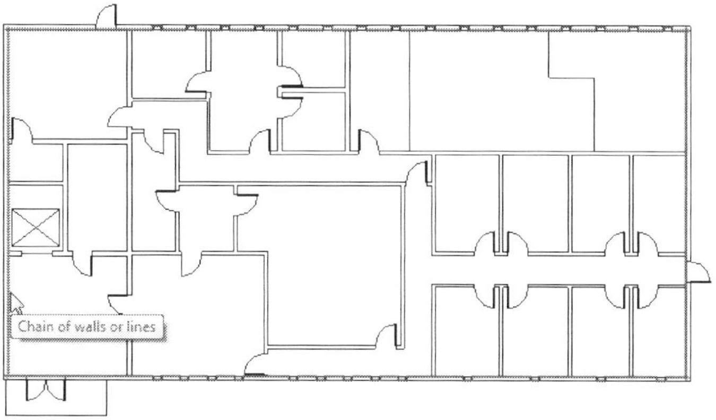

Figure 2–31

4. Open the *Visibility/Graphic Overrides* dialog box, expand *Areas*, and select **Interior Fill**. While you are still in the dialog box, toggle off **Rooms** completely to ensure that you do not select them by mistake.
5. Click **OK**.
6. In the *Architecture* tab>*Room & Area* panel, click (Area Boundary). Use (Pick Lines) and select the walls shown in Figure 2–32. (Only the new lines are shown.) Modify the lines as needed to create closed boundaries.

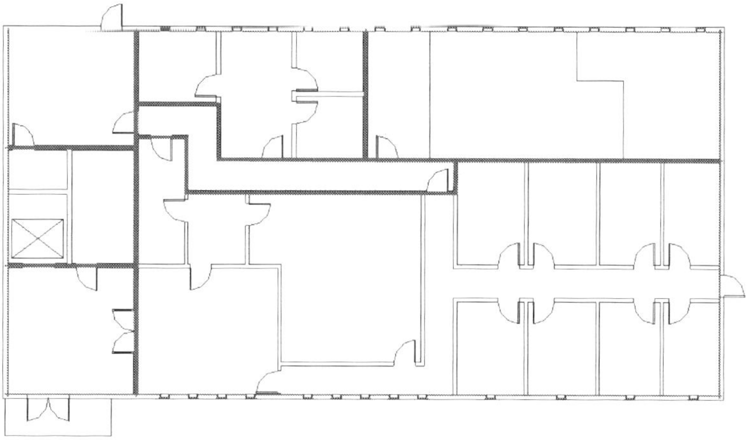

Figure 2–32

7. In the *Architecture* tab>*Room & Area* panel, expand (Area) and click (Area). Place areas and rename them, as shown in Figure 2–33.

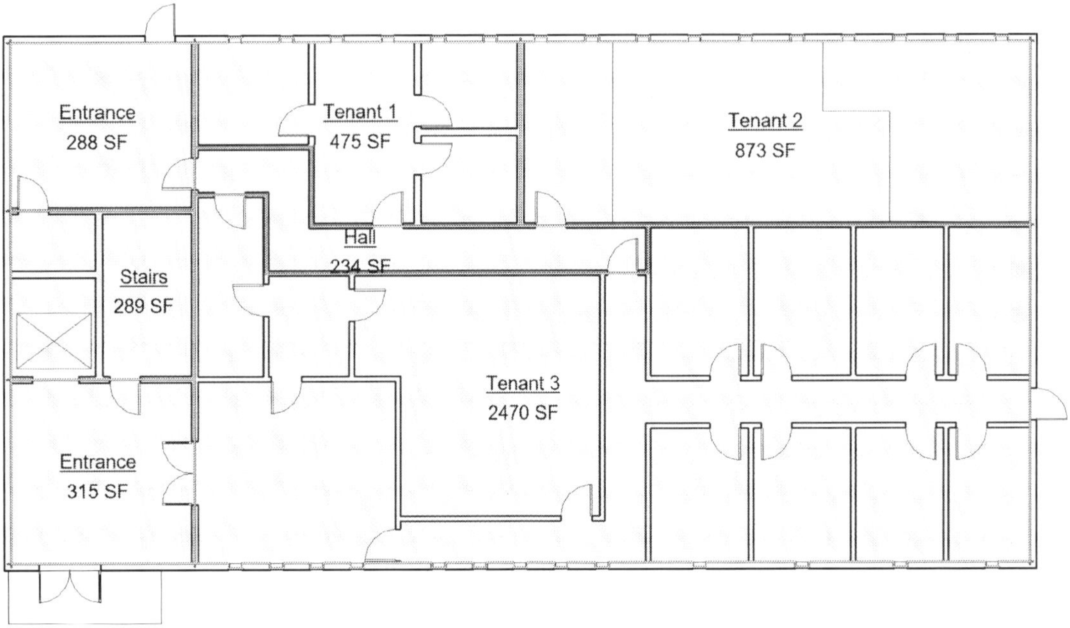

Figure 2–33

8. Save the project.

Task 3: Change area types using a schedule.

1. Open the **Schedules/Quantities: Area Schedule (Rentable)** view. The areas are listed but all of the *Area Types* are set to the default **Building Common Area**, as shown in Figure 2–34.

<Area Schedule (Rentable)>

A	B	C
Name	Area Type	Area
Entrance	Building Common Area	288 SF
Entrance	Building Common Area	315 SF
Hall	Building Common Area	234 SF
Stairs	Building Common Area	289 SF
Tenant 1	Building Common Area	475 SF
Tenant 2	Building Common Area	873 SF
Tenant 3	Building Common Area	2470 SF

Figure 2–34

2. Change the area types in the schedule, as shown in Figure 2–35. The *Area* values change as the *Area Type* is modified.

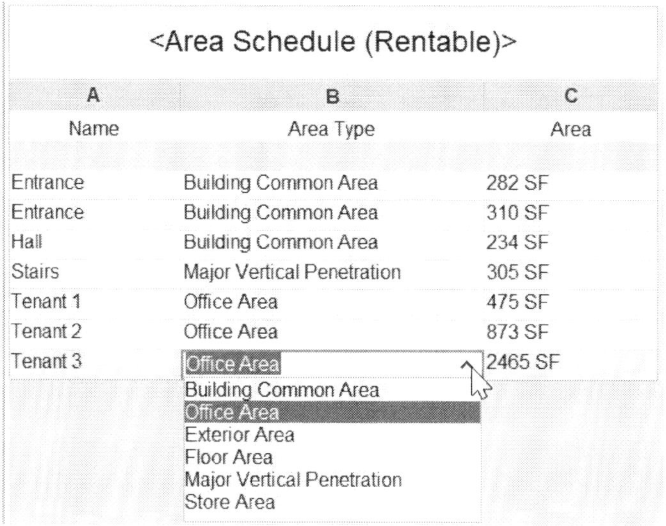

Figure 2–35

3. Save the project.
4. If you have time, create an additional Rentable area plan for Level 2.
5. Add area boundaries to define several areas on Level 2, and add areas to them.

Task 4: Add the schedules to a sheet.

1. Create a new sheet file using the default title block.
2. Add the area plans and schedule to the sheet, as shown in Figure 2–36.
   - Toggle off the elevation markers in the area plans before you add them to the sheet so that they will fit.
   - Toggle off the area interior fill (this does not typically need to print).

Figure 2–36

3. Save and close the project.

End of practice

2.3 Creating Color Schemes

Color schemes added to views show information about rooms and areas. For example, if you add data to the room properties, such as Department or Occupancy, you can create a color scheme showing the groups using rooms. If you are using areas, you can identify the area types on an area plan, as shown in Figure 2–37.

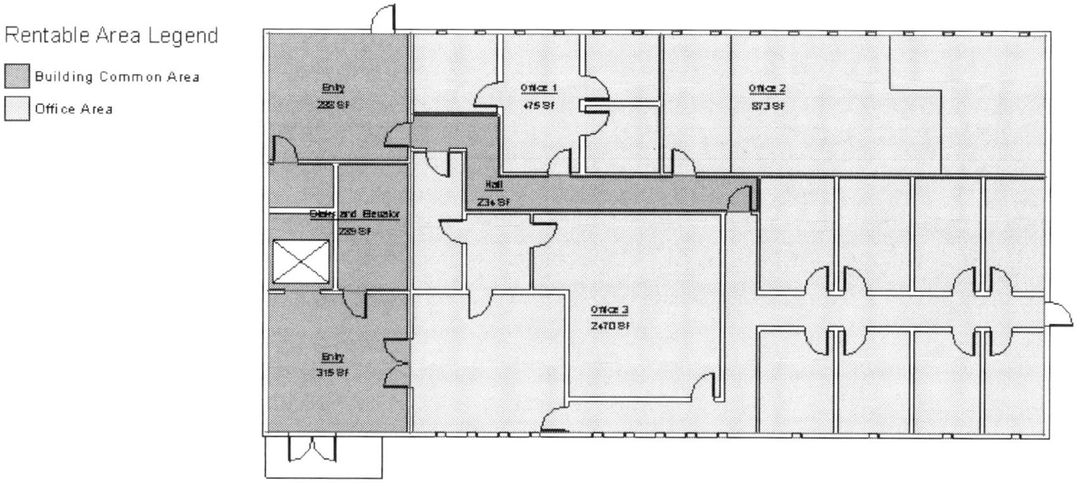

Figure 2–37

How To: Set Up a Color Scheme in a View

1. Create or duplicate a view for the color scheme.
2. In the *Annotate* tab>*Color Fill* panel, click (Color Fill Legend) and place the legend in the view.

3. In the dialog box, select the *Space Type* and *Color Scheme* (as shown in Figure 2–38) and click **OK**. The color scheme is applied to the view, as shown in Figure 2–39.

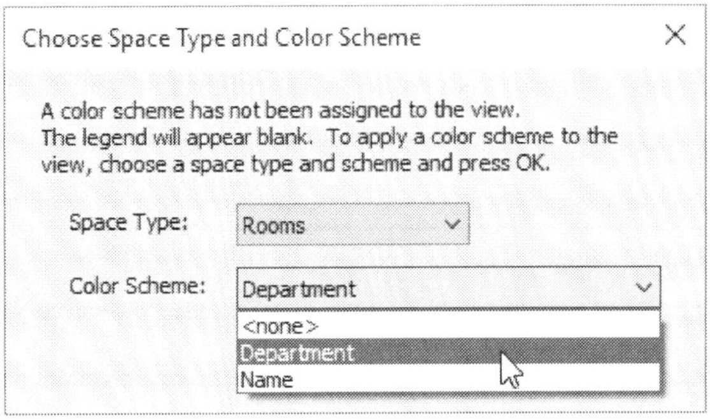

Figure 2–38

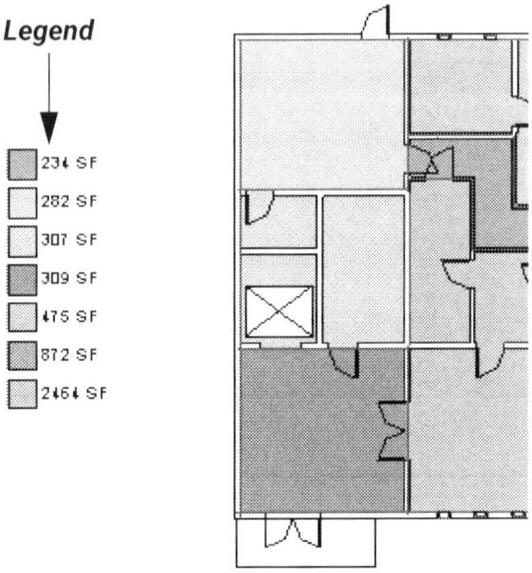

Figure 2–39

- You can also select a color scheme and place the legend later. In Properties, click the button next to the *Color Scheme*, as shown in Figure 2–40. Then, in the *Edit Color Scheme* dialog box, in the *Schemes* area, select the *Category* and an existing scheme.

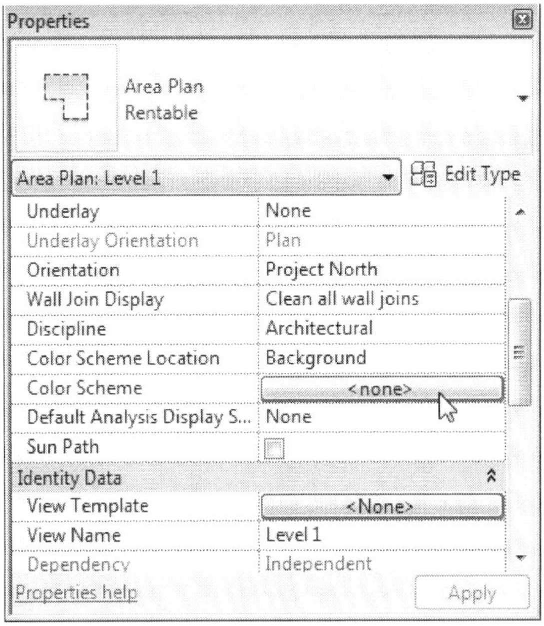

Figure 2–40

- If you change the **Color Scheme** in the *View Properties* dialog box, it also updates the associated legend.
- You can edit the color scheme through properties or select the **Color Fill Legend** and, in the *Modify | Color Fill Legend* tab>*Scheme* panel, click (Edit Scheme).

  Note: *You can set the Color Scheme Location in Properties.*

- The color fill of the scheme can display in background or the foreground of the view, as shown in Figure 2–41. This impacts how components display as well as whether or not the color fill stops at the walls.

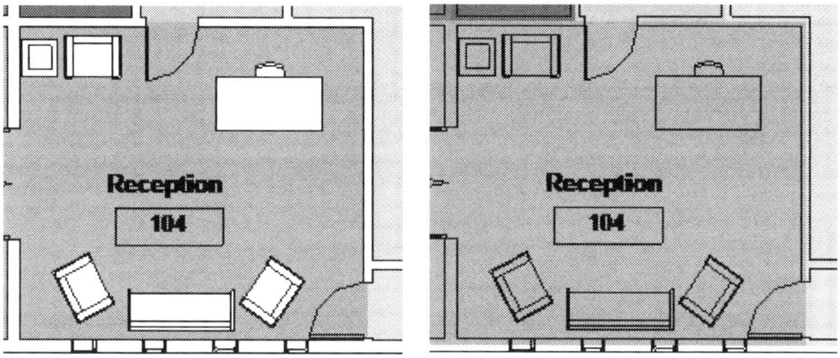

Color fill in background ***Color fill in foreground***

Figure 2–41

How To: Define a Color Scheme

1. In View Properties, click the button next to the *Color Scheme* parameter, or in the *Architecture* tab>*Room & Area* panel, expand the panel title and click (Color Schemes).
2. In the *Edit Color Scheme* dialog box, *Schemes* area, select a *Category*: **Areas (Gross Building)**, **Areas (Rentable)**, or **Rooms**, as shown in Figure 2–42.

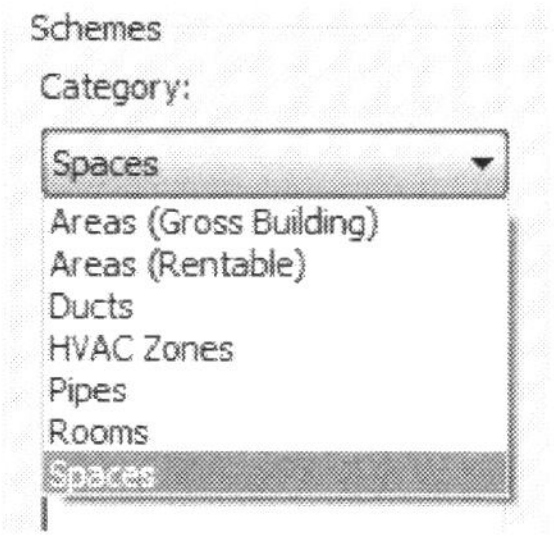

Figure 2–42

- Additional options for MEP related elements may also be available, including Ducts, HVAC Zones, Pipes, and Spaces.

3. Select an existing scheme and click (Duplicate).
4. In the *New Color Scheme* dialog box, enter a new name and click **OK**.
5. In the *Edit Color Scheme* dialog box, in the *Scheme Definition* area, enter a name for the *Title* of the color scheme. This displays when the legend is placed in the view.
6. In the *Color* drop-down list, select an option, as shown in Figure 2–43. The available parameters depend on the type of scheme you are creating.

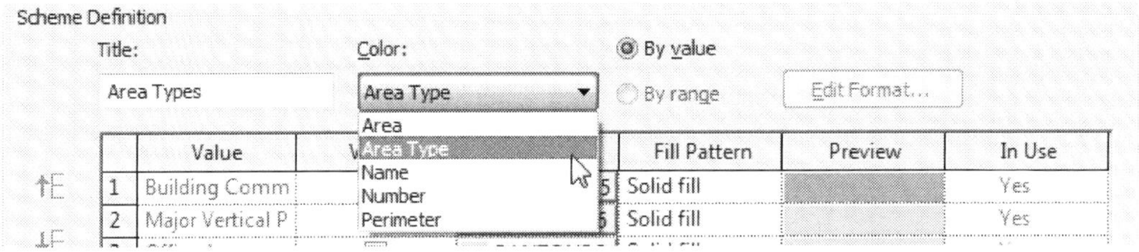

Figure 2–43

7. Select the **By value** or **By range** option to set how the color scheme displays.
8. Click (Add Value) to add more rows to the scheme, as shown in Figure 2–44. Modify the visibility (*Visible* column), *Color*, and *Fill Pattern* as required.

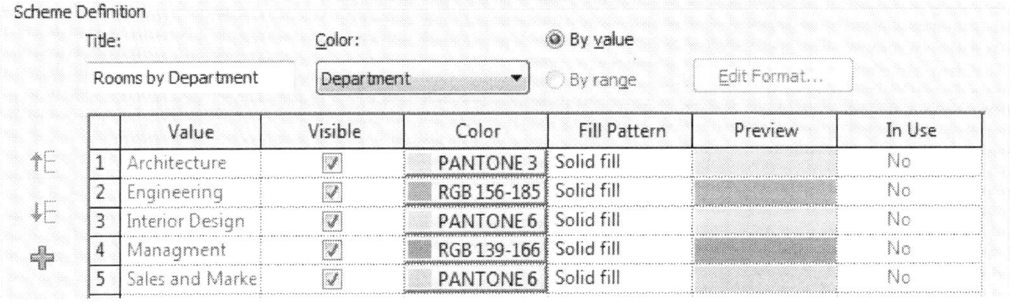

Figure 2–44

9. In the *Options* area, select **Include elements from linked files** if you are using linked files.
10. Click **OK** to finish.

- Click (Move Rows Up) or (Move Rows Down) to change the order of rows in the list.
- To remove a row, select it and click (Remove Value). This option is only available if the parameter data is not being used in the room or area elements in the project.

Color Schemes By Value

If you select the **By value** option, you can modify the visibility, color, and fill pattern of the scheme. The value is assigned by the parameter data in the room or area object.

- Values are automatically updated when you add data to the parameters used in the color scheme. For example, if you create a color by room *Name* and then add another room name in the project, it is also added to the color scheme.

Color Schemes By Range

If you select the **By range** option, you can modify the *At Least* variable and the *Caption*, as well as the visibility, color, and fill pattern, as shown in Figure 2–45.

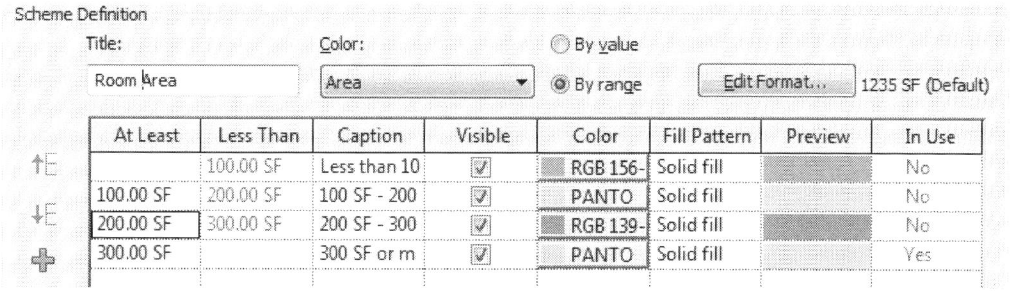

Figure 2–45

- Only the **Area** and **Perimeter** parameters can be set by range.
- Click **Edit Format...** to modify the units display format.
- When you add rows, the new row increments according to the previous distances set or double the value of the first row.

Practice 2c
Create Color Schemes

Practice Objectives

- Apply a color scheme to a view.
- Add a color scheme legend.
- Create By value and By range color schemes.

In this practice, you will add an existing color scheme and a legend to a view, as shown in Figure 2–46. You will also create and apply color schemes **By value** for room names and **By range** for rentable area sizes.

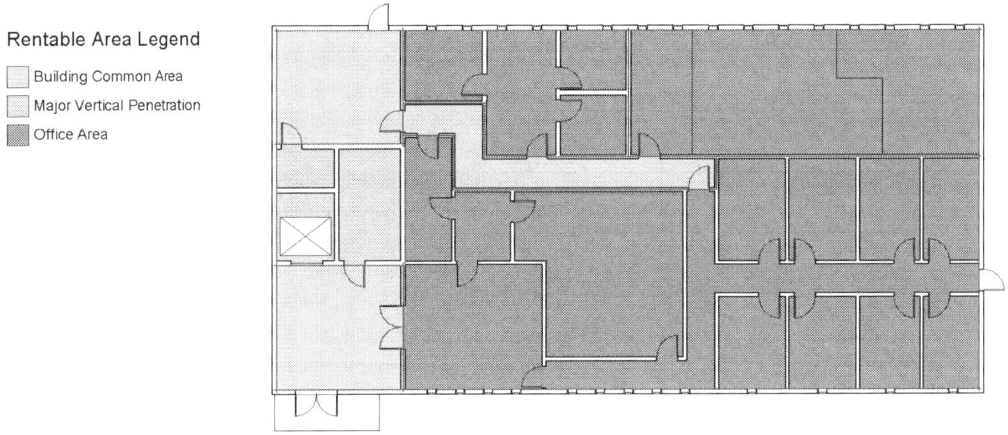

Figure 2–46

Task 1: Apply a color scheme.

1. In the practice files folder, open **Medical-Office-Colors.rvt**.
2. Duplicate the **Area Plans (Rentable): Level 1** view and name it **Level 1 - Rentable Area**.
3. In the *Annotate tab>Color Fill* panel, click (Color Fill Legend) and click to the left of the building to place the legend.
4. In the *Choose Space Type and Color Scheme* dialog box, set the *Space Type* to **Areas (Rentable)** and the *Color Scheme* to **Rentable Area**. Click **OK**.
5. The Legend and floor plan are set to the appropriate color fill, as shown above in Figure 2–46.
6. Save the project.

Task 2: Create a color scheme.

1. Duplicate with detailing the **Area Plans (Rentable): Level 1 - Rentable Area** view and name it **Level 1 - Rentable Area by Size**.
2. Select the legend and in the *Modify | Color Fill Legends* tab>*Scheme* panel, click (Edit Scheme).
3. In the lower-left corner of the *Edit Color Scheme* dialog box, click (Duplicate) to create a copy of the existing area color scheme. Name it **Rentable Area by Size** and click **OK**.
4. In the *Scheme Definition* area, enter **Rentable Area by Size** for the *Title* and select **Area** in the *Color* drop-down list.
   - Whenever a warning about colors not being preserved displays, click **OK**.
5. Select **By range**. The default ranges display, as shown in Figure 2–47.

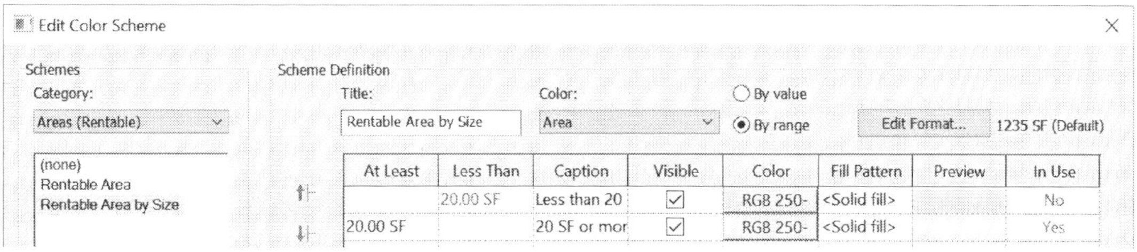

Figure 2–47

6. In the second row, set the *At Least* value to **200 SF**.
7. Click (Add Value). This should create a value of **400 SF**.
8. Select **400 SF** and click (Add Value) again. Continue working down the menu until you have **1000 SF** in the *At Least* value list, as shown in Figure 2–48.

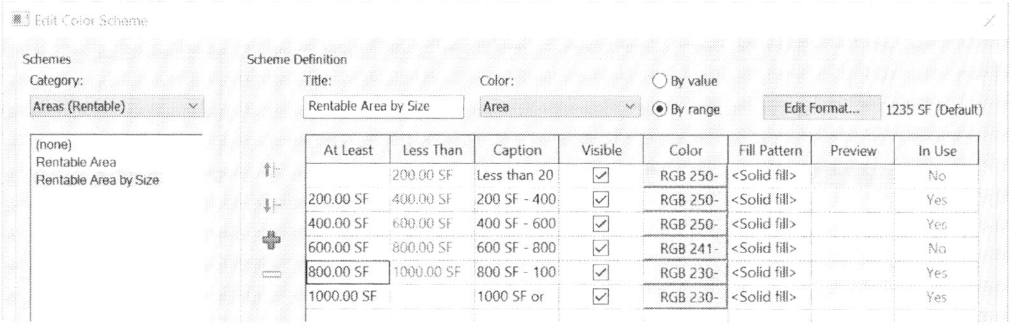

Figure 2–48

9. Click **OK** to close the dialog box. The new color scheme is applied to the view, as shown in Figure 2–49.

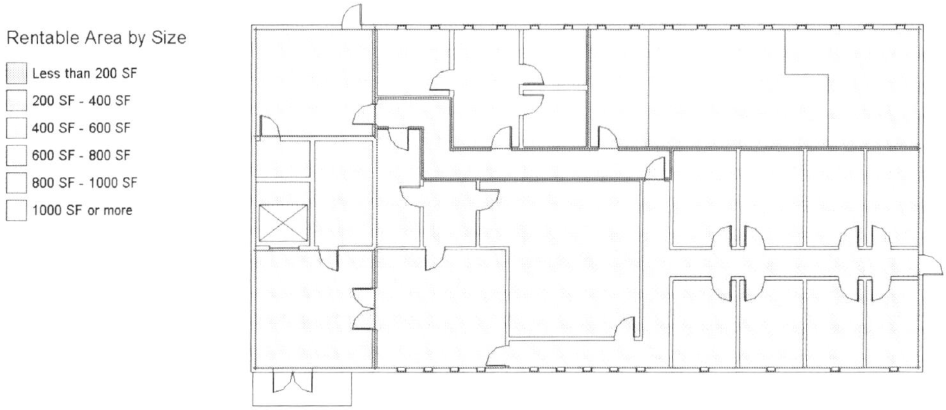

Figure 2–49

10. Save the project.

Task 3: Create a room color scheme.

1. In the *Architecture* tab>*Room & Area* panel, expand the panel title and select (Color Schemes).
2. In the *Edit Color Scheme* dialog box, set the *Category* to **Rooms**.
3. Select **Department** and click (Duplicate) to create a copy of the existing room color scheme. Name it **Room Names**.
4. Click **OK**.
5. In the *Scheme Definition* area, enter **Room Names** for the *Title* and select **Name** in the *Color* drop-down list.
6. The values are automatically applied according to the room names used in the project, as shown in part in Figure 2–50.

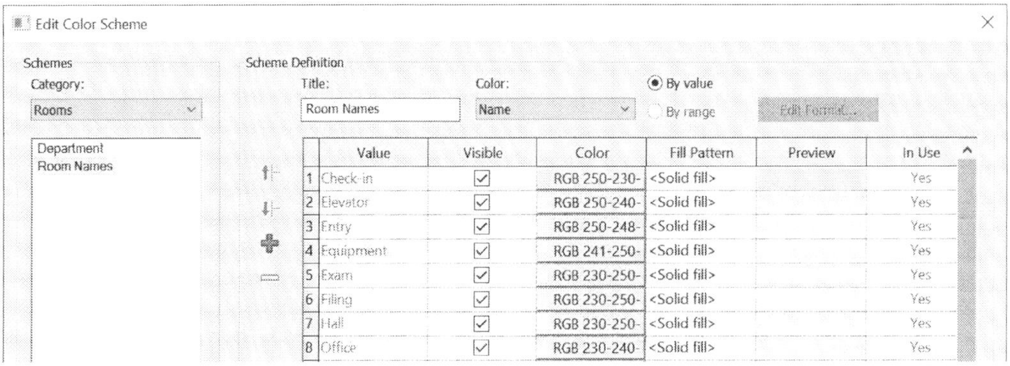

Figure 2–50

7. Click (Add Value) and create a new value named **Lab**. The new Lab value is set to **No** in the *In Use* column, as shown in Figure 2–51.

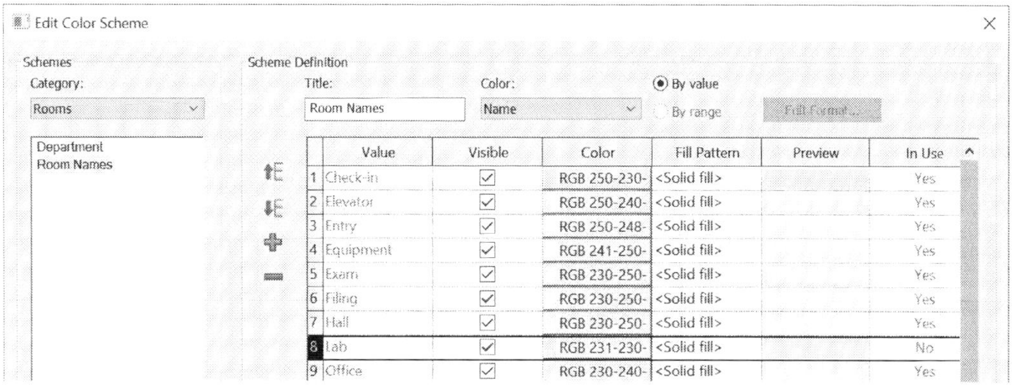

Figure 2–51

8. Modify the color for the **Lab** by clicking on the RGB value in the *Color* column to open the *Color* dialog box. Change the colors to *Red:* **193**, *Green:* **191**, and *Blue:* **242**, as shown in Figure 2–52.

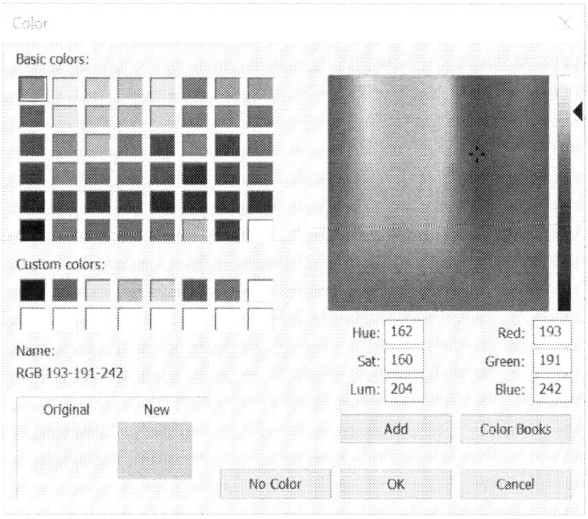

Figure 2–52

9. Click **OK** twice. The scheme is not applied to the current view when you create it this way.
10. Open the **Floor Plans: Level 1 - Rooms** view.
11. In Properties, select the **Color Scheme** button.
12. In the *Edit Color Scheme* dialog box, set the *Category* to **Rooms**, select the **Room Names** color scheme, and click **OK**.
13. In the *Annotate* tab>*Color Fill* panel, click (Color Fill Legend).

14. Place the legend to the side of the building. It automatically displays using the current color scheme, as shown in Figure 2–53.

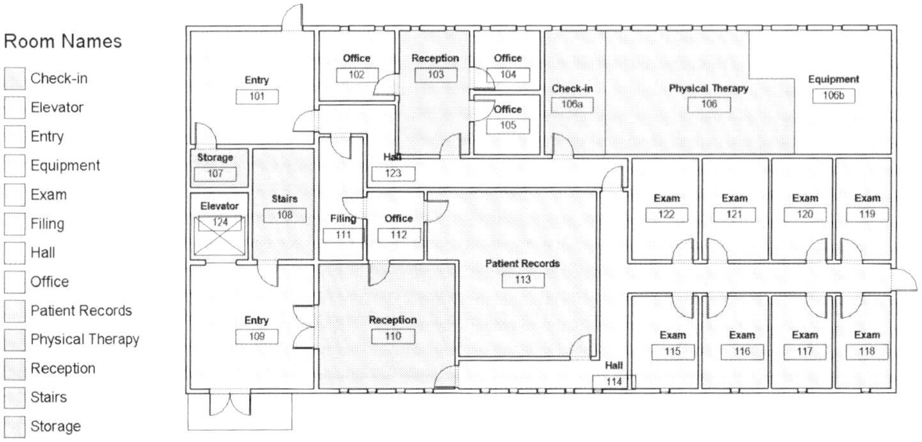

Figure 2–53

15. Change the name of one of the offices to **Lab**. The color updates to match the Lab value you added to the color scheme.

16. Change the name of one of the exam rooms to **Mechanical**. A new value is automatically added to the color scheme, as shown in Figure 2–54.

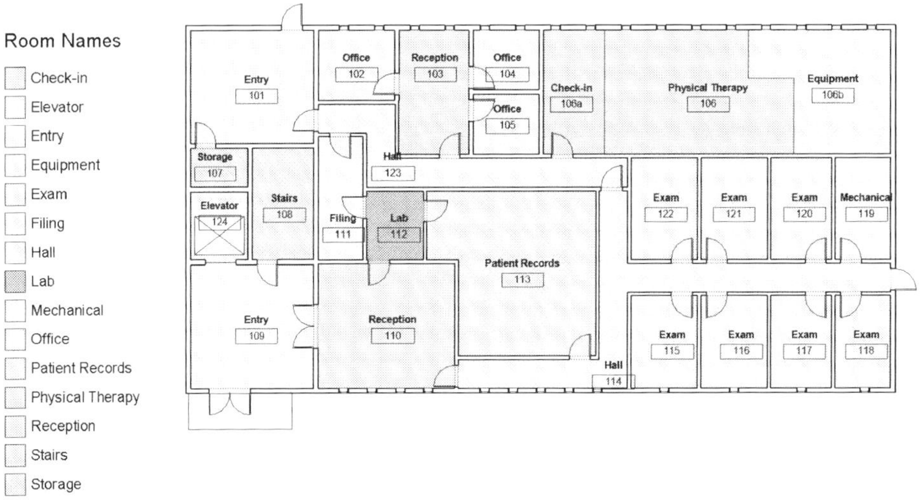

Figure 2–54

17. Save and close the project.

End of practice

Chapter Review Questions

1. Which of the following element types can define the boundaries of a room? (Select all that apply.)
    a. Walls
    b. Retaining Walls
    c. Floors
    d. Roofs

2. Where can you set the height of a room, as shown in Figure 2–55? (Select all that apply.)

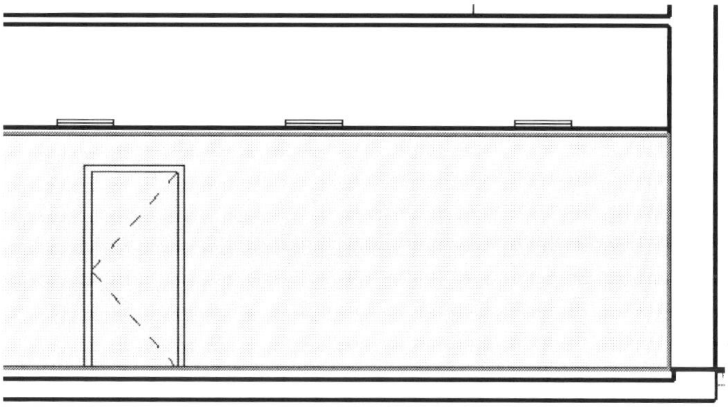

Figure 2–55

    a. In Properties, before or after you place the room.
    b. In a section, after you place the room.
    c. In a 3D view.
    d. In the Options Bar, before you place the room.

3. In which type of view do you place areas?
    a. Floor Plans
    b. Sections
    c. Area Plans
    d. Elevations

4. Which of the following need to be in place before you add areas to an area plan, as shown in Figure 2–56?

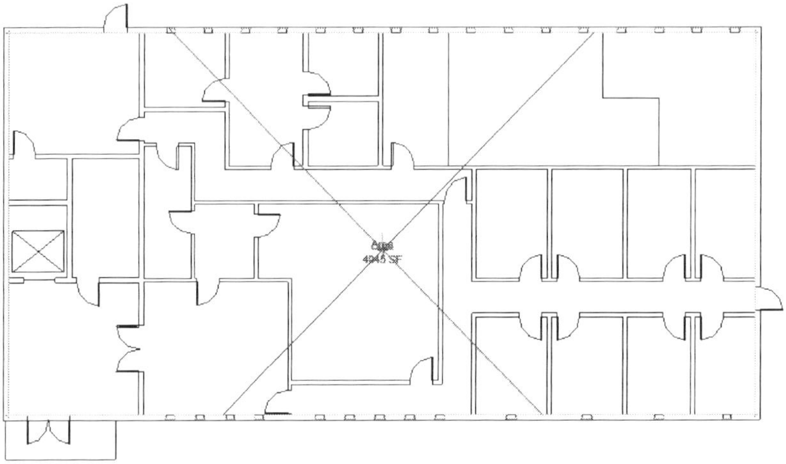

Figure 2–56

   a. Room boundaries
   b. Room separation lines
   c. Area separation lines
   d. Area boundaries

5. If you want to have more than one color scheme that uses the same level and rooms, you need to create a view for each scheme.

   a. True
   b. False

6. If you are creating a color scheme to display the individual area of each room, as shown in Figure 2–57, which of the following do you use?

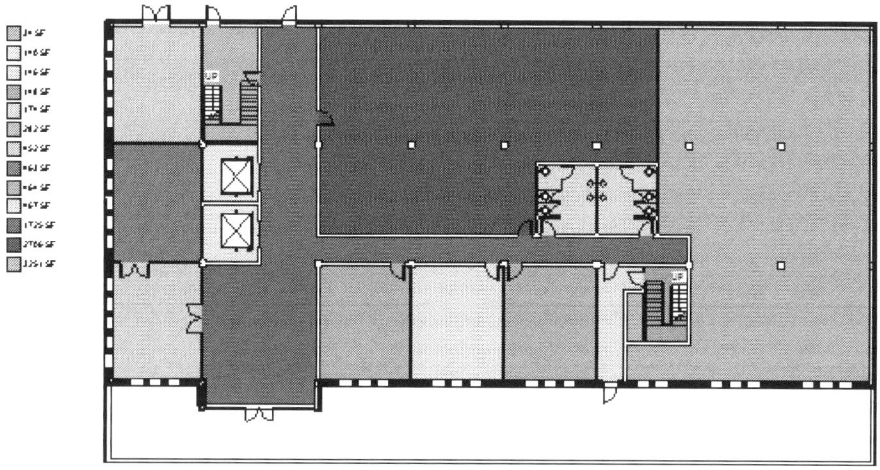

Figure 2–57

a. By value

b. By range

Command Summary

Button	Command	Location
	**Area**	• **Ribbon:** *Architecture* tab>*Room & Area* panel, expand Area
	**Area and Volume Computations**	• **Ribbon:** *Architecture* tab>*Room & Area* panel, expand panel title
	**Area Boundary**	• **Ribbon:** *Architecture* tab>*Room & Area* panel
	**Area Plan**	• **Ribbon:** *Architecture* tab>*Room & Area* panel, expand Area
	**Color Fill Legend**	• **Ribbon:** *Annotate* tab>*Color Fill* panel
	**Color Schemes**	• **Ribbon:** *Architecture* tab>*Room & Area* panel, expand panel title
	**Room**	• **Ribbon:** *Architecture* tab>*Room & Area* panel • **Shortcut:** RM
	**Room Separator**	• **Ribbon:** *Architecture* tab>*Room & Area* panel
	**Tag All Not Tagged**	• **Ribbon:** *Architecture* tab>*Room & Area* panel, expand Tag Room or Tag Area
	**Tag Area/Area Tag**	• **Ribbon:** *Architecture* tab>*Room & Area* panel or *Annotate* tab>*Tags* panel
	**Tag Room/Room Tag**	• **Ribbon:** *Architecture* tab>*Room & Area* panel or *Annotate* tab>*Tags* panel • **Shortcut:** RT

Chapter 3

Visualization

For the architectural community, one of the most powerful features of Revit® is the ability to create views that enable you to display the building design in its full 3D expression. Not only can you create perspective views, but you can also make any 2D or 3D view look realistic or like it was hand-sketched. You can create exploded orthographic views – each of which can help others understand your design. You can also visually test the design using sun studies that show exactly how sun and shadows would impact the building.

Learning Objectives

- Create perspective views using the Camera tool.
- Modify a view using graphic display options, such as Sketchy Lines and Depth Cueing.
- Displace elements in a view to create an exploded view.
- Set True North and the project location to prepare a project for solar studies.
- Graphically display sun locations and their impact on the project using the sun path with shadows.
- Create solar studies, including Still, Single Day, and Multi-Day studies.

3.1 Creating Perspective Views

Perspectives, as shown in Figure 3–1, provide more realistic views of buildings that can help designers visualize and pass on information to others who might not understand plans and elevations. They are easily created using the **Camera** command by specifying a camera location and a target.

Figure 3–1

- You can add, delete, modify, and move elements in 3D perspective views.
- Perspective views can be placed on sheets.

How To: Create a Perspective

1. Open a plan view.
2. In the Quick Access Toolbar (or the *View* tab>*Create* panel), expand (3D View) and click (Camera).
3. In the Options Bar, select **Perspective** and set an *Offset* for the camera *From* one of the levels, as shown in Figure 3–2. This is the height of the camera.
   - To create orthographic views, clear the **Perspective** option and select a scale for the view.

Figure 3–2

4. Select a point on the drawing to place the camera.

5. Select another point for the target location, as shown in Figure 3–3.

   Note: *To create an interior perspective, place the camera inside the room.*

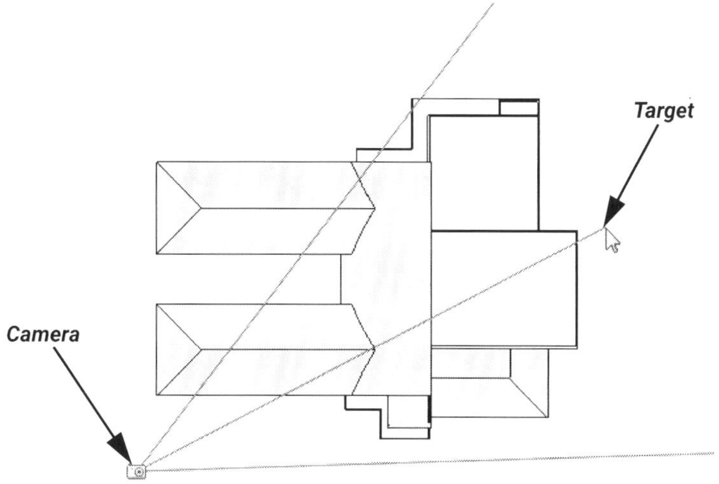

Figure 3–3

6. A new 3D view is created and opened, as shown in Figure 3–4.

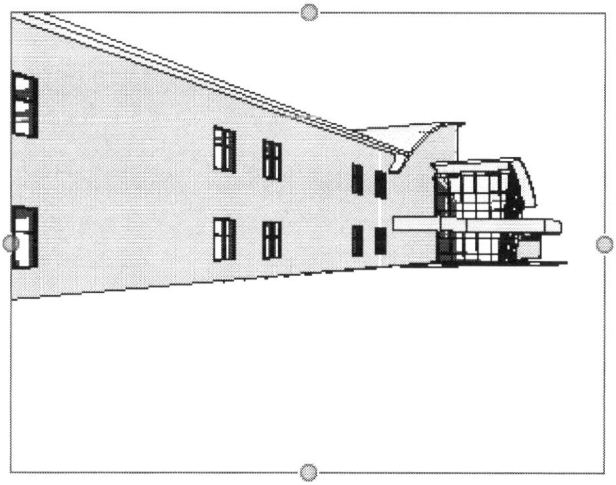

Figure 3–4

7. In the Project Browser, right-click on the new 3D view and rename it.

- If you do not want the 3D View to be cropped, in the View Control Bar, click (Do Not Crop View).

Modifying Perspectives

Perspectives can be modified by changing the camera information using controls or the camera properties. You can also modify the view size through a dialog box.

- Use the ViewCube or the mouse (<Shift>+middle mouse button) to rotate the view.
- You can switch between Perspective and Isometric mode by right-clicking on the ViewCube and selecting **Perspective** or **Orthographic**. You can also change this in the view properties.
- To change the field of view, select the shape handles of the crop region and manipulate them so that they show the required part of the building, as shown in Figure 3–5.

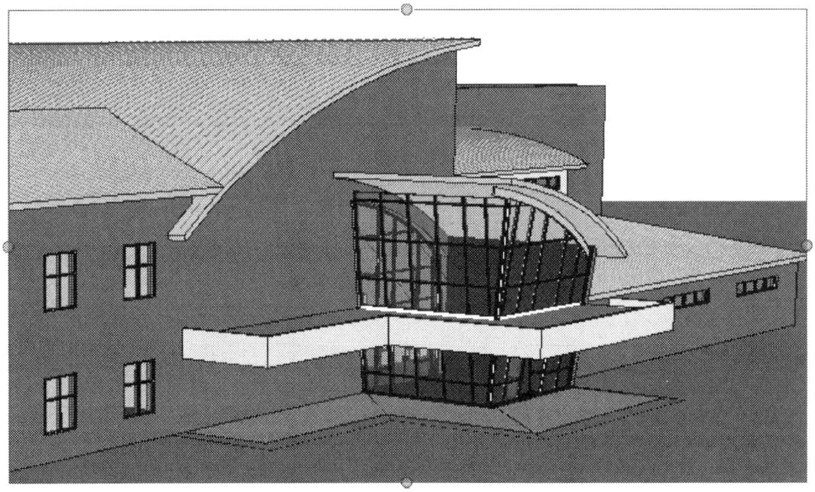

Figure 3–5

- To toggle off the box around the perspective, in Properties, clear the **Crop Region Visible** option or in the View Control Bar, click (Hide Crop Region).
- Change the *Visual Style* to **Shaded**, **Consistent Colors**, **Textures**, or **Realistic** to see a representation of the materials.
  - The (Realistic) visual style is ideal for managing light exposure, shadows, and Rich Photorealistic Content (RPC) components.

How To: Modify the Camera

1. Open the 3D camera view and one other view and tile them.
2. Select the edge of the camera view crop region and the camera displays in the other view.
   - Another way to make a camera display in a plan view: right-click on the perspective view in the Project Browser and select **Show Camera**.
3. Drag the controls for the camera, target, and far clip plane, as shown in Figure 3–6, to new locations.

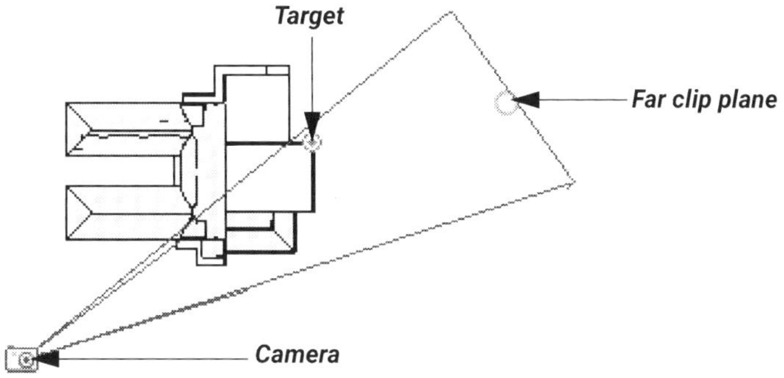

Figure 3–6

- The target is what the eye sees. The far clip plane needs to be located beyond the information you want to see in the view.

- You can make changes to cameras in Properties by scrolling down to the *Extents* and *Camera* sections, as shown in Figure 3–7.

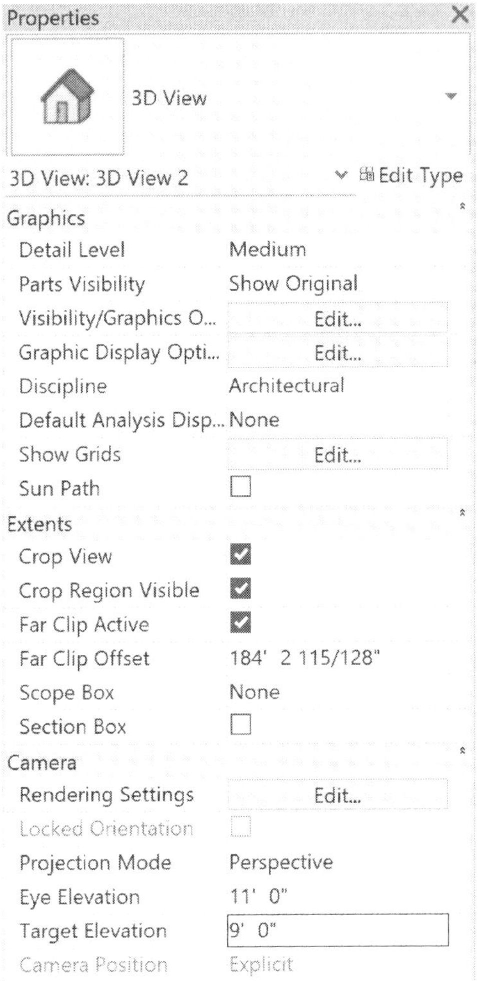

Figure 3–7

- For a true 2-point perspective, ensure that both the *Target Elevation* and *Eye Elevation* are the same height.

How To: Modify View Size

1. In the *Modify | Cameras* tab>*Crop* panel, click  (Size Crop).
2. In the *Crop Region Size* dialog box (shown in Figure 3–8), specify an exact *Width* and *Height* for the view.

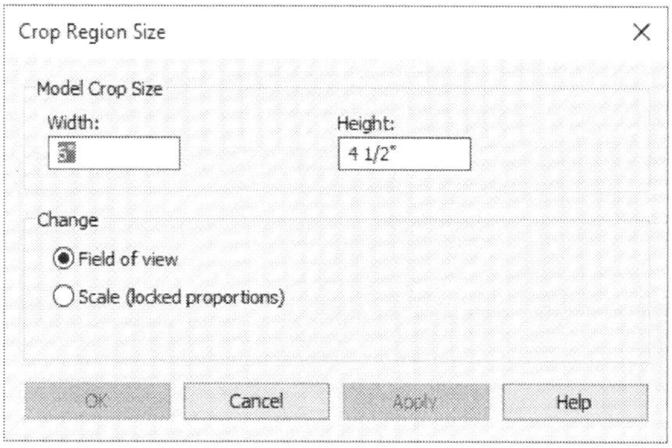

Figure 3–8

- Select **Field of view** to resize both the *Height* and *Width* of the crop region.
- Select **Scale (locked proportions)** to lock the proportions of the crop region. When you change the width, the height adjusts proportionally.
- Alternatively, in the view you can use the control grips to resize the crop view, as shown in Figure 3–9.

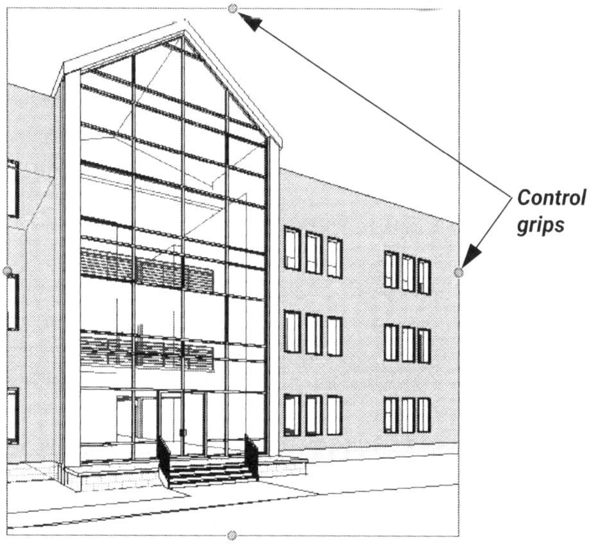

Figure 3–9

Hint: Surface Transparency Sliders

While creating a perspective view, you are sometimes required to see behind a wall. You can toggle off an individual wall using **Hide in View>Elements,** or make the wall transparent as shown Figure 3–10.

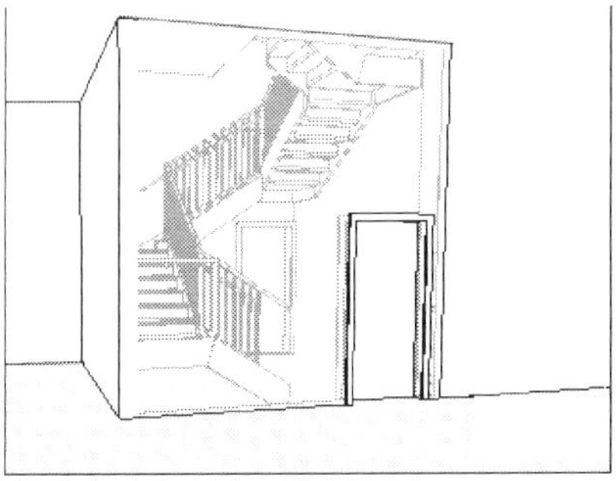

Figure 3–10

How To: Adjust Transparency

1. Select the element(s), right-click, and select **Override Graphics in View>By Element...**.
2. In the *View Specific Element Graphics* dialog box, expand the *Surface Transparency* area and adjust the slider bar as required, as shown in Figure 3–11.

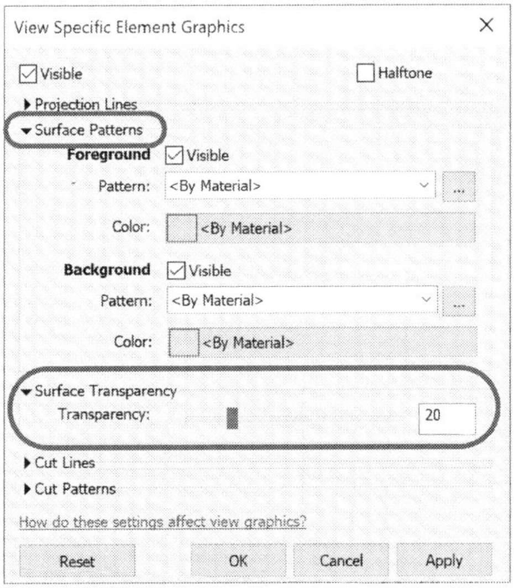

Figure 3–11

- Surface patterns (such as brick) are not affected by the transparency setting; so, you may want to toggle them off in the *Surface Patterns* area, when working with transparency.

Practice 3a
Create Perspective Views

Practice Objective

- Create exterior and interior perspective views.

In this practice, you will create an interior perspective and an exterior perspective, as shown in Figure 3–12.

Figure 3–12

Task 1: Create an exterior perspective view.

1. In the practice files folder, open **Midrise-Perspective.rvt**.
2. Open the **Floor Plans: Level 1** view.
3. In the *View* tab>*Create* panel, expand (3D View) and click (Camera).

4. Create an exterior perspective showing the front of the building (as shown in Figure 3–13).

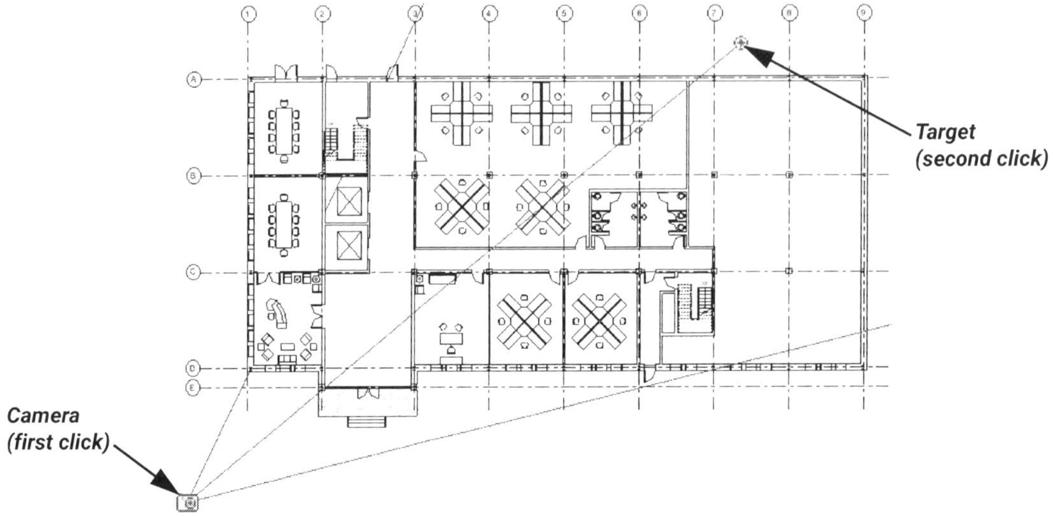

Figure 3–13

5. In the Project Browser, rename the *3D View 1* to **Front Perspective**. Set the *Visual Style* to **Consistant Colors**.
6. Using the crop region controls, modify the camera to see the entire building. Hold <Shift>+middle mouse button to rotate the view.
7. Manipulate the camera view by adjusting the *Eye Elevation* and *Target Elevation* parameters in the *Camera* section in Properties as needed to modify the view. Figure 3–14 shows an example of adjusting the various options for a camera view.

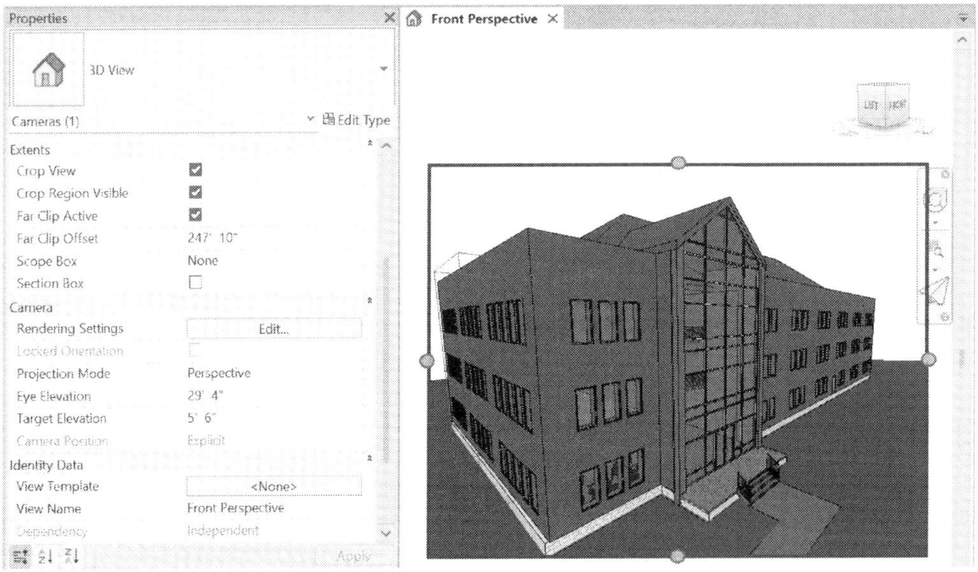

Figure 3–14

Task 2: Create an interior perspective view.

1. Return to the **Level 1** view. Repeat the **Camera** command and create an interior perspective view, as shown in Figure 3–15. Name it **Office Perspective**.

   Note: If the corner of the room does not display, change the far clip view.

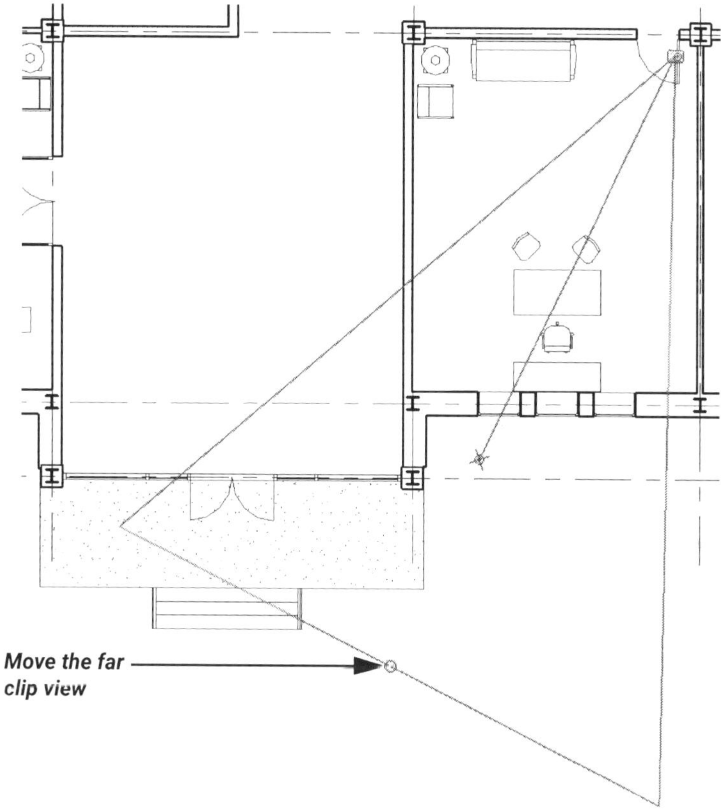

Figure 3–15

2. Adjust the crop region and Properties as needed. Figure 3–16 shows an example of the Office Perspective view.

Figure 3–16

3. Save the project.

End of practice

3.2 Working with Graphic Display Options

Even without creating a rendering, you can set up striking views using graphic display options. These include tools for setting up the model display of surfaces and edges, shadows, sketchy lines for preliminary views, and added depth cueing for automatic lineweight control, and backgrounds as shown in Figure 3–17.

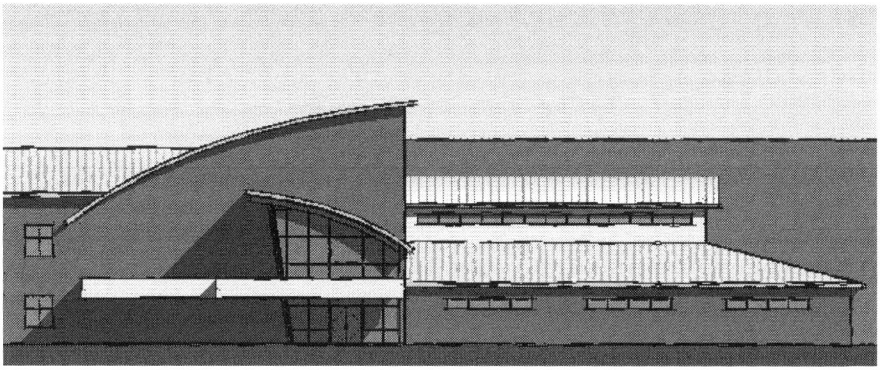

Figure 3–17

- In the View Control Bar, expand the *Visual Style* drop-down list and select **Graphic Display Options...**, as shown in Figure 3–18. Alternatively, you can type **GD** to open the *Graphic Display Options* dialog box.

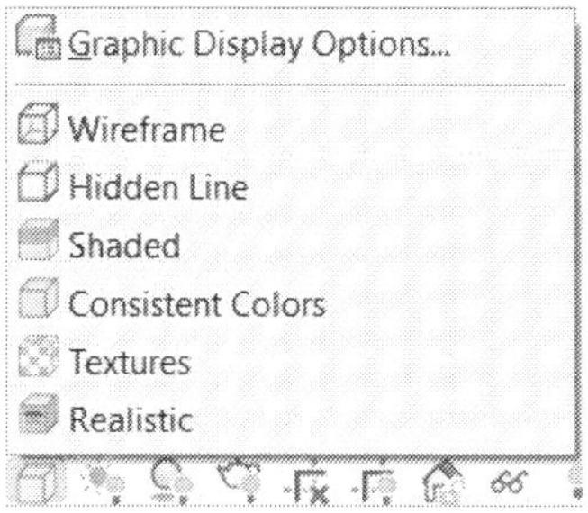

Figure 3–18

- The *Graphic Display Options* dialog box displays, as shown in Figure 3–19.

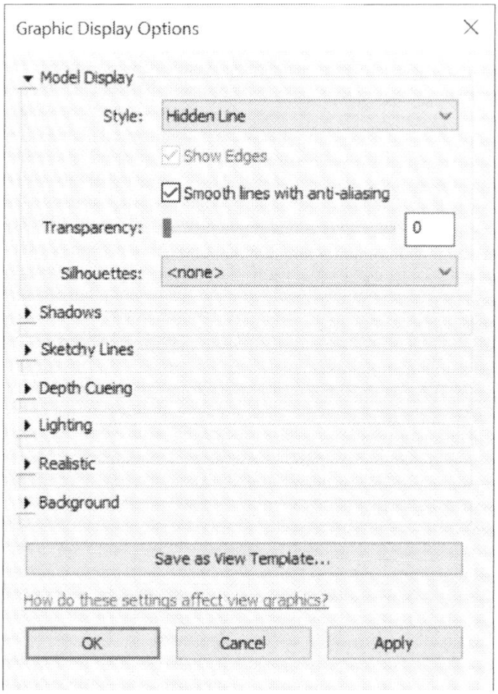

Figure 3–19

- The settings that are selected in the *Graphic Display Options* dialog box can be saved as a view template.

Model Display

In the *Graphic Display Options* dialog box, in the *Model Display* area, you can set the visual *Style* and *Transparency* (for all objects in the view) and select a linetype from the *Silhouettes* drop-down list. This override enables you to specify the type of lines used to outline various parts of a building in a view, as shown in Figure 3–20.

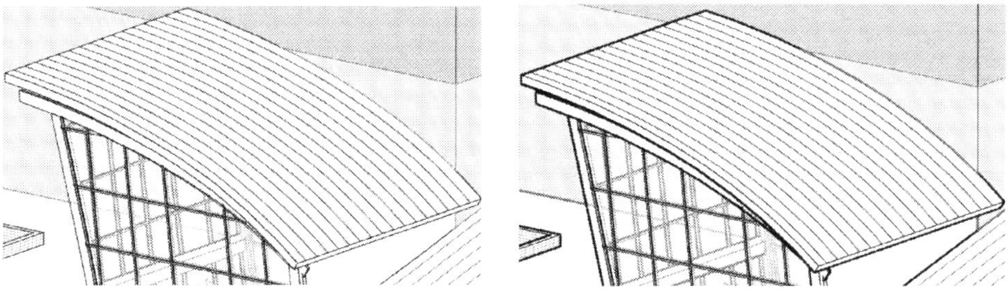

Default silhouette ***Silhouette override***

Figure 3–20

Hint: Adjusting Linework

To emphasize a particular line or change the look of a line in elevations and other views, modify the lines using the **Linework** command. If there is linework that you do not want to see, you can set the linework's line style to **<Invisible lines>**. These changes are view-specific, applying only to the view in which you make them, as shown in Figure 3–21.

Figure 3–21

- The **Linework** command can be used on project edges and cut edges of model elements, edges in imported CAD files, and edges in linked Revit models.

How To: Adjust Linework

1. In the *Modify* tab>*View* panel, click (Linework), or type the shortcut **LW**.
2. In the *Modify | Linework* tab>*Line Style* panel, select the line style you want to use from the list.
3. Move the cursor and highlight the line you want to change. Use <Tab> to toggle through the lines as required.
4. Click on the line to change it to the new line style.
5. Click on other lines as required, or return to the **Modify** command to finish.

If the line is too long or short, you can modify the length using the controls at the end of the line.

- The **Linework** tool overrides any other graphic changes to the view.

Shadows

In the *Graphic Display Options* dialog box, in the *Shadows* area, select **Cast Shadows**, as shown Figure 3–22. You can also select **Show Ambient Shadows**. Ambient shadows look more realistic as shadows are added to corners and other dark areas, but they make the view much darker.

Figure 3–22

Sketchy Lines

Revit models can look polished even at the conceptual stage. Some people prefer to show clients a presentation that looks like it is hand-drawn. To do this, you can set up a view using sketchy lines, as shown in Figure 3–23.

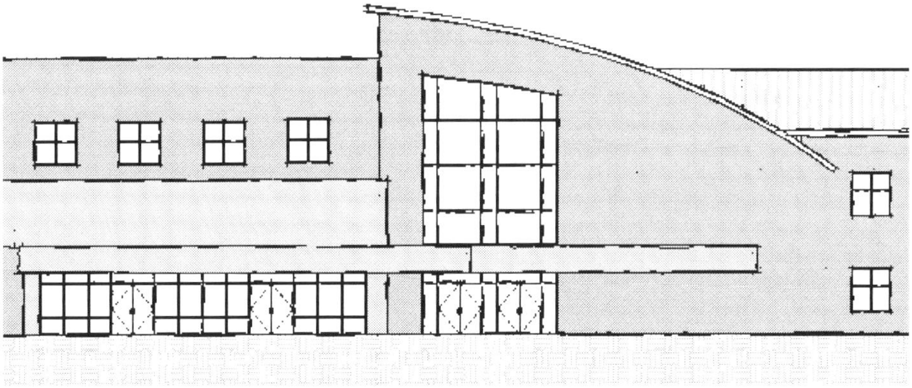

Figure 3–23

- Sketchy lines can be used in all types of views, including: plans, elevations, sections, 3D orthographic, and perspective views.
- Datums (levels and grids) and annotation items are not impacted by sketchy lines.

- Views using sketchy lines can be exported to an image file, printed, and put on sheets.

How To: Modify a View Using Sketchy Lines

1. Set up a view where you want to apply a hand-drawn look.
2. In the View Control Bar, expand the *Visual Style* drop-down list and select **Graphic Display Options...**. Alternatively, in Properties, beside *Graphic Display Options...*, click **Edit...**.
3. In the *Graphic Display Options* dialog box, expand the *Sketchy Lines* area.
4. Select **Enable Sketchy Lines** and move the sliders for *Jitter* and *Extension*, as shown in Figure 3–24. Alternatively, you can type in a number in the box next to the slider bar.

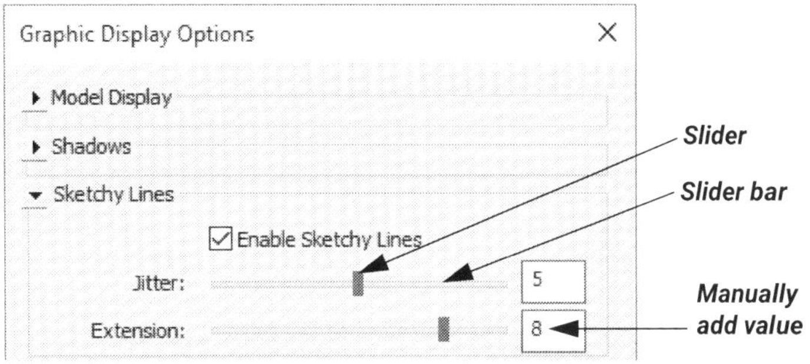

Figure 3–24

- *Jitter* controls how wavy the lines are and how many layers of lines there are. It varies from 0, where the lines are perfectly straight, to 10, which has multiple layers of wavy lines, as shown in Figure 3–25.
- *Extension* controls the length of the line beyond the end point. It varies from 0, where there is no extension, to 10 where the extension is longer, as shown in Figure 3–26.

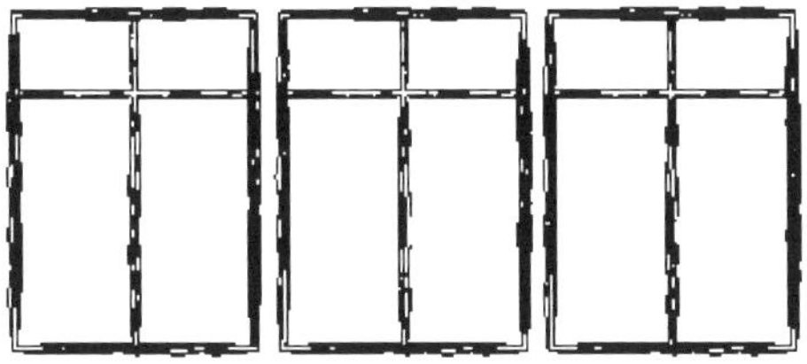

Figure 3–25

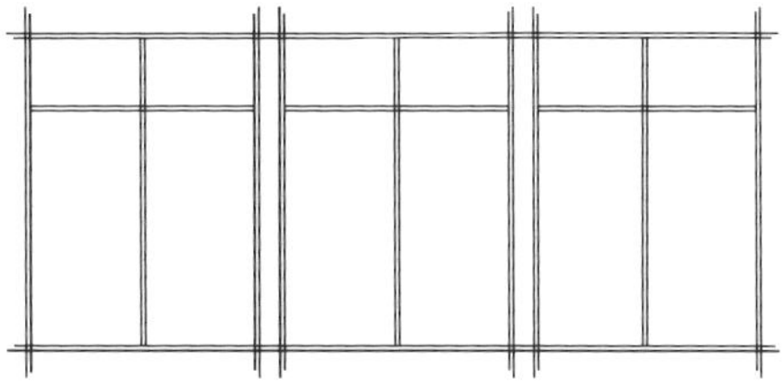

Figure 3–26

5. Click **Apply** to see the change to the view.
6. When you are satisfied with the look, click **OK**.

Depth Cueing

Another important visual aid, called depth cueing, gives you a sense of depth by fading elements in the distance, as shown in Figure 3–27. This is set up in the *Graphic Display Options* dialog box.

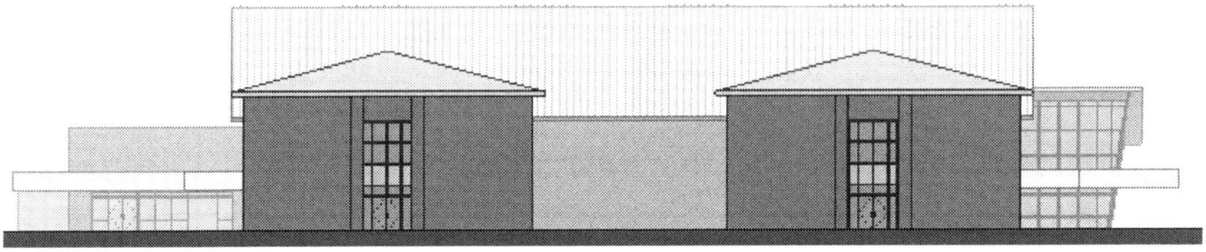

Figure 3–27

- Depth cueing is specifically used for elevations and sections and does not work in plan or 3D views.
- The *Far Clipping* and *Far Clip Offset* parameters, which are set up in Properties (as shown in Figure 3–28), impact how depth cueing works. In the *Far Clipping* dialog box, select one of the clip methods, as shown in Figure 3–29, and click **OK**. Then, set a useful *Far Clip Offset* for the building.

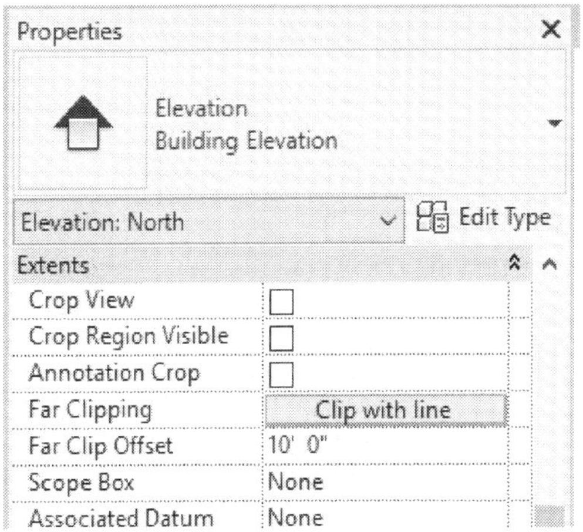

Figure 3–28

Figure 3–29

- You can try changing the *Far Clip Offset* before adjusting the view in the *Graphic Display Options* dialog box, as depth cueing is based on the location of the front and back view clip planes.

How To: Establish a Sense of Depth in a View

1. Set up a view where you want to apply depth cueing.
2. In Properties, set up a *Far Clipping* method and a *Far Clip Offset*.
3. Open the *Graphic Display Options* dialog box and expand *Depth Cueing*.
4. Select **Show Depth** and click **Apply** to see how the default settings work.
5. Move the sliders for *Fade Start/End Location* and *Fade Limit (%)* as required, as shown in Figure 3–30.

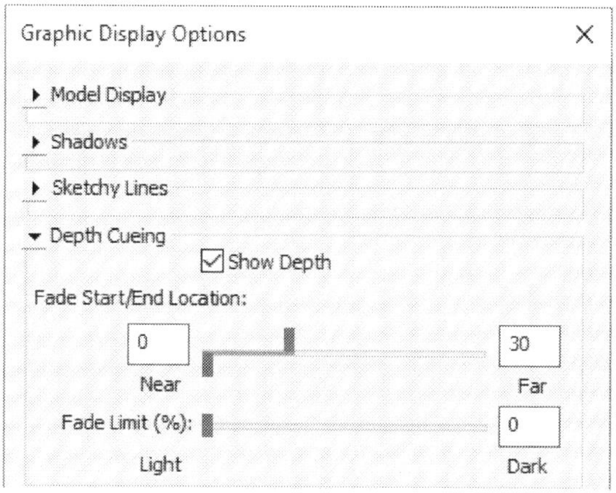

Figure 3–30

- *Fade Start/End Location* controls the start and end of the fading. *Near* and *Far* are the percentage away from the front and back view clip planes.
- The *Fade Limit (%)* intensity can be set from *Light* to *Dark*.

6. Click **Apply** to see the change to the view.
7. When you are satisfied with the look, click **OK**.

Background

In the *Background* area, in the *Background* drop-down list, select one of the following four options: **None**, **Gradient** or **Sky** (which give a default sky appearance and enable you to specify a ground color, as shown in Figure 3–31 and Figure 3–32), or **Image** (which enables you to select a custom background image).

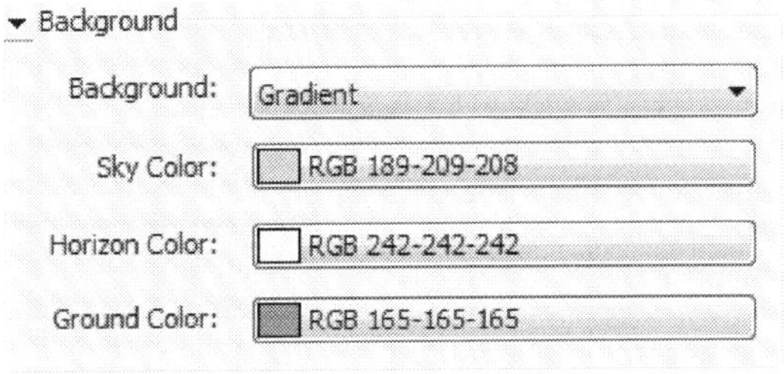

Figure 3–31

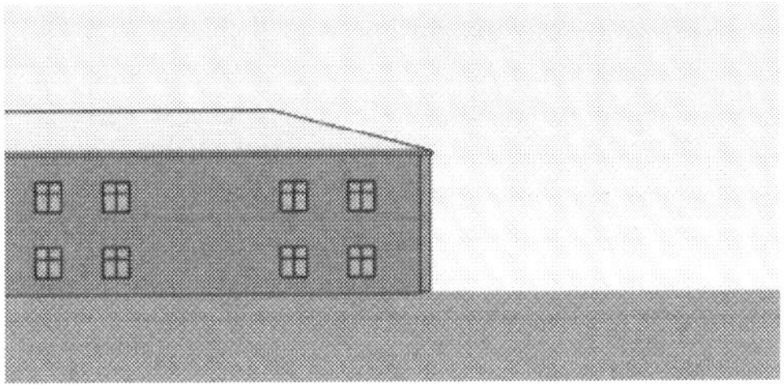

Figure 3–32

Lighting and Realistic Settings

When you are in the **Realistic** visual style, in the *Lighting* area (shown in Figure 3–33), you can set the *Sun Settings* and specify the intensity of the *Sun*, *Ambient Light*, and *Shadows*. You can also specify *Artificial Lights* if you have lighting fixtures in the project and want to specify which ones will be used in the view.

> ***Note:*** *The concepts in the Lighting and Realistic areas are covered in more depth in Sun Studies and Rendering.*

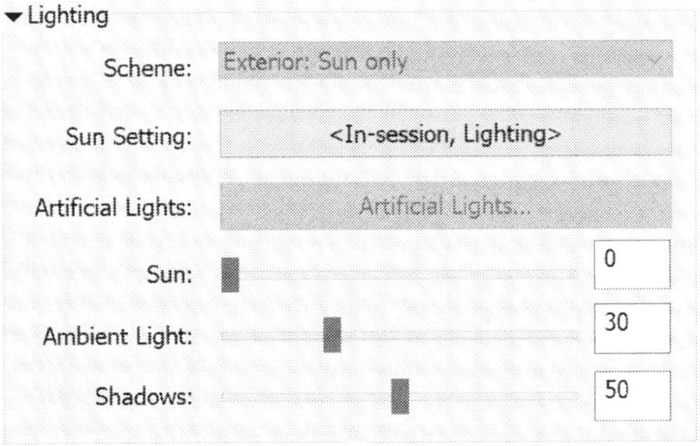

Figure 3–33

In the *Realistic* area (shown in Figure 3–34), you can modify the artificial lights to set the best exposure to a scene.

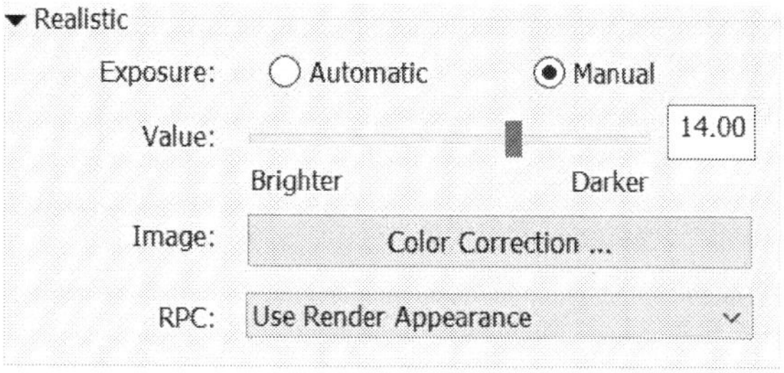

Figure 3–34

Practice 3b
Work with Graphic Display Options

Practice Objectives

- Use Sketchy Lines and other graphic display options.
- Set up a 3D view oriented to a 2D view.
- Investigate Depth Cueing.

In this practice, you will set up an elevation view of the front entrance and modify the look using Sketchy Lines. You will then duplicate the view and set it up to look more realistic, as shown in Figure 3–35. You will also create a 3D elevation view and modify another view using Depth Cueing and how the Far Clip plane and offset impacts the view.

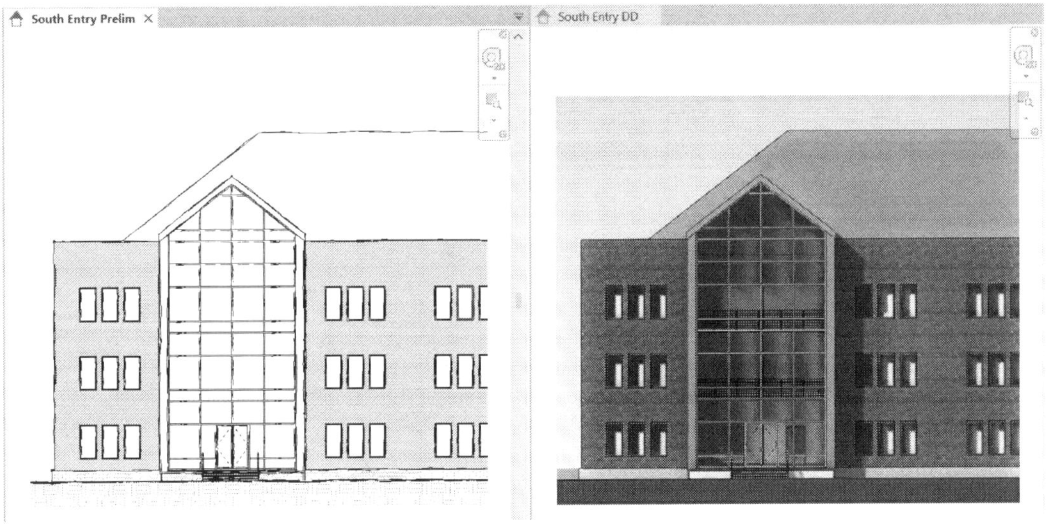

Figure 3–35

Task 1: Set up a view using Sketchy Lines.

1. In the practice files folder, open **Midrise-Display.rvt**.
2. In the Project Browser, duplicate the **Elevations (Building Elevation): South** view and rename it to **South Entry Prelim**.
3. Hide the level lines. (Select a level and type **VH** to hide the category.)
4. In the View Control Bar, click (Show Crop Region).

5. Modify the crop region so you are only seeing the entry area of the building, as shown in Figure 3–36.

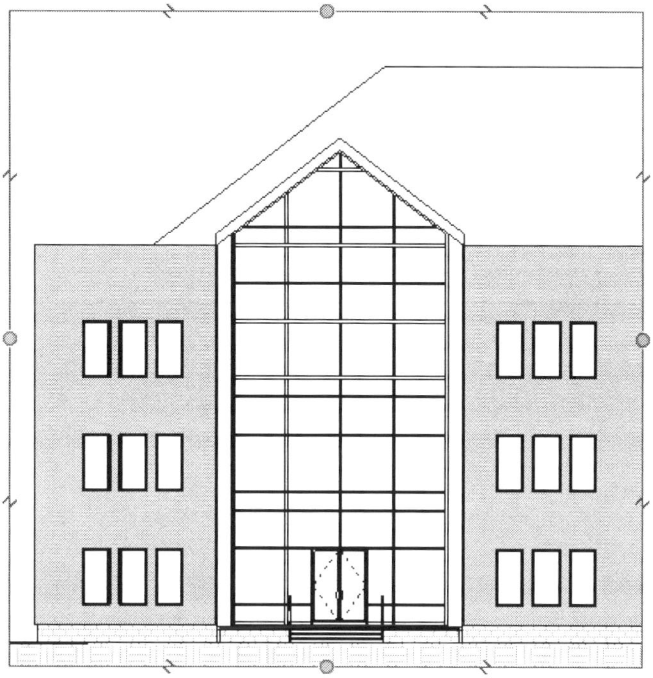

Figure 3–36

6. In the View Control Bar, click  (Hide Crop Region).
7. In Properties, beside *Graphic Display Options...*, click **Edit...**.
8. In the *Graphic Display Options* dialog box, expand the *Sketchy Lines* area and select **Enable Sketchy Lines**.
9. Move the dialog box over to the side so you can see the view as you make changes, and click **Apply**.

10. Slide the *Jitter* bar to around **6** and click **Apply**. (You can also type 6 in the box next to the slider bar.) The lines take on a sketch-like look, as shown in Figure 3–37.

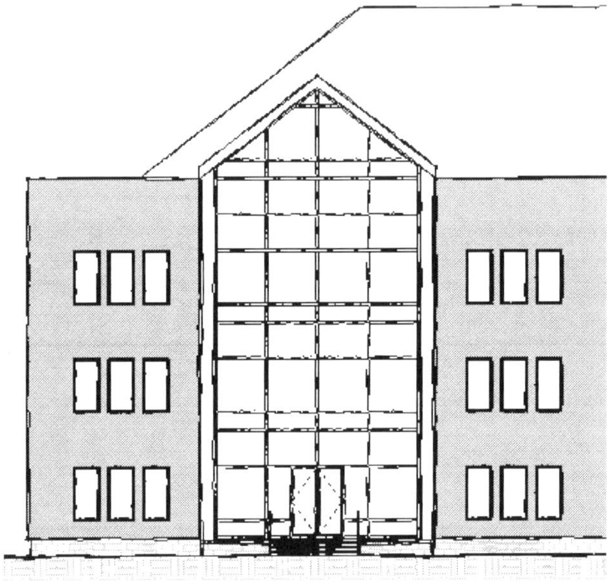

Figure 3–37

11. Try several different looks by manipulating the *Jitter* and *Extension* slider bars. Click **Apply** after each change to see the variations.
12. Click **OK** when you have the desired look.
13. Save the project.

Task 2: Set up a view using shadows and the Realistic visual style.

1. Duplicate the **South Entry Prelim** view and name it **South Entry DD**.
2. Open the *Graphic Display Options* dialog box. (**Hint:** Type **GD**).
3. In the *Graphic Display Options* dialog box, set the following. Click **Apply** after every change to see the the view update.
    - In the *Sketchy Lines* area, toggle off **Sketchy Lines**.
    - In the *Model Display* area, set the *Style* to **Realistic** and select both **Show Edges** and **Smooth lines with anti-aliasing**.
    - In the *Shadows* area, select both **Cast Shadows** and **Show Ambient Shadows**.
    - In the *Background* area, expand the *Background* drop-down list and test out several different options. Click **Apply** and the background is applied, such as the gradient shown in Figure 3–38.

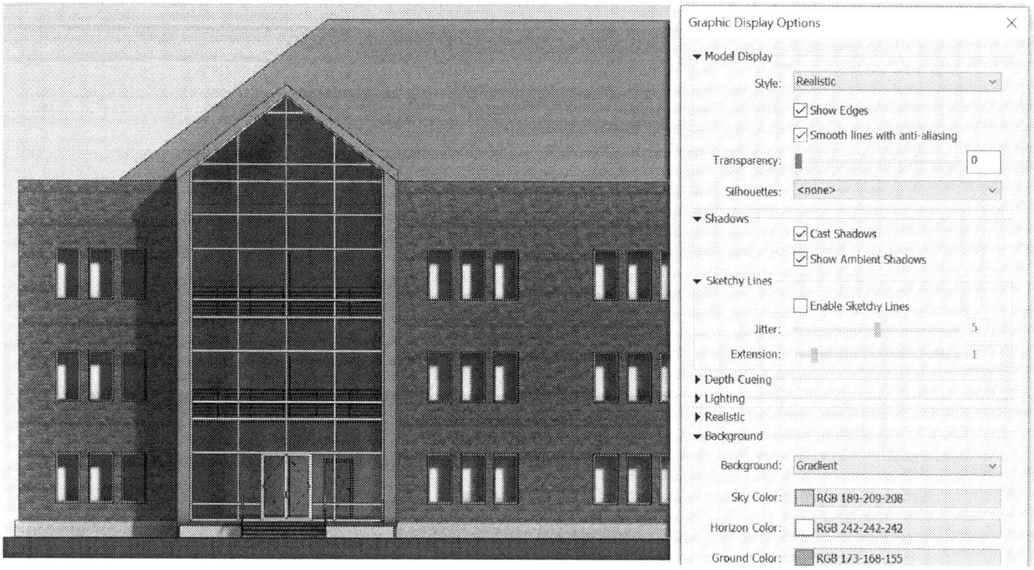

Figure 3–38

Note: *If you select the* ***Image*** *option, there are several image files you can use in the practice files Images folder.*

4. Stay in the *Graphic Display Options* dialog box.

Task 3: Apply lighting to the view.

1. Expand the *Lighting* area. Next to *Sun Setting*, click **<In-session, Lighting>**.
2. In the *Sun Settings* dialog box, in the *Presets* section, select **Sunlight from Top Left**. Click **Apply** to see the light direction display on the building in the view, as shown in Figure 3–39.

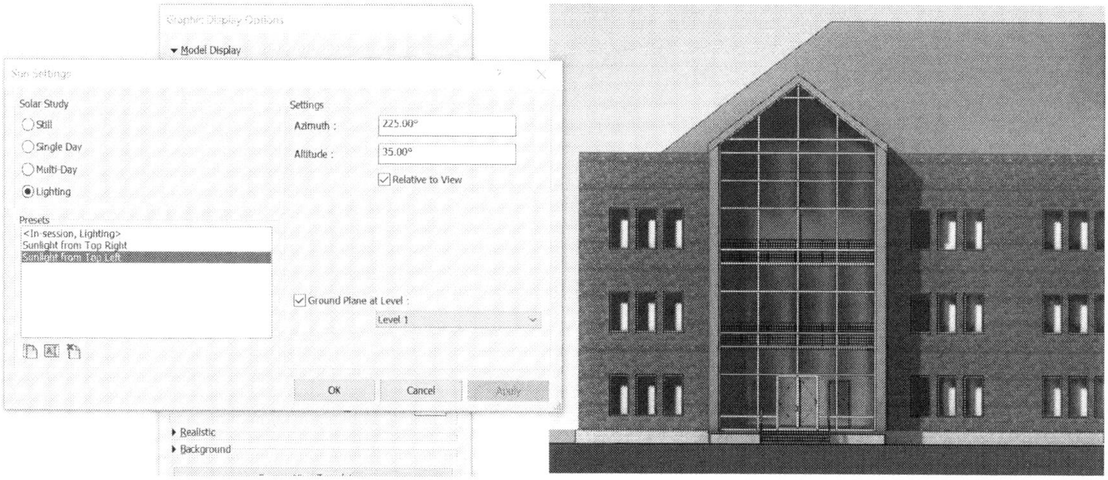

Figure 3–39

3. Click **OK** twice to get back to the view.
4. Save the project.

Task 4: Create a 3D elevation view

1. Open the default 3D view.
2. Rename it **South Entry**.
3. Right-click on the ViewCube and select **Orient to View> Elevations>Elevation: South Entry DD**, as shown in Figure 3–40.
4. Turn off the grids and levels.
5. Test out several different visual styles and graphic display options with this view, as shown in Figure 3–41.

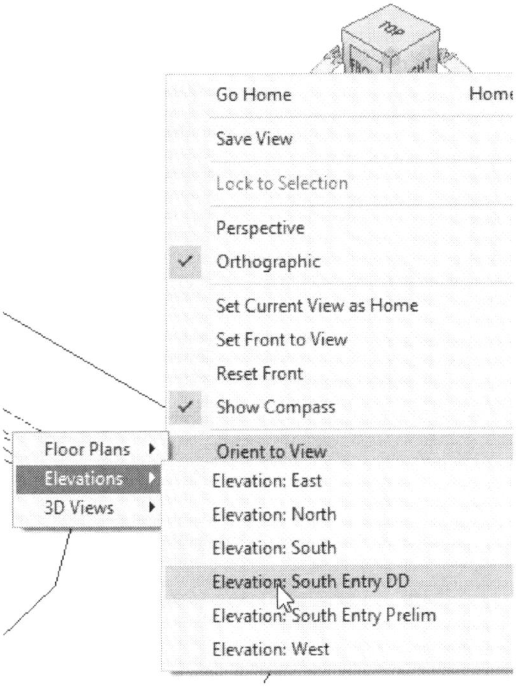

Figure 3–40

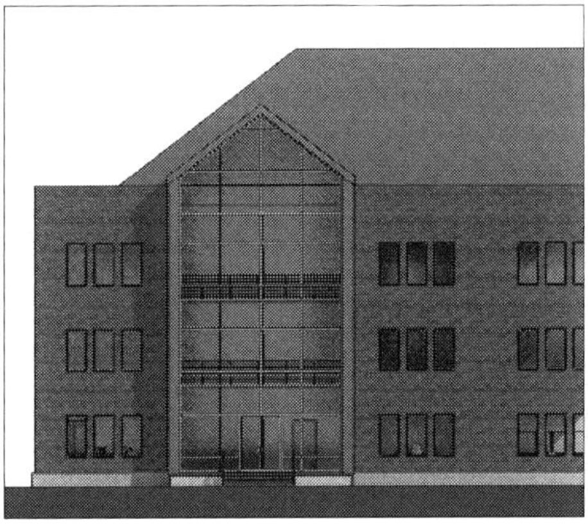

Figure 3–41

- While in the Realistic visual style, you cannot enable Depth Cueing but all other graphic display options are available.

6. Close the dialog box.
7. Save the project.

Task 5: Apply Depth Cueing to a view.

1. Open the **Elevations: South** view.

   Note: You may need to open Floor Plans Level 1 and adjust the elevation markers clipping.

2. Set the *Visual Style* to **Shaded**.
3. Open the *Graphic Display Options* dialog box and expand *Depth Cueing*.
4. Toggle on **Show Depth**, but do not make any changes yet. Click **OK**.
5. In Properties, set *Far Clipping* to **Clip with line**. By default, the *Far Clip Offset* is set to **10'-0"**. This distance is not deep enough to show the building so only the toposurface displays as shown in Figure 3–42.

Figure 3–42

6. In Properties, test several *Far Clip Offset* distances in increments of 10 (e.g., 20', 30', 40') and finish with **100'-0"**. The building displays with a shaded roof.
7. Open the *Graphic Display Options* dialog box and make changes to the *Depth Cueing* **Fade Limit (%)**, and **Fade Start/End Location** options to fade the roof, as shown in Figure 3–43.

Figure 3–43

8. Save and close the project.

End of practice

3.3 Adding Exploded Views

You can use displacement sets to create exploded views that can be used to explain a project or detail a complex detail. These views update as you work on a project, any other view does. They can be created in 3D perspective or orthographic views, such as that shown in Figure 3–44.

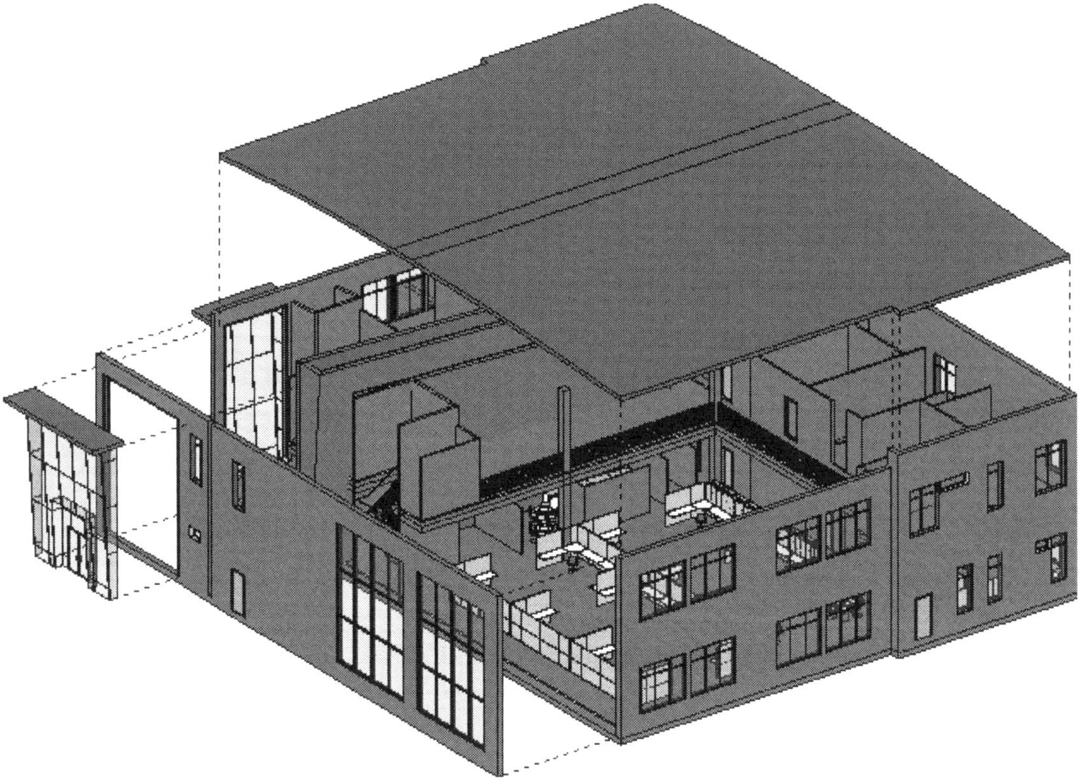

Figure 3–44

- Displaced views are full 3D views and can be rotated using the mouse or ViewCube.

How To: Displace Elements

1. Select the element or elements that you want to displace.
2. In the *Modify | <element type>* tab>*View* panel, click (Displace Elements).

3. In Properties, set the *X*, *Y*, and/or *Z Displacement* or use the drag controls on the face of the element, as shown in Figure 3–45.

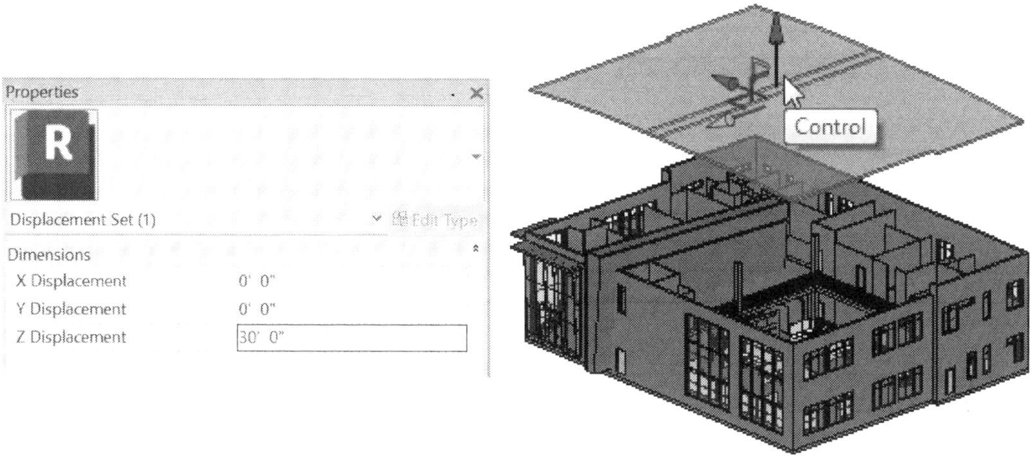

Figure 3–45

4. To display projection lines from the original location to the displacement, in the *Modify | Displacement Set* tab>*Displacement Set* panel, click (Path).
5. Select the corner of the displaced element where you want to locate the path.

- When displacing a wall, elements (such as doors and windows) are also displaced. You can displace them separately by using <Tab> to select them once you have displaced the wall.
- Storefront curtain wall elements are not displaced with the walls in which they are located. You can add them to the displacement set or displace them separately.
- If you want to displace a door or window separately from a wall, press <Tab> until the element is highlighted and then follow the steps for displacing elements.
- If you no longer want an element to be displaced, select it, and in the *Modify | Displacement Set* tab>*Displacement Set* panel, click (Reset).

- In a view that displays the displacements sets, in the View Control Bar, click (Highlight Displacement Sets). The displacement sets display in color with a rim around the edge of the view, as shown in Figure 3–46.

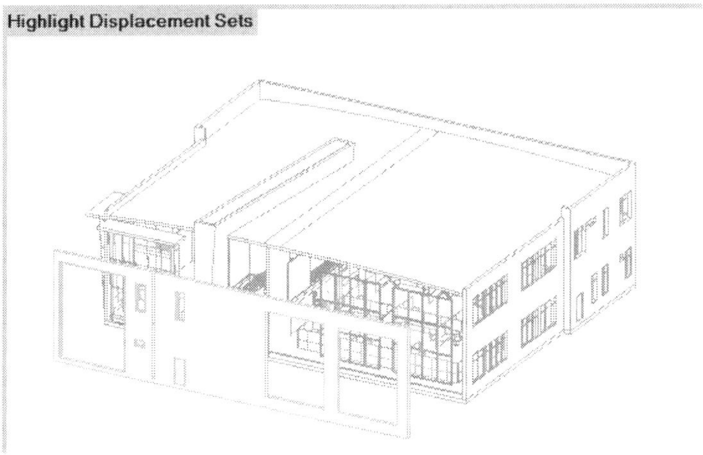

Figure 3–46

How To: Edit Displaced Elements

1. Select a displaced element.
2. In the *Modify | Displacement Set* tab>*Displacement Set* panel, click (Edit). The existing displacement set is highlighted.
3. In the floating *Edit Displacement Set* panel, verify that (Add) is selected and select the elements you want to include in the displacement set, as shown in Figure 3–47.

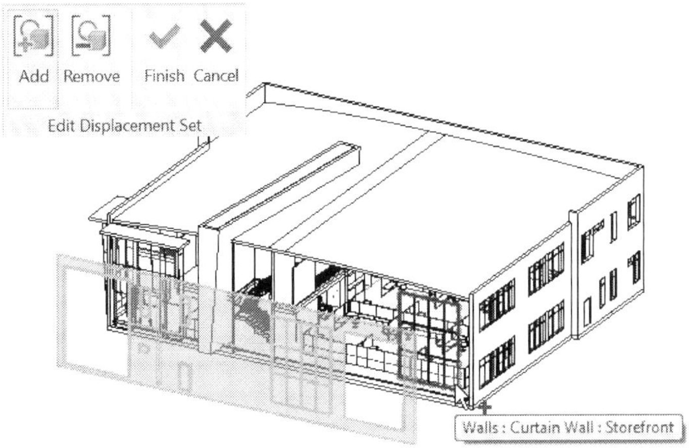

Figure 3–47

4. As you select the elements, they are moved into place and highlighted.
5. If you do not want an element to be in the displacement set, click (Remove) and select the element. The element returns to place.
6. Click (Finish).

- It is sometimes easier to displace one element (such as a wall) and then add other elements to the set.

Practice 3c
Create an Exploded View

Practice Objectives

- Displace elements in a view to create an exploded view.
- Add elements to a displacement set.

In this practice, you will create a 3D view in which you will set up several displacement sets to create an exploded view of the building. You will also add an element to a set and place paths that display the location. An example of a finished view is shown in Figure 3–48 with the displacement sets highlighted.

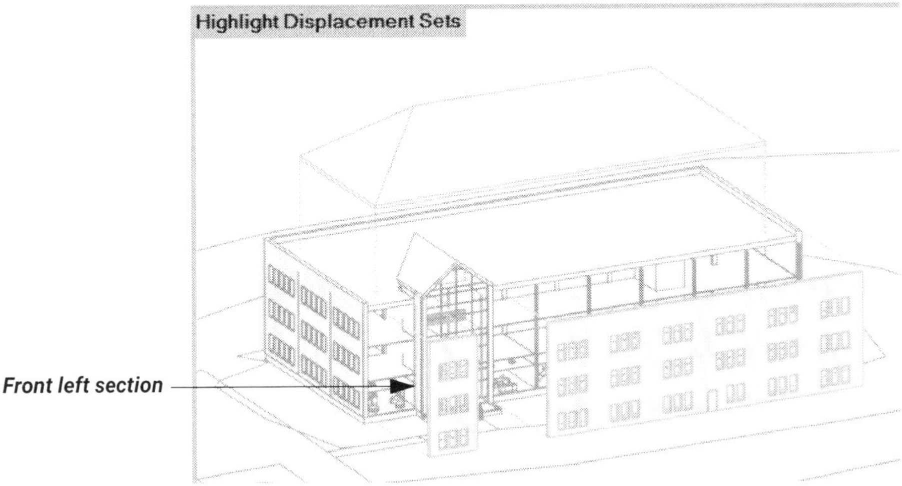

Figure 3–48

1. In the practice files folder, open **Midrise-Exploded.rvt**.
2. Open the **3D Views: 3D-Exploded** view.
3. Rotate the view so it is similar in orientation to that shown above in Figure 3–48.
4. Select the brick wall on the front left. Do not select the right section at this time.
5. In the *Modify | Walls* tab>*View* panel, click (Displace Elements).
6. Use the green control to drag it away from the building, as shown in Figure 3–49.

   Note: *In this case, you need to move the control in the direction opposite to the arrow.*

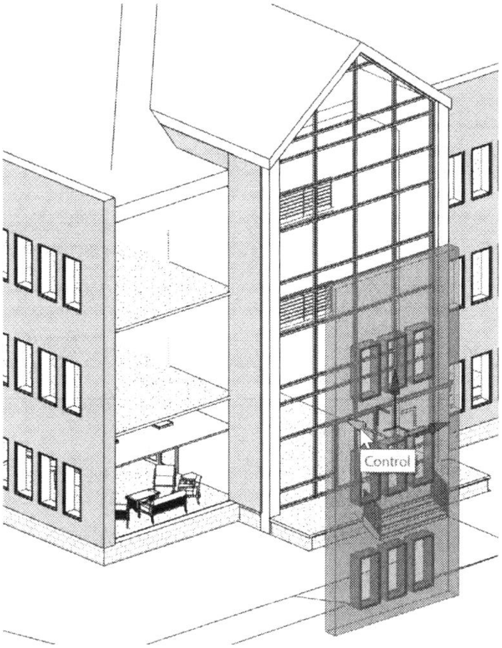

Figure 3–49

7. Select the hipped roof, click (Displace Elements), and move it up using the blue control or Properties.
8. Select the first wall that you displaced. In the *Modify | Displacement Set* tab>*Displacement Set* panel, click (Edit).
9. In the floating *Edit Displacement Set* panel, ensure that (Add) is selected and click on the longer front brick wall. It moves to match the location, as shown in Figure 3–50.

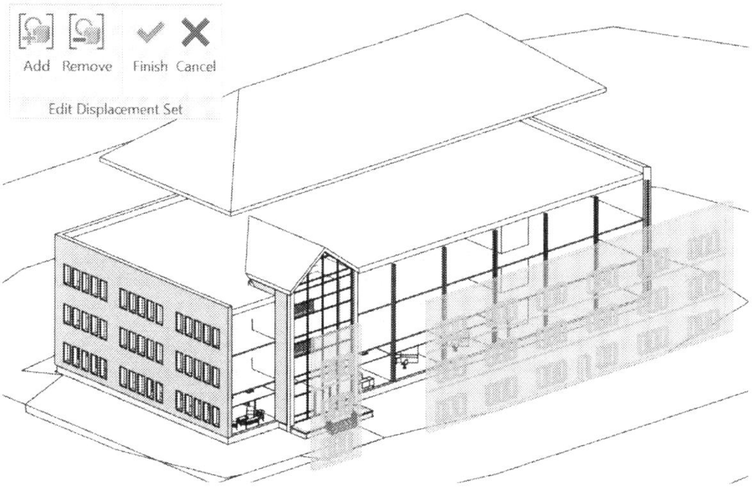

Figure 3–50

10. Click (Finish).
11. With the elements still selected, click (Path).
12. Select the corners of each wall and the corners of the roof to place the lines, as shown in Figure 3–51.

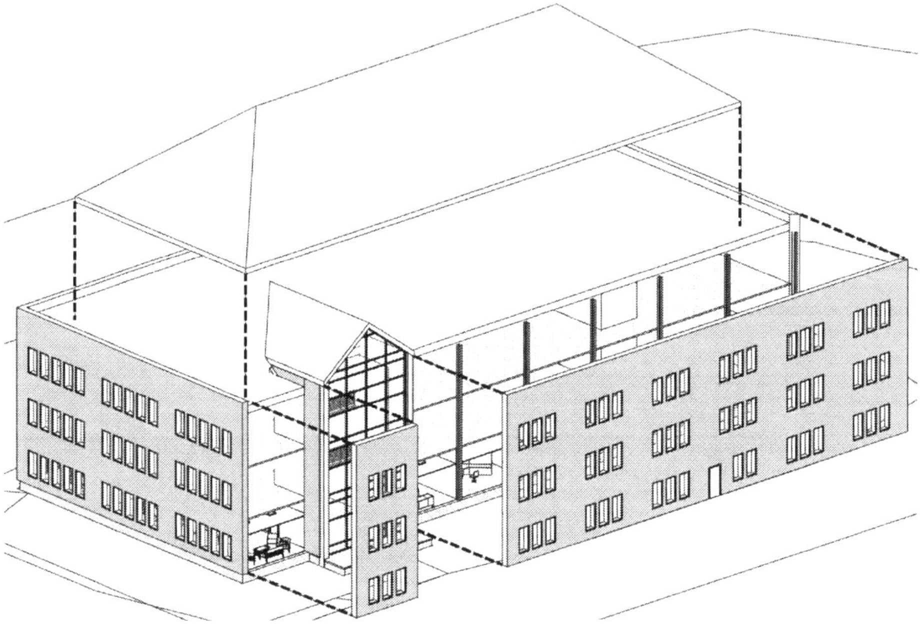

Figure 3–51

13. Displace other elements of the building, if time permits.
14. Save and close the project.

End of practice

3.4 Setting Up Solar Studies

The next step in enhancing your views is to get the sun in the correct place so that you can see how shadows impact your project. First, you need to establish the geographical location of the project and the true north direction. Then, you can graphically set year and time of day using the sun path, as shown in Figure 3–52. From there, you can create still, single day, and multi-day solar studies that show more accurate time settings.

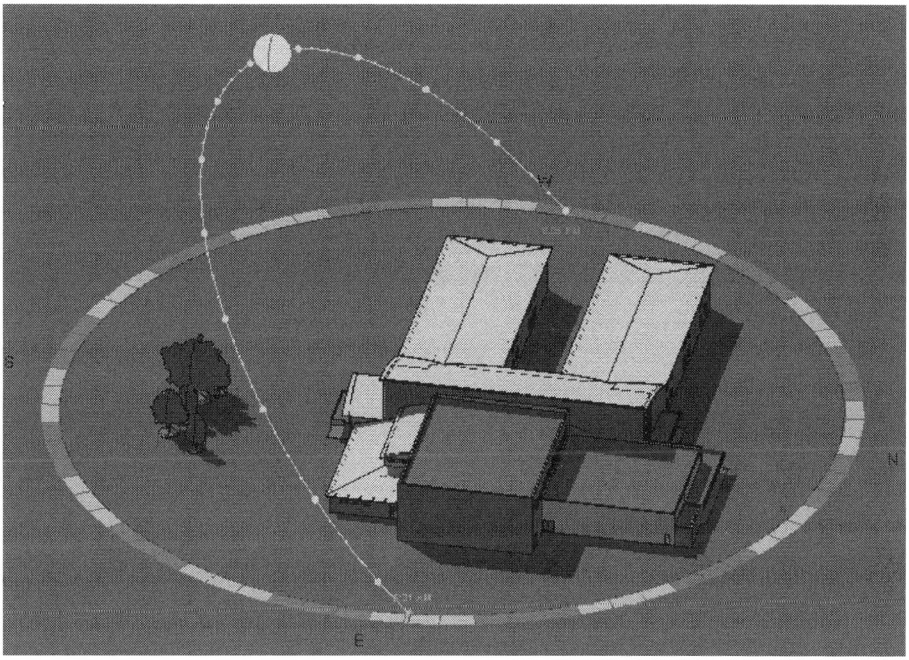

Figure 3–52

In the View Control Bar, toggle on **Sun Path** and **Shadows**, as shown in Figure 3–53.

Note: *Toggle shadows off when you do not need them to conserve memory resources.*

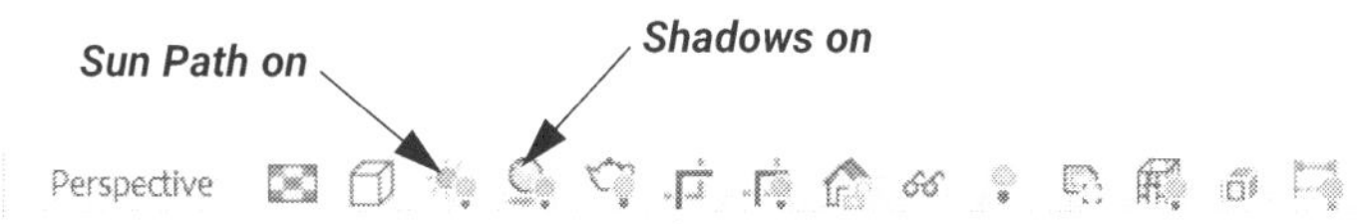

Figure 3–53

- The sun path and shadows can be used in 2D and 3D views.

Preparing for Solar Studies

The geographic location of a project and the true north orientation of the model on the site impact solar studies. Most buildings are modeled with north at the top of the primary axis, as shown in Figure 3–54. True north can be set in a site plan view, as shown in Figure 3–55.

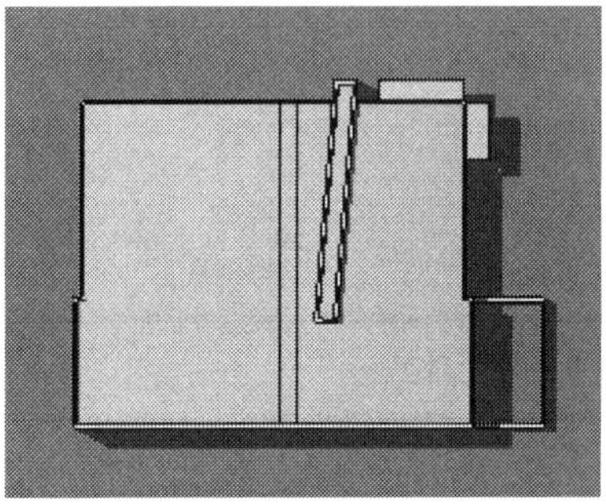

Figure 3–54

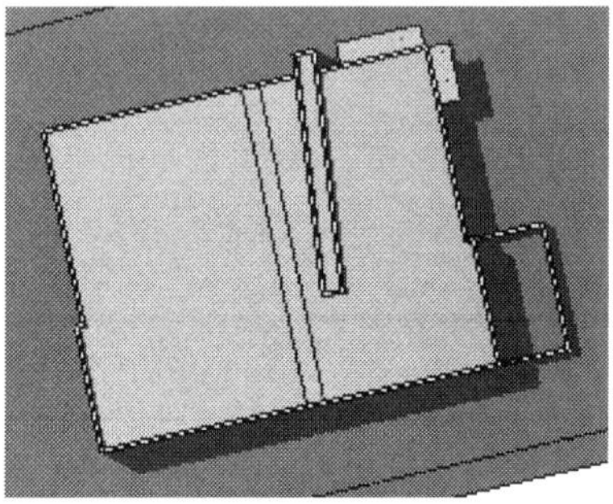

Figure 3–55

- If you are working with a linked DWG file, you can use the geographic data stored in that file.

How To: Set True North

1. Duplicate the **Floor Plans: Site** view and rename it **Site - True North**.
2. In Properties, set the *Orientation* to **True North**, as shown in Figure 3–56.

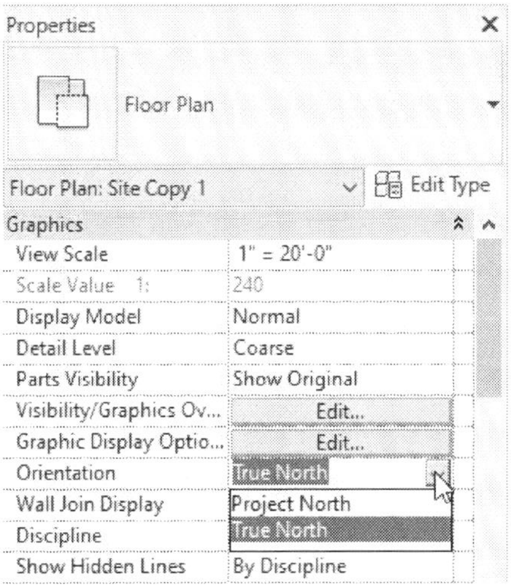

Figure 3–56

3. In the *Manage* tab>*Project Location* panel, expand (Position) and click (Rotate True North).

4. In the Options Bar, enter a value for *Angle from Project to True North*, or select two points on the screen to define the angle (similar to the **Rotate** command). The entire project rotates, as shown in Figure 3–57.

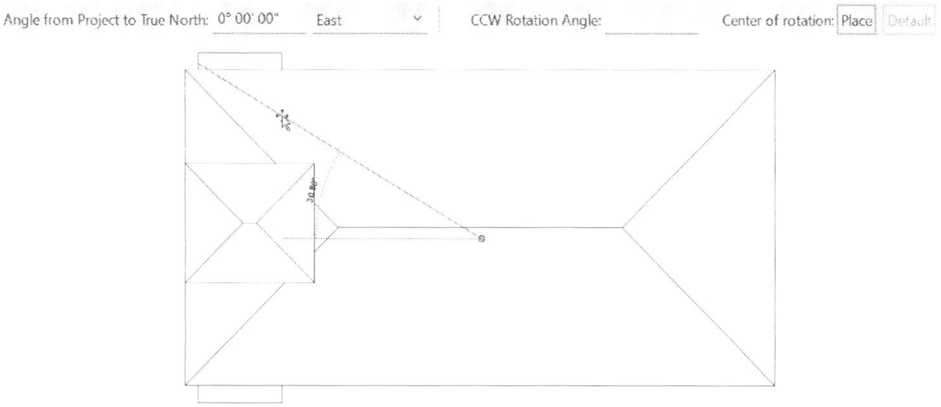

Figure 3–57

How To: Manage the Location for a Project

1. In the *Manage* tab>*Project Location* panel, click (Location).
2. In the *Location and Site* dialog box, on the *Location* tab, you can set the *Define Location by:* drop-down list to **Default City List** (typically used for HVAC sizing), as shown in Figure 3–58, or **Internet Mapping Service** (typically used for energy analysis), as shown in Figure 3–59.

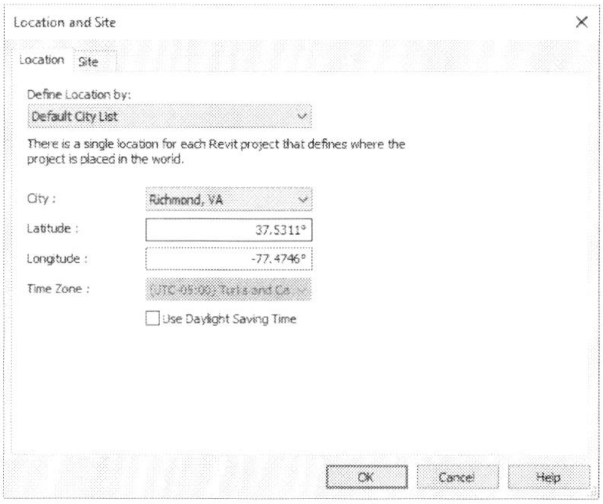

Figure 3–58

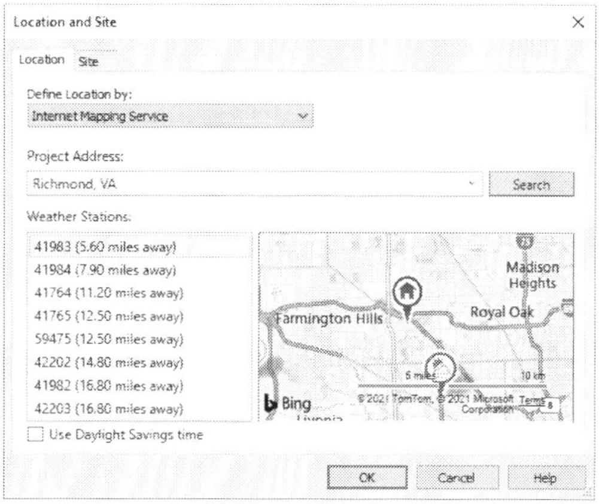

Figure 3–59

Using the Sun Path

If you want to graphically set the sun locations, you can use the sun path to specify the date and time of day by dragging the sun icon around the path or analemma, as shown in Figure 3–60.

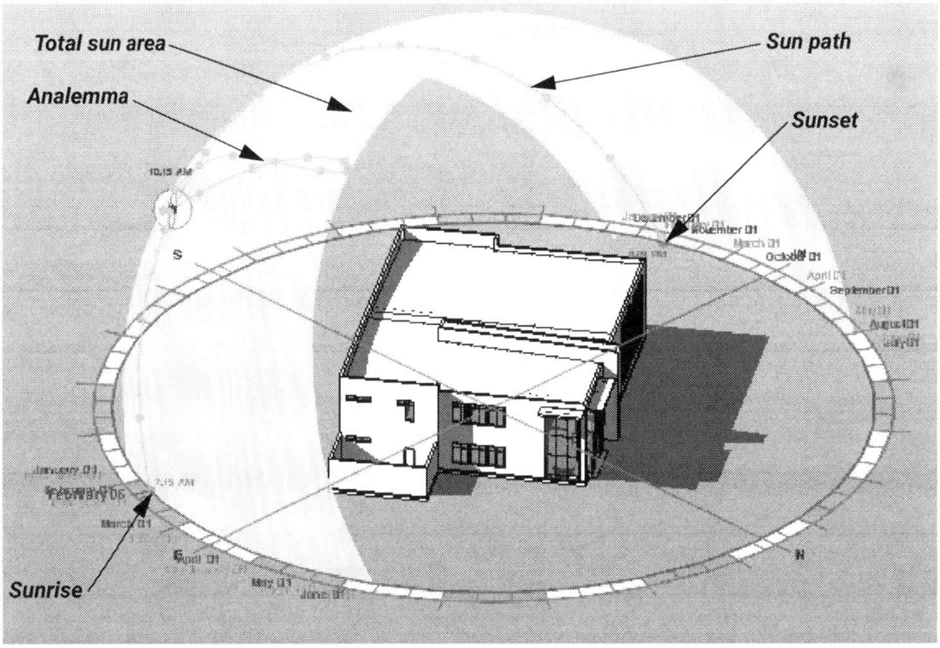

Figure 3–60

How To: Use the Sun Path

1. In the View Control Bar, expand (Sun Path Off) and click (Sun Path On).
   - If you have not already applied the appropriate sun settings, an alert box displays. Select **Use the specified project location, date, and time instead** to apply the default settings. The other option will not display the sun.
2. Move the sun along the path to change the time of day.
3. Move the sun along the analemma to retain the time of day but change the month.

4. Click on the time of day or the month and change the number, as shown in Figure 3–61.

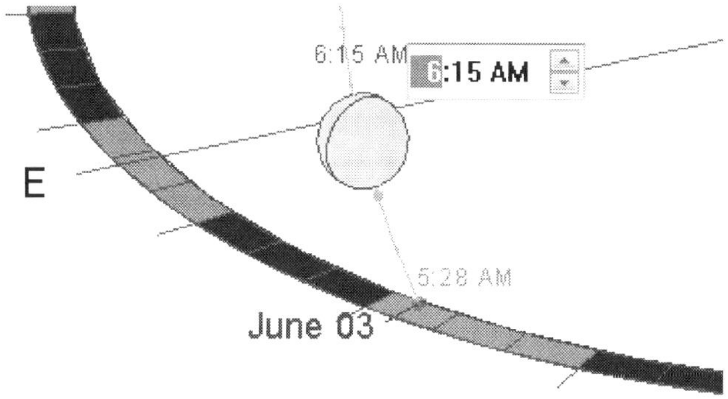

Figure 3–61

Creating Solar Studies

To create solar studies you will use the *Sun Settings* dialog box, where you can set up the information for still, single day, and multi-day options. Additionally, you can use several preset studies. At least one solar study is always available.

- Shadows need to be on to display the solar studies.

How To: Create Solar Studies

1. In the View Control Bar, expand the *Sun Path* drop-down list and click **Sun Settings**, as shown in Figure 3–62. You can also access the Sun Settings in Properties, through the *Graphic Display Options* dialog box.

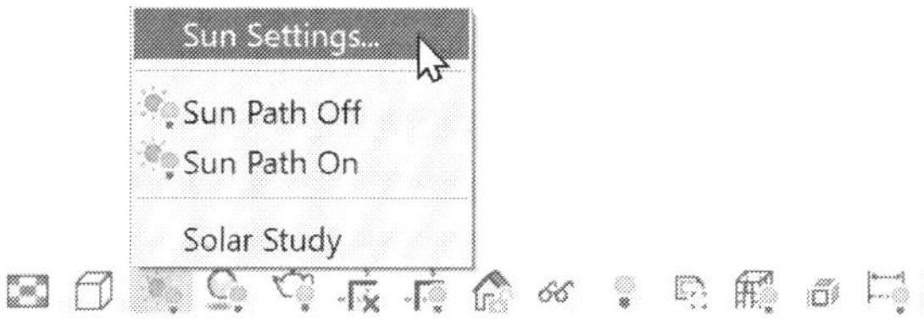

Figure 3–62

2. In the *Sun Settings* dialog box, *Solar Study* area, select the type of study you want to create: **Still**, **Single Day**, or **Multi-Day**.
3. In the *Presets* area, select an existing study and click (Duplicate).
4. In the *Name* dialog box, enter a name for the study and click **OK**.

- For **Still** studies, in the *Settings* area, specify the *Location*, *Date*, and *Time*, as shown in Figure 3–63.

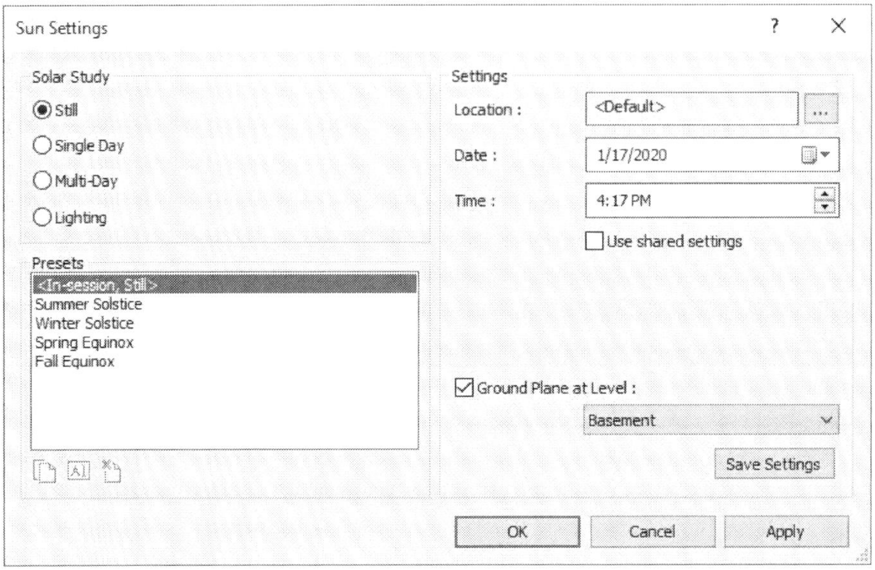

Figure 3–63

Note: *The* ***Sunrise to sunset*** *option automatically calculate the times based on the date.*

- For **Single Day** studies, in the *Settings* area (shown in Figure 3–64), specify the *Location*, *Date*, and *Time* (start and end). Select the *Time Interval* (**15**, **30**, **45 minutes** or **One hour**). The *Frames* value is read-only.

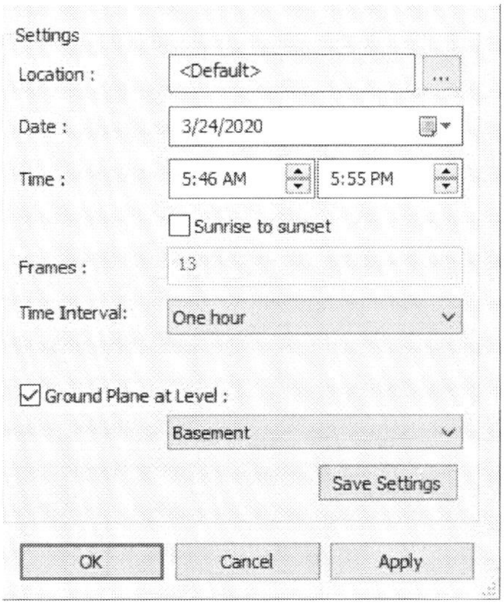

Figure 3–64

- For **Multi-Day** studies, in the *Settings* area, specify the *Date* range, and the *Time* and the *Time Interval*, which is typically set to **One day** or more, as shown in Figure 3–65.

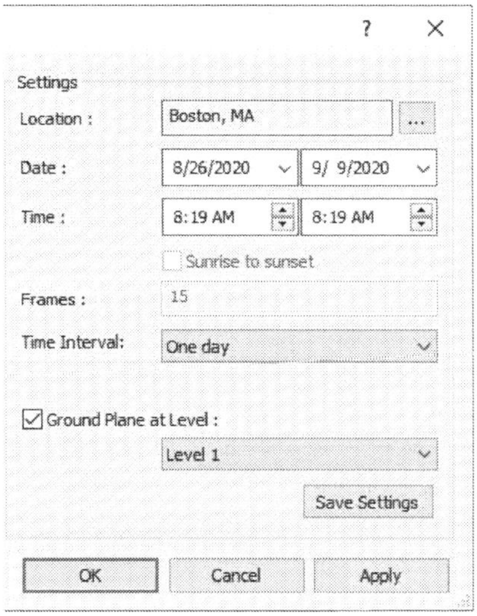

Figure 3–65

5. Click **OK** to close the dialog box and apply the still solar study to the view.

Hint: Setting the Ground Plane

In each type of solar study, you can set the **Ground Plane at Level**, as shown on the left in Figure 3–66, or leave this option cleared. If you do not have site information in the drawing or you are working with an interior view, specify a level. If you have site information (topography) in the drawing, do not specify a level for the ground plane so that the shadows flow over the contours, as shown on the right in Figure 3–66.

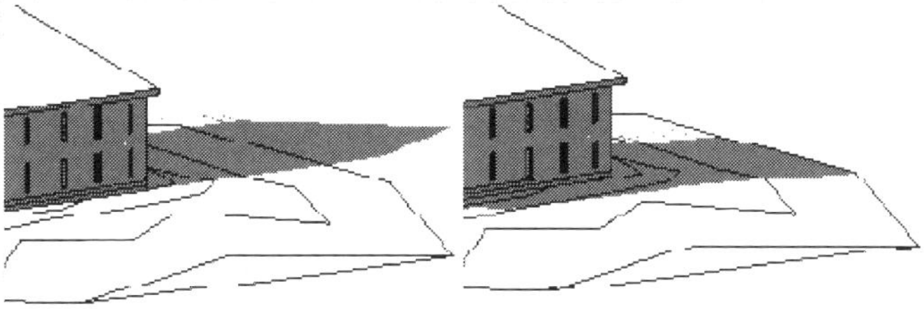

Ground plane at Level 1 ***Ground plane on site***

Figure 3–66

How To: View Solar Studies

1. Toggle on shadows and ensure that you are in either a **Single Day** or **Multi-Day** solar study type.
2. In the View Control Bar, click (Sun Path Off) and select **Solar Study**, as shown in Figure 3–67.

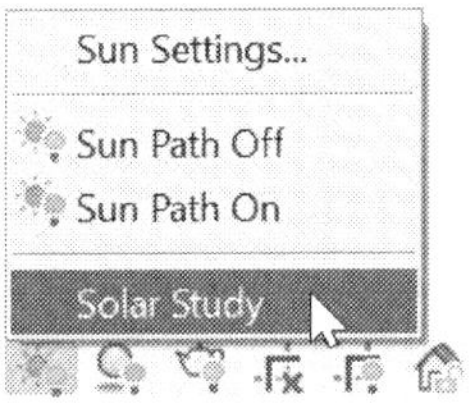

Figure 3–67

3. Set the required options in the *Solar Study* contextual tab. The tab is divided into four panels with the following features, as shown in Figure 3–68:
   - **Preview and Play:** Contains controls to play the entire study, or move forward or backward. You also have the option of playing the solar study continuously in a loop.
   - **Display:** You can adjust the speed, sunlight, and shadow intensity of the solar study.
   - **Study Type:** You can change the type of the solar study, choosing from **Still Image**, **Single Day**, **Multi-day**, or **Lighting**.
   - **Presets and Data:** Contains miscellaneous controls that are dependent on the type of study being played.
4. In the *Solar Study* contextual tab (shown in Figure 3–68), specify the frame at which you want to start and click (Play Preview).

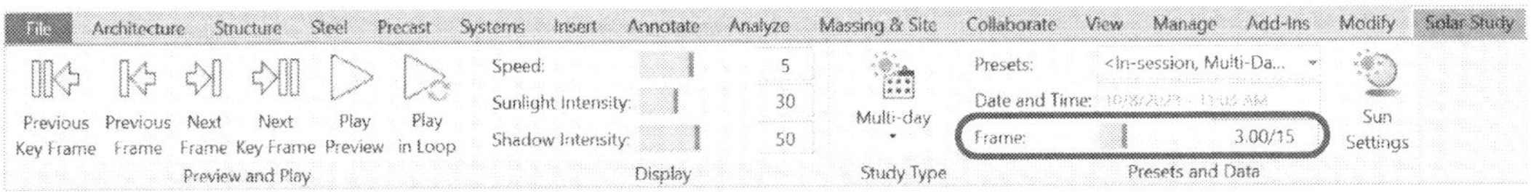

Figure 3–68

5. Press the <Esc> key on the keyboard to close the *Solar Study* contextual tab.

How To: Export Solar Studies

1. Toggle on shadows and ensure that you are in either a **Single Day** or **Multi-Day** solar study type.
2. In the *File* tab, expand (Export)> (Images and Animations) and click (Solar Study).
3. In the *Length/Format* dialog box, specify the *Output Length* and *Format*, as shown in Figure 3–69.

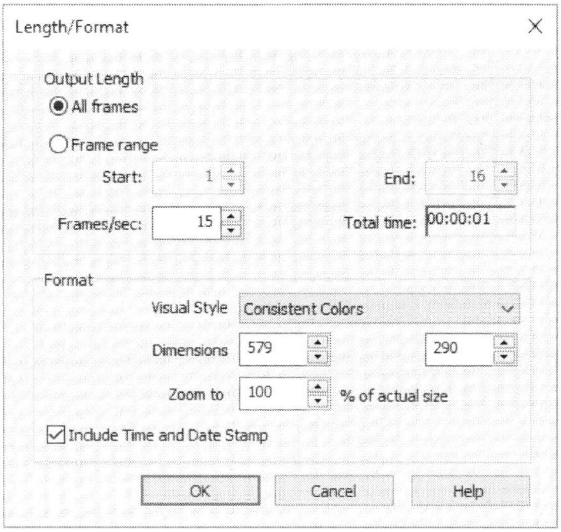

Figure 3–69

4. Click **OK**.
5. In the *Export Animated Solar Study* dialog box, navigate to a folder and specify a file name.
   - By default, the file name is the name of the project plus the name of the Solar Study.
6. Specify the file format, as shown in Figure 3–70, and click **Save**.

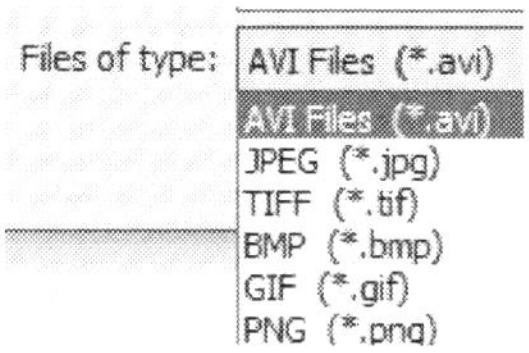

Figure 3–70

7. In the *Video Compression* dialog box, select the type of *Compressor*, as shown in Figure 3–71, and specify any other options. Click **OK**.

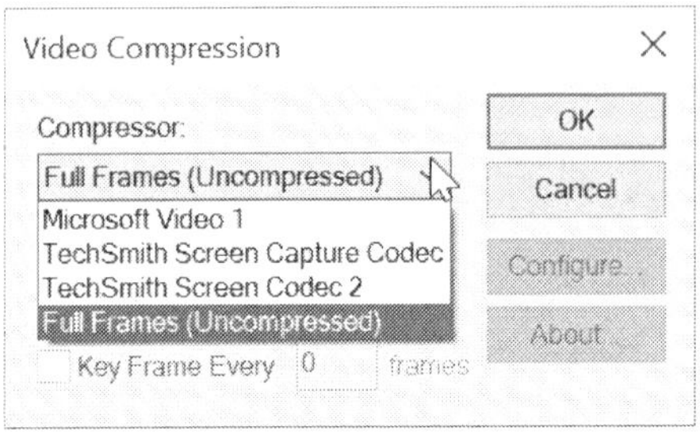

Figure 3–71

- The new animation is processed and can be viewed using the related video software.

Practice 3d
Set Up Solar Studies

Practice Objectives

- Set the True North and establish the project location to prepare a project for solar studies.
- Create a Still solar study, a Single Day solar study, and a Multi-Day solar study.

In this practice, you will create solar studies for your location using the three methods: **Still** (as shown in Figure 3–72), **Single Day**, and **Multi-Day**.

Figure 3–72

Task 1: Prepare the project for solar studies.

1. In the practice files folder, open **Midrise-Solar.rvt**.
2. Duplicate the **Floor Plans: Site** view and rename it **Site-True North**. Open the new view.
3. In Properties, set the *Orientation* to **True North**.
4. In the *Manage* tab>*Project Location* panel, expand (Position) and click (Rotate True North).

5. In the Options Bar, set the *Angle from Project to True North* to **23°** from **East** and press <Enter> for it to take effect. The site plan rotates, as shown in Figure 3–73.

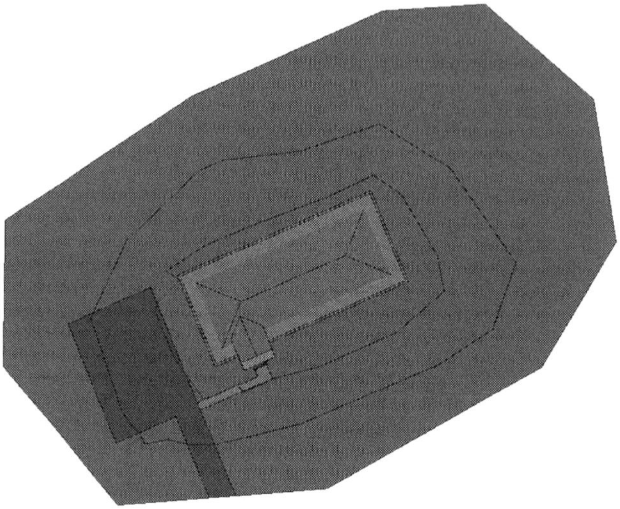

Figure 3–73

6. In the *Manage* tab>*Project Location* panel, click (Location).
7. In the *Location and Site* dialog box, on the *Location* tab, expand the *Define Location by:* drop-down list and select either **Default City List** to select a city from a drop-down list or **Internet Mapping Service** to select a location using the map. Select your city or one close to you. At the bottom of the dialog box, check the checkbox for **Use Daylight Saving Time**, if this applies. Click **OK**.

Task 2: Create a Still solar study.

1. Open the default 3D view and rotate it to show the front of the building and the site. Rename the view to **Still Solar Study**.
2. In the View Control Bar, set the *Model Graphics Style* to (Consistant Colors) and enable (Shadows On).
3. In the View Control Bar, enable (Sun Path On). When the *Sun Path - Sun Not Displayed* dialog box opens, select **Use the specified project location, date and time instead**.
4. Expand (Sun Path On) and select **Sun Settings...**.
5. In the *Sun Settings* dialog box, in the *Solar Study* area, select **Still**.
6. In the *Settings* area, specify today's date and time. To easily get to today's date, expand and click **Today**, as shown in Figure 3–74. Set the time to **11:00 am**.

   Note: *The date and location may vary depending on when and where you modify these settings.*

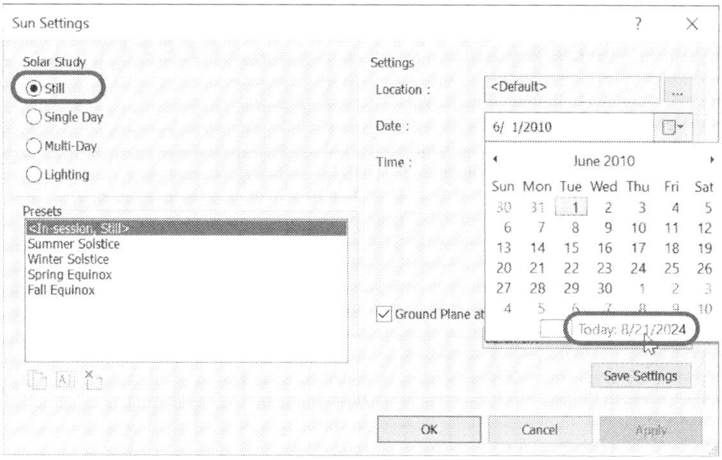

Figure 3–74

7. Choose **Level 1** for *Ground Plane at Level*.
8. Click **OK** to close the dialog box. The solar study displays according to your location and time, similar to that shown in Figure 3–75.
   * In the view, click on the various graphic tools, such as the date and time, or drag the sun to change to another day and time.

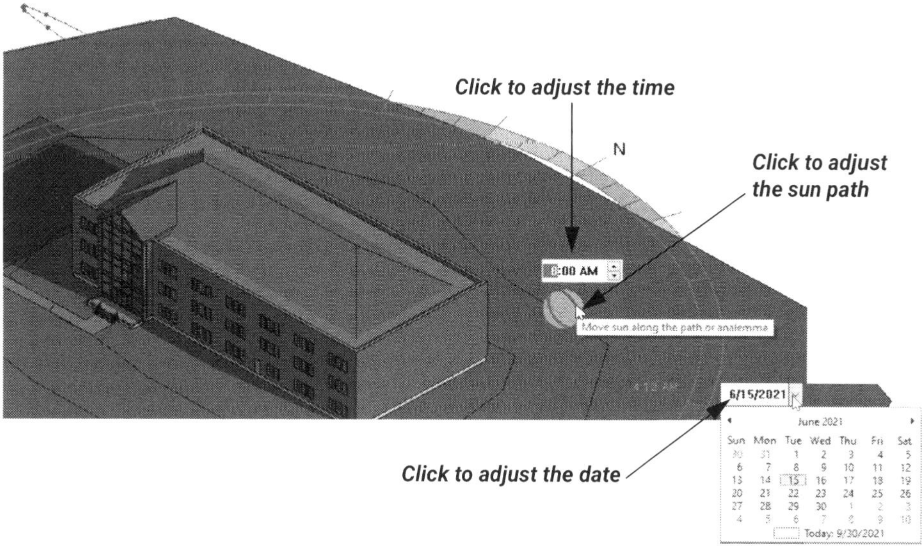

Figure 3–75

9. Save the project.

Task 3: Create a Single Day solar study.

1. Duplicate the **Still Solar Study** view.
2. Rename the new view to **Single Day Solar Study**.
3. Toggle off the sun path.
4. Open the *Sun Settings* dialog box and create a new **Single Day** solar study for today's date, from sunrise to sunset, with a *Time Interval* of **15 minutes**, and *Ground Plane at Level* set to **Level 1**.
5. Click **OK** to close the dialog box.
6. In the View Control Bar, click (Sun Path Off) and select **Solar Study**. (If this is not available, verify that the shadows are on.)
7. In the *Solar Study* contextual tab, slide the **Shadow Intensity** slider back and forth and note how the shadows lighten or darken. Settle the slider somewhere near **85%**.
8. Click (Next Frame) a few times. The shadows jump across the building, as shown in Figure 3–76. (Your shadow may differ from what is shown in the image based on several factors, like the date, time, and preset type selected.)

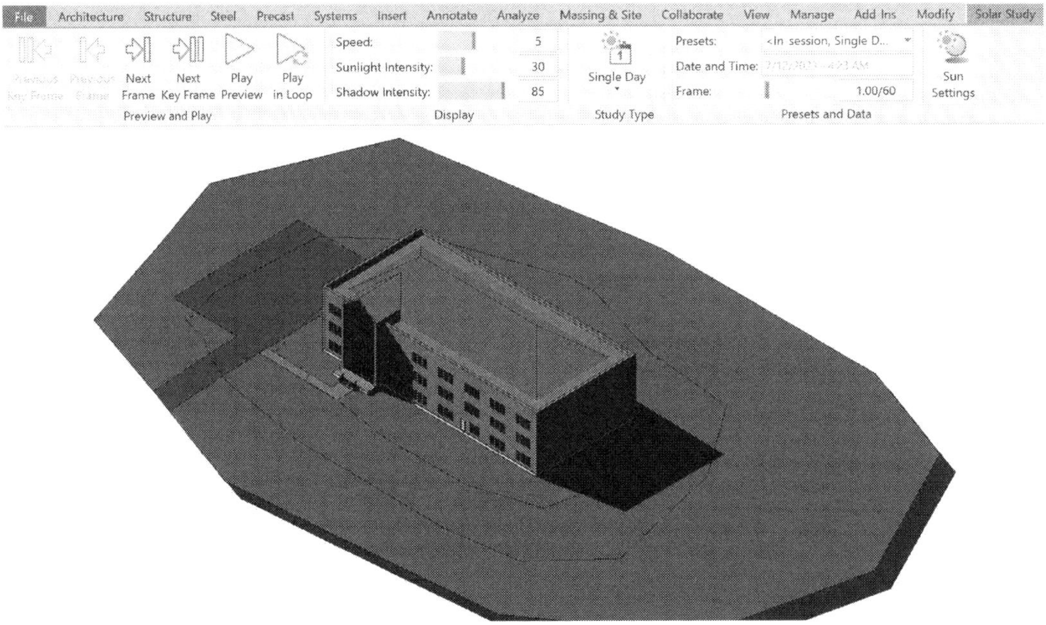

Figure 3–76

9. Click (Play Preview).The animation plays from start to end.

Task 4: Create a Multi-Day solar study.

1. Duplicate the **Single Day Solar Study** view.
2. Rename the new view as **Multi-Day Solar Study**.
3. Open the *Sun Settings* dialog box and create a new **Multi-Day** solar study for one year at noon with a *Time Interval* of **One month** and the *Ground Plane at Level* set to **Level 1**.
4. Click **OK** and preview the solar study animation.
5. Use  (Next Frame) and step through each month.
6. Click  (Play in Loop). The animation plays continuously. While it is playing, adjust the **Speed** slider to change the rate it is playing. Click  (Play in Loop) again to stop playback.
7. Press the <Esc> key on the keyboard. This closes the *Solar Study* contextual tab.
8. Save and close the project.

End of practice

Chapter Review Questions

1. How do you create a perspective view, as shown in Figure 3–77?

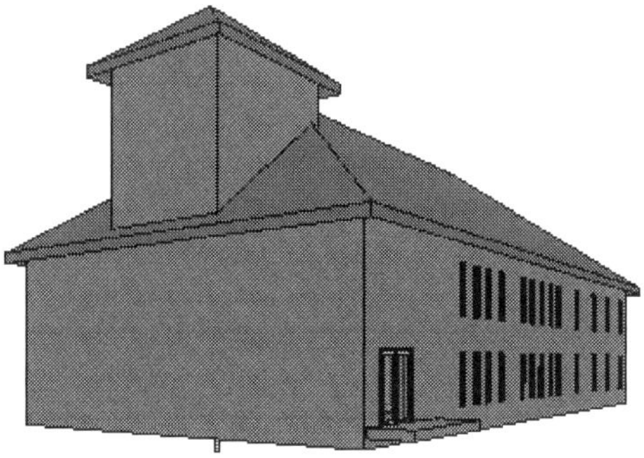

Figure 3–77

   a. Create a Default 3D view and, in Properties, modify the Camera settings.
   b. Create a Camera view.
   c. Create a Default 3D view and, in Properties, select Perspective.
   d. Create a Camera view and, in Properties, select Perspective.

2. Where can you set the Eye and Target Elevations of a camera?
   a. In Properties.
   b. In the Options Bar.
   c. In the View Control Bar.
   d. In the *Modify | Camera* tab in the ribbon.

3. Which of the following types of views can you customize to resemble a hand-drawn sketch? (Select all that apply.)
   a. Floor Plans
   b. Perspectives
   c. 3D Orthographic Views
   d. Elevations

4. When creating an exploded view, how do you add the dashed lines that connect to the origins, as shown in Figure 3–78?

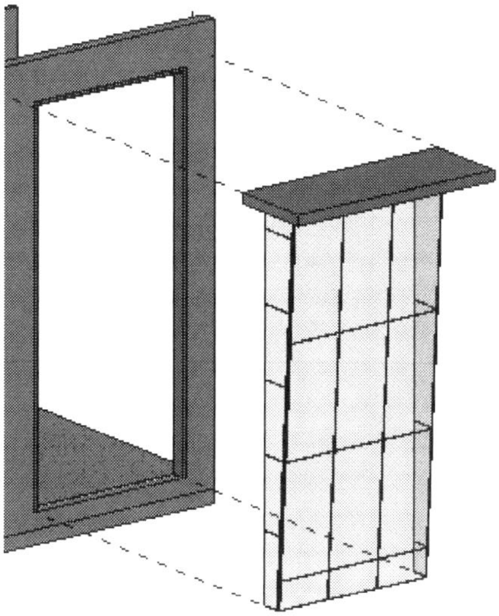

Figure 3–78

a. Draw them using (Detail Line).

b. Draw them using (Model Line).

c. Select the displaced element, click (Edit), and draw them.

d. Select the displaced element, click (Path), and select the corners of the displaced element.

5. How do you change the time of day when working with the sun path shown in Figure 3–79? (Select all that apply.)

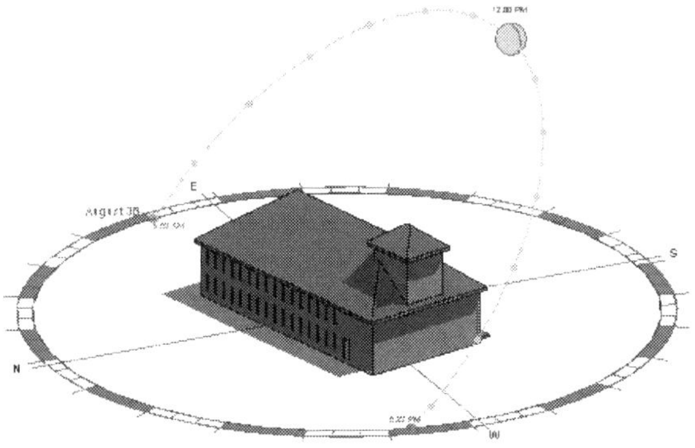

Figure 3–79

a. Modify the sun path Properties.

b. Drag the sun along the path.

c. Change the time in the Options Bar.

d. Click on the time control.

6. To get the most accurate view of how the sun impacts your project, which of the following must be set before a solar study is produced?

a. The geographic location of the project site and the project's orientation to True North.

b. Nothing needs to be set.

c. The rotation of the building to Project North.

7. When creating a Multi-Day sun study, the *Time Interval* can be set to every 15 minutes.

a. True

b. False

Command Summary

Button	Command	Location
	Camera	• **Ribbon:** *View* tab>*Create* panel, expand 3D View • **Quick Access Toolbar:** Expand 3D View
N/A	**Graphic Display Options**	• **Properties** • **View Control Bar:** Expand *Visual Styles* • **Shortcut:** GD
	Location	• **Ribbon:** *Manage* tab>*Project Location* panel
N/A	**Preview Solar Study**	• **View Control Bar:** Expand *Sun Path*
	Rotate True North	• **Ribbon:** *Manage* tab>*Project Location* panel, expand Position
	Shadows On	• **View Control Bar**
	Shadows Off	• **View Control Bar**
	Sun Path On	• **View Control Bar**
	Sun Path Off	• **View Control Bar**
N/A	**Sun Settings**	• **View Control Bar:** Expand *Sun Path*
Exploded Views		
	Displace Elements	• **Ribbon:** *Modify <elements type>* tab>*View* panel
	Edit	• **Ribbon:** *Modify | Displacement Set* tab>*Displacement Set* panel
	Highlight Displacement Sets	• **View Control Bar**
	Path	• **Ribbon:** *Modify | Displacement Set* tab>*Displacement Set* panel
	Reset	• **Ribbon:** *Modify | Displacement Set* tab>*Displacement Set* panel

Chapter

4

Rendering

The most powerful way to show off a design is to create a rendering. Renderings provide a "real world" view that typical floor plans and elevations cannot match. Using a rendering, you can show materials, lighting, daylight, people, furniture, and plants as part of your design. You can use graduating levels of quality in your rendering as you prepare the view for a final, photorealistic rendering.

Learning Objectives

- Create a rendering of a view or a portion of a view.
- Set the rendering options.
- Add light fixtures and view light sources.
- Set up groups of lights so that you can control the lights that display in a rendering.
- Add people, plants, and other components to enhance your renderings.

4.1 Producing Basic Renderings

Rendering is a powerful tool where you display a photorealistic view of the model you are working on, such as the example shown in Figure 4–1. This can be used to help clients and designers alike to understand the building design in better detail. Renderings can be used as presentations for everything from code compliance to color schemes.

Figure 4–1

- While you can produce fairly elaborate renderings directly in Revit®, more extensive renderings are typically created in other software such as Autodesk® Navisworks®, Twinmotion®, or Autodesk® 3ds Max®.
- Twinmotion is a powerful real-time visualization tool that allows you to create stunning visual assets from your design data. It instantly reflects any changes you make, providing a dynamic and immersive experience. You can seamlessly transfer your Revit models to Twinmotion using the built-in Datasmith Exporter for Revit commands. This integration allows for a smooth transition and easy continuation of the design process.
- If you have an Autodesk Subscription, you can also render in the cloud using Autodesk® A360 Rendering. The service will notify you when the rendering is complete. You can view, download, and modify completed renderings in the Render Gallery.
- All rendering done in Revit is created using Autodesk® Raytracer. This rendering engine accurately represents real-world materials by calculating light and its impact on materials as accurately as possible.
- If you are upgrading a model from previous versions, any Mental Ray settings are automatically mapped to the appropriate Raytracer settings. These settings are not maintained when upgrading.

Importing a Revit Project into Twinmotion

With Twinmotion's real-time capabilities and seamless integration with Revit, it is perfect for creating captivating visualizations, engaging VR experiences, and delivering interactive presentations. As your Revit model evolves, you can effortlessly synchronize changes back into Twinmotion, keeping your design up-to-date with the latest revisions.

How To: Import a Revit Project into Twinmotion

1. Open Revit and open a Revit project.
2. Open a 3D view within the project. The visual style of the 3D view does not need to be set to any specific style.
3. In the *View* tab>*Presentation* panel, expand (Twinmotion) and click on (Open in Twinmotion).
4. In the *Direct Link* dialog box (shown in Figure 4–2), click **OK** to apply the default settings.

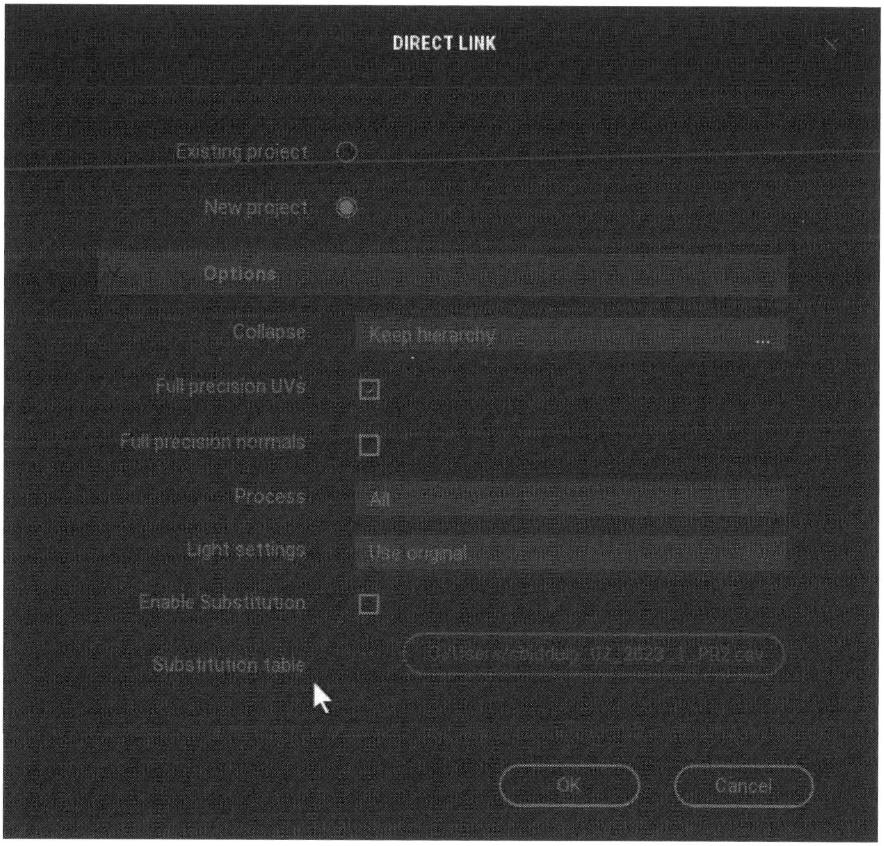

Figure 4–2

5. Twinmotion opens. You will see your Revit project, as shown in Figure 4–3.

Figure 4–3

Preparing Views for Rendering

To prepare a view for rendering, you need to:

- Create the 3D view.
- Verify that the materials you want are applied to the model elements.
- Toggle on shadows.
- Add lights and/or specify sun settings.
- Apply a background.
- Add Rich Photorealistic Content (RPC) components (such as plants, people, and cars).

Hint: Rendering 2D Views

Although only 3D views can be rendered, you can create a 3D view that looks like a 2D view. In a 3D view, right-click on the ViewCube and select **Orient to View** or **Orient to a Direction**. Set the view up using shadows and materials and render it, as shown in Figure 4–4.

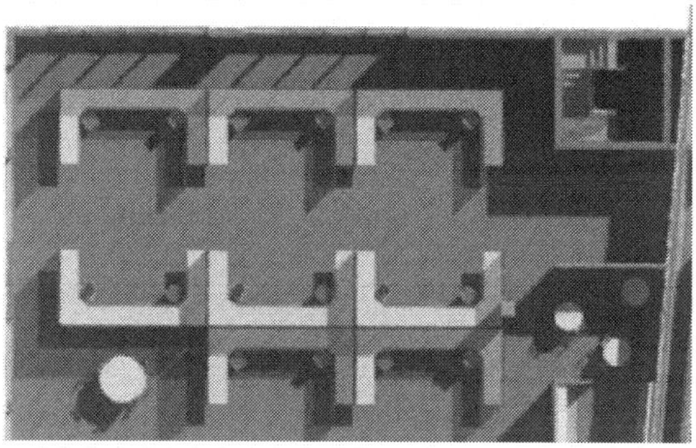

Figure 4–4

- Materials and lighting are built into many of the elements in the Revit model, including walls, windows, and light fixtures.
- The (Realistic) visual style gives you a sense of what the rendered view might actually look like. It includes any RPC you might have added.

How To: Render a View – Basic Steps

1. In the View Control Bar, click (Show Rendering Dialog), type **RR**, or in the *View* tab> *Presentation* panel, click (Render).

   Note: *This option only displays if you are in a 3D view.*

2. In the *Rendering* dialog box shown in Figure 4–5, set up the rendering settings for *Quality*, *Output Settings*, *Lighting*, and *Background*.

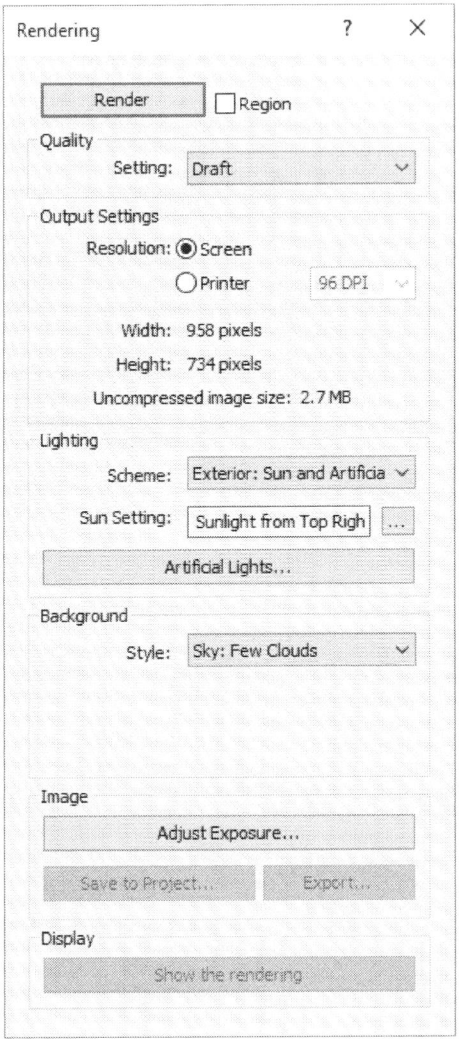

Figure 4–5

3. Click **Render**.

4. The *Rendering Progress* dialog box opens, as shown in Figure 4–6. It closes when the rendering is complete if that option is selected.

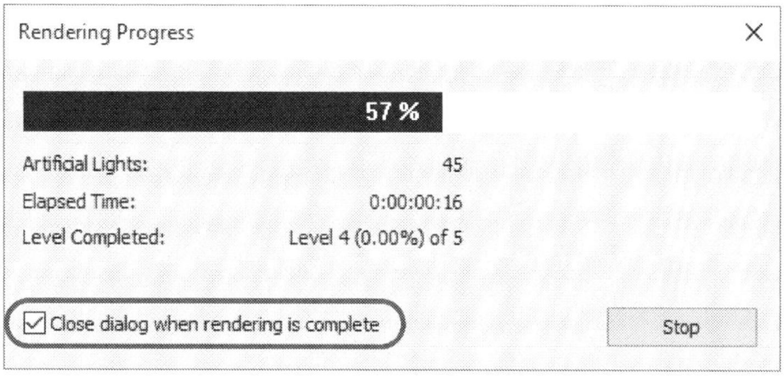

Figure 4–6

5. In the *Image* area of the *Rendering* dialog box, click **Adjust Exposure...** to modify the brightness and other options.

Note: Saving a rendering to a project significantly increases the file size.

6. Click **Save to Project...** to keep a copy of the rendering. Enter a name in the *Save To Project* dialog box (as shown in Figure 4–7) and click **OK**.

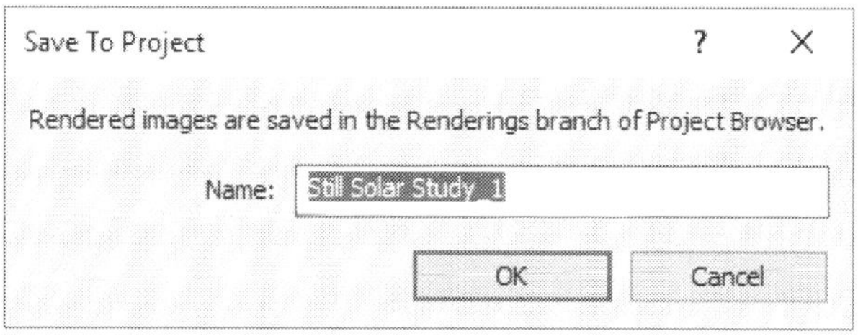

Figure 4–7

*Note: The **Save to Project...** and **Export...** options are not available until a view is rendered.*

- Rendered views saved to the Project Browser can be printed and placed on sheets.

7. Click **Export...** to export a rendering as .BMP, .JPG, .JPEG, .PNG, or .TIFF files.
   - The new file can be brought back into the project using the **Image** command.

8. When you are finished with an on-screen rendering, click **Show the model** in the *Display* area to remove the rendering from the view.

- Rendering information is saved with the 3D view used to create the rendering. In Properties, in the *Camera* area beside *Rendering Settings*, click **Edit...** to bring up the *Rendering Settings* dialog box, as shown in Figure 4–8. You can modify the *Quality*, *Lighting*, *Background*, and adjust the exposure of the *Image*.

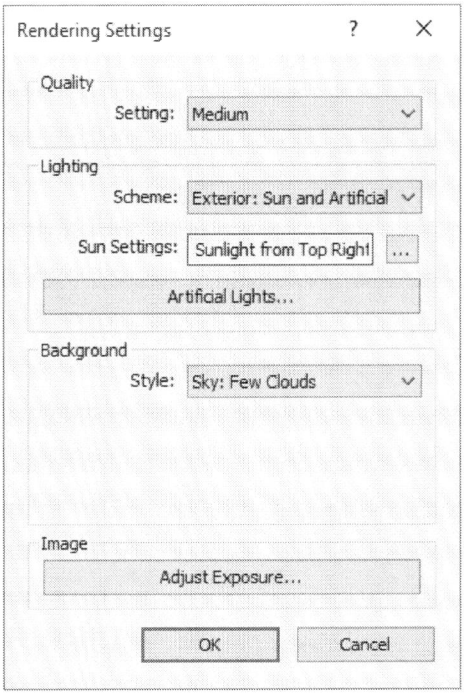

Figure 4–8

- Rendering settings can be included in a View Template and applied to other views.

Hint: Best Practices: Rendering a Region

The amount of time required to render an image is directly related to the complexity of the model and of the materials, the number of artificial lights, and the size or resolution of the image. To save time when you are developing the image, in the *Render* dialog box, select **Region** and place a region around some of the elements, as shown in Figure 4–9. It is also beneficial to go into Visibility/Graphic Overrides and turn off elements that are not seen in your rendering.

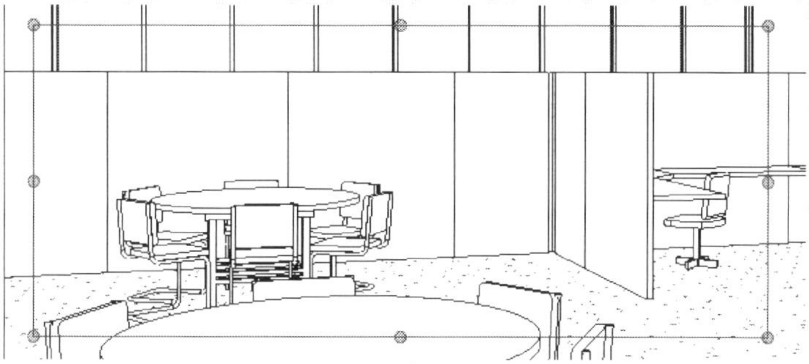

Figure 4–9

- Drag the box to move the entire region or drag the controls to resize the region.
- If some elements do not render as expected, check the materials. The material might be set to **<By Category>** rather than using a specific material.

Rendering Settings

Quality

The first setting you need to specify for a rendering is the *Quality*. You can select from a preset list (as shown in Figure 4–10) or create your own Custom (view specific) settings.

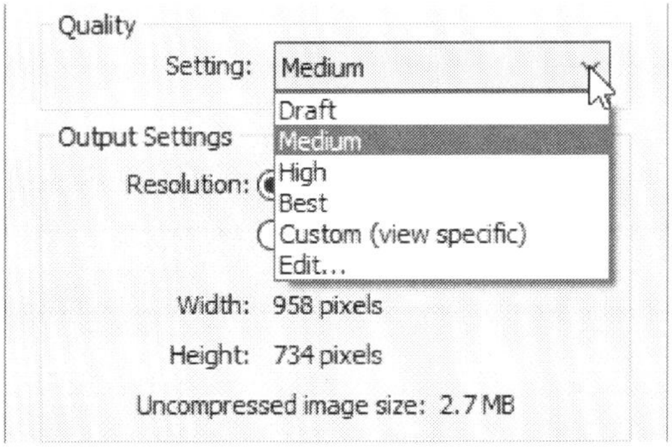

Figure 4–10

- Start with a draft quality image to verify that the materials and lights appear as you expect. Then, modify these elements and other settings and move to a higher quality output as you create a more realistic image. Only use high quality settings when you know you have the image you want.

Output Settings

Renderings can be set to the screen or to a printer. If you select the **Printer** option, you can select from a list of DPI (dots per inch) options. The *Width* and *Height* of the view are displayed in pixels and the image size is displayed in megabytes (MB), as shown in Figure 4–11.

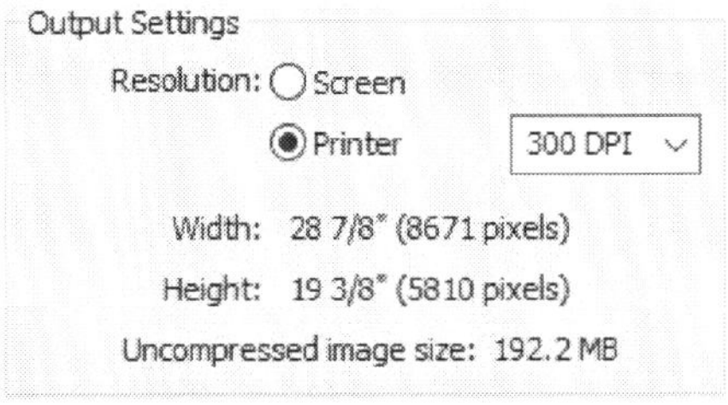

Figure 4–11

Lighting

In the *Lighting* area in the *Rendering* dialog box, you can select a *Scheme* that defines the use of the sun and artificial light, set up the *Sun* settings, and work with the artificial lights in the model, as shown in Figure 4–12.

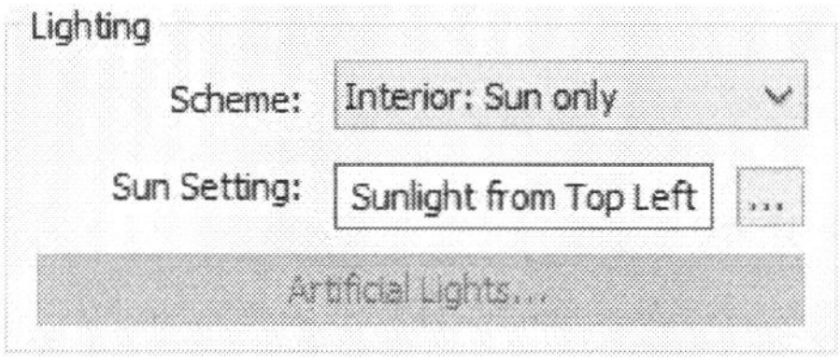

Figure 4–12

- Select from a variety of lighting schemes including **Exterior: Sun only**, **Exterior: Sun and Artificial**, **Exterior: Artificial only**, **Interior: Sun only**, **Interior: Sun and Artificial**, and **Interior: Artificial only**.
- For the *Sun Setting*, click  (Browse) to access the dialog box to select, make, or edit other solar studies.

  ***Note:** The Artificial Lights button is grayed out if you are set to one of the Sun Only lighting schemes.*

- Click **Artificial Lights...** to set up the lights and light groups used in the rendering.

Background

In the *Background* area in the *Rendering* dialog box, you can set the *Style* for the sky. Select from several levels of cloud cover, a color, or an image, and specify the *Haze* level for any amount of clouds, as shown in Figure 4–13.

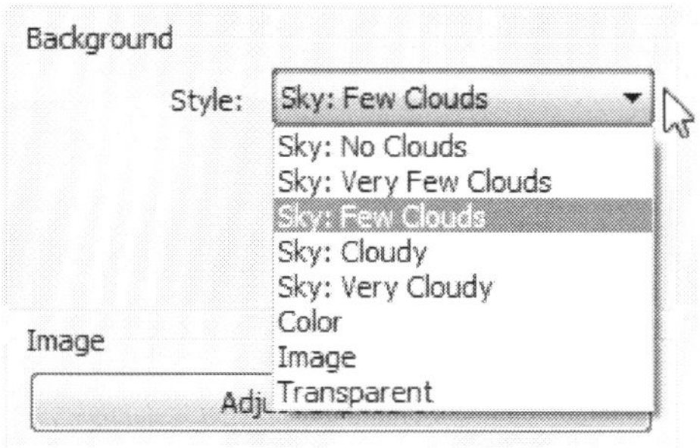

Figure 4–13

- The amount of clouds in a background impacts the overall quality of light in the rendering.
- When you select **Image**, you can specify any image file as the background.
- The **Transparent** option enables you to create a PNG or TIFF file that leaves the background transparent.

Image

Click **Adjust Exposure...** to open the *Exposure Control* dialog box, as shown in Figure 4–14. You can make the rendering brighter or darker, cooler or warmer, and more gray or more intense.

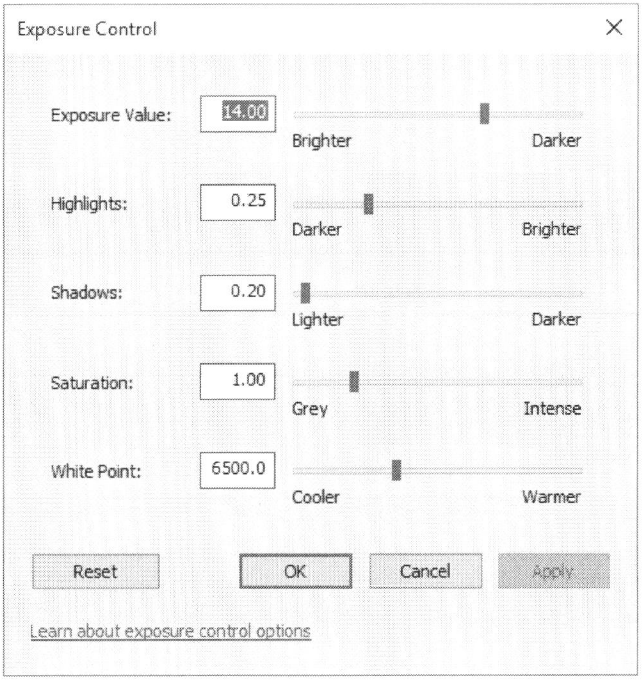

Figure 4–14

- Once you adjust the exposure, Revit remembers the settings for the current view the next time you repeat the rendering process.

Display

The *Display* area in the *Rendering* dialog box presents a button for **Show the model** when a rendering is active or **Show the rendering** when a rendering has been saved to the view. If it's grayed out, it means no rendering has been done in the active view.

Hint: Saving Custom Rendering Settings

If you have modified the rendering settings quality, you can save the settings to a view template, which can be used in another view or project.

1. Set up the 3D view with the rendering settings. Only 3D views display Render Settings.
2. Right-click on the view name in the Project Browser and select **Create View Template From View....**
3. Enter a new name for the view template and click **OK**.
4. In the *Apply View Template* dialog box, verify that the *Rendering Settings* are correct.
5. Click **OK**.

- To use the view settings for another view in the current project, right-click on the view name in the Project Browser and select **Apply Template Properties**.
- To use the view settings in another project, in the *Manage* tab>*Settings* panel, click  (Transfer Project Standards). You must be in a plan view to transfer the standards.

Practice 4a
Produce Basic Renderings

Practice Objectives

- Render a region of a view in Draft mode to test the materials.
- Modify materials and render at Medium mode.

In this practice, you will set up and render a test region of a view. You will also modify the materials of some elements and test the rendering again at a slightly higher quality.

Task 1: Render a region of the view.

1. In the practice files folder, open **Midrise-Rendering.rvt**.
2. Open the 3D Views: **Front Perspective** view.
3. Set the *Visual Style* to  (Shaded) to see the materials that come with the element styles (such as the brick walls, glass curtain wall and windows, and grass on the site), as shown in Figure 4–15.

   Note: *Your view might look slightly different.*

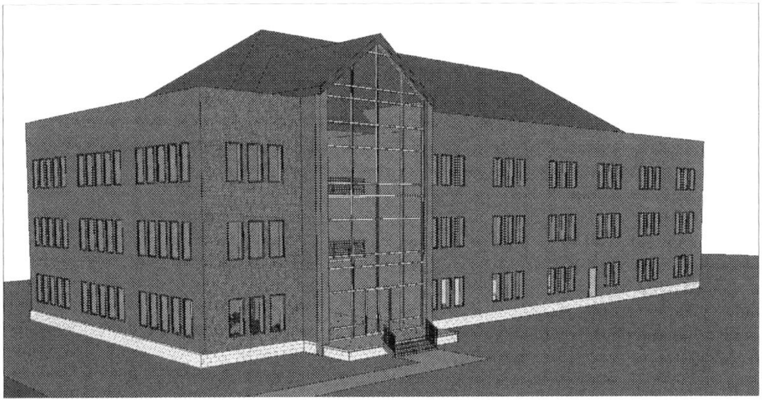

Figure 4–15

4. In the View Control Bar, click  (Show Rendering Dialog).

5. In the *Rendering* dialog box, select **Region**. Modify the existing region in the view by the grips so it is similar to Figure 4–16.

Figure 4–16

6. Set the following options in the *Rendering* dialog box:
   - *Quality:* **Draft**
   - *Output Settings:* **Screen**
   - *Lighting:* **Exterior: Sun only**
   - *Background:* **Sky: Few Clouds**
7. Click **Render**.

Task 2: Modify materials and render the view again.

Using the Draft quality setting displays the materials, but is not clear enough to provide a good view of the building, especially the mullions of the curtain wall. However, you can see that the stairs are made of brick, where they should be showing a stone material.

1. Click **Show the model** to return to the unrendered perspective. Keep the *Rendering* dialog box open and move it off to the side.
2. Select the stairs. In Properties, click (Edit Type).

3. Set the *Tread*, *Riser*, and *Stringer Material* for the stairs to **Masonry-Stone**, as shown in Figure 4–17.

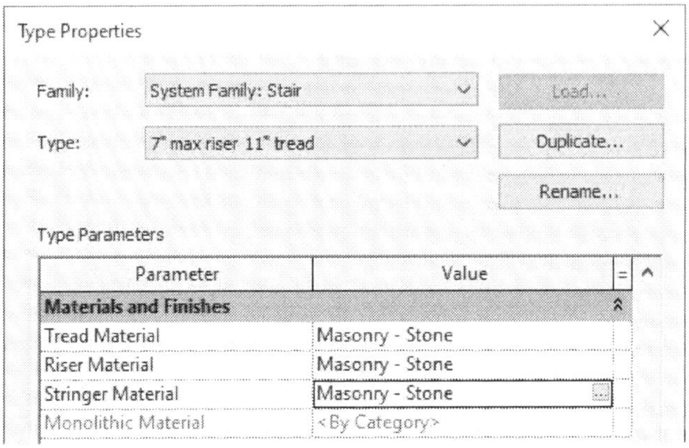

Figure 4–17

4. Click **OK** to close the *Type Properties* dialog box.
5. In the *Rendering* dialog box, set the *Quality Setting* to **Medium** and click **Render**.
6. The stairs display the correct color and the medium setting displays the curtain wall mullions more precisely, as shown in Figure 4–18.
7. In the *Rendering* dialog box, click **Adjust Exposure...**. In the *Exposure Control* dialog box, adjust the exposure to brighten the rendering. Click **Apply** to update the rendering. When finished, click **OK**.

Figure 4–18

8. In the *Rendering* dialog box, click **Save to Project...**. In the *Save To Project* dialog box, type **Entry-Medium** for the name and click **OK** to save the rendering to the project.
9. Click the X in the upper-right corner of the *Rendering* dialog box to close it.
10. Save the project and keep it open for the next practice.

End of practice

4.2 Working with Lighting

A crucial component of rendering is setting up lights —both sunlight and light fixtures that radiate light, as shown in Figure 4–19. Sunlight is controlled by the location, time of day, and cloud cover. Artificial light comes from lighting components that are added to the reflected ceiling plan or floor plan.

Figure 4–19

Light Fixture Families

Light fixtures are families that are placed with (Component). Many of the light fixture families included in Revit have multiple options for the type of lamp in the fixture, as shown in Figure 4–20.

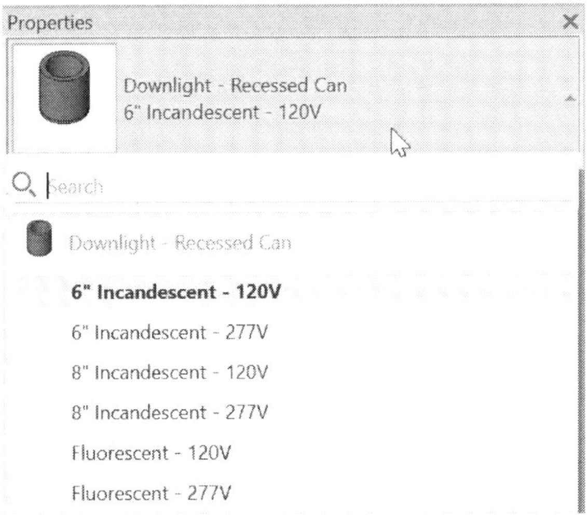

Figure 4–20

Viewing Light Sources

As you place light fixtures, especially spotlights, sconces, or downlights illuminating specific objects, it is helpful to toggle on the light sources, as shown in Figure 4–21.

Figure 4–21

How To: Toggle On Light Sources

1. Open the *Visibility/Graphic Overrides* dialog box.
2. In the *Model Categories* tab, expand **Lighting Fixtures** and select **Light Source**, as shown in Figure 4–22.

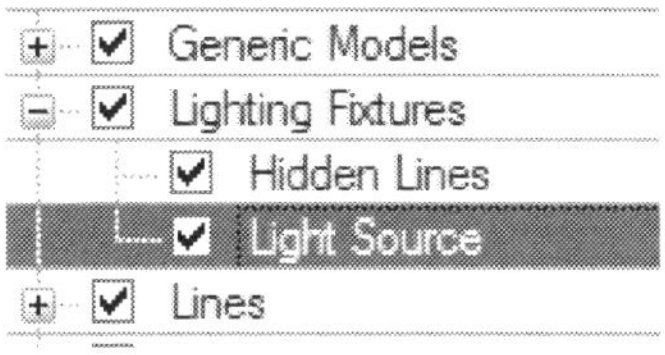

Figure 4–22

3. Click **OK**.

- Toggle on the  (Shaded) visual style to get the best view of the light sources. Shading displays the difference between the beam angle and the field angle for spotlights.
- To have even more accurate lighting in a rendering, you can specify photometric light sources. These sources use an IES file from the lighting manufacturer. This file describes the light intensity for points on a spherical grid and how the light comes from the fixture. Light sources are specified in the lighting fixture family.

Setting Up Light Groups

While a project might include hundreds of light fixtures in the building, only some of them impact the rendering you are working on. To save time, limit the light fixtures to those that are used in the current view by creating and setting up light groups.

How To: Create Light Groups

1. Open the view that displays the lights you want to group.
2. Select at least one of the lights.
3. In the Options Bar, in the *Light Group:* drop-down list, select **Edit/New...** to create a new group, as shown in Figure 4–23.

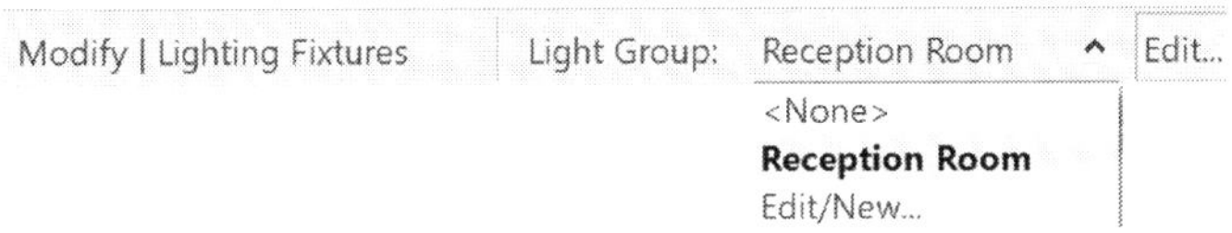

Figure 4–23

4. The *Artificial Lights* dialog box opens, as shown in Figure 4–24.

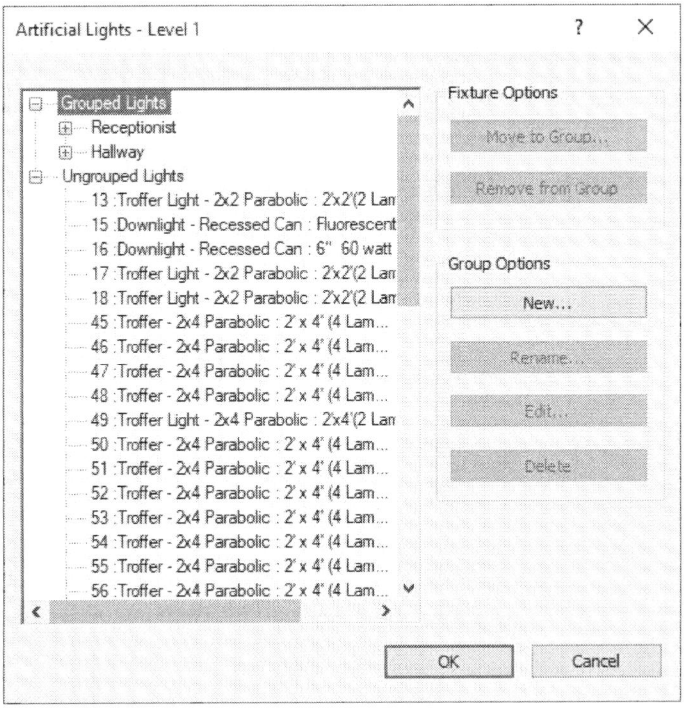

Figure 4–24

5. In the *Group Options* area in the dialog box, click **New** to create a new group.
6. In the *New Light Group* dialog box, enter a name for the light group and click **OK**.
7. Select the new group name and in the *Group Options* area, click **Edit...**.
8. The floating *Light Group* panel displays. Select  (Add) and click on each light that you want to add to the light group, as shown in Figure 4–25.

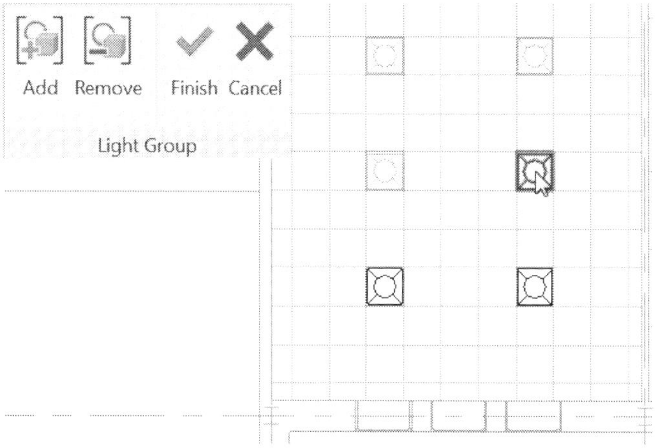

Figure 4–25

9. Click  (Finish), then click **OK**.

- When you need to edit a light group, select at least one light. In the Options Bar, select a light group from the *Light Group:* drop-down list (as shown in Figure 4–26) and click **Edit...**.

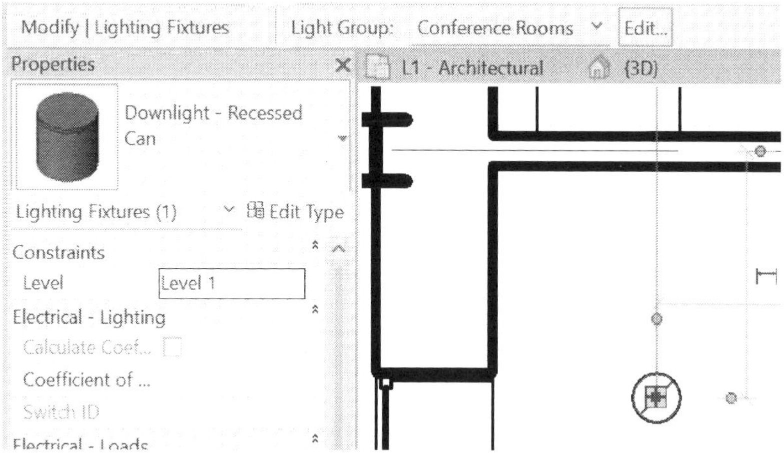

Figure 4–26

- If you select a light that is already part of another group, you will get the message that you are about to move the light to a new group, as shown in Figure 4–27.

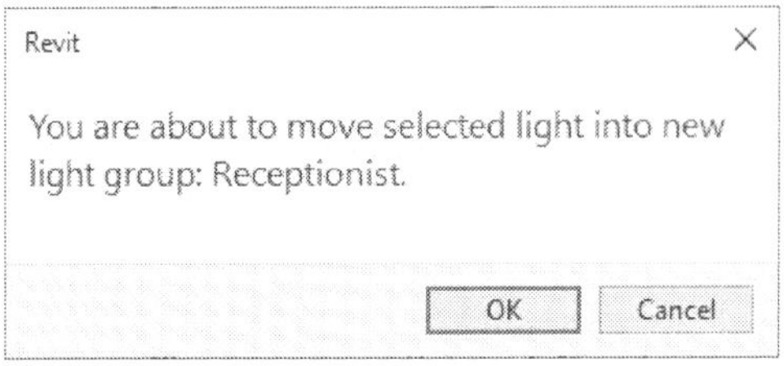

Figure 4–27

How To: Add Lights to a Light Group

1. Open the view that displays the lights you want to add to a group.
2. Select at least one of the lights.
3. In the Options Bar, in the *Light Group:* drop-down list, select an existing group.
4. An alert box opens prompting you that you are about to move the selected light(s) to a new light group. Click **OK** or **Cancel**.

How To: Use Light Groups in a Rendering

1. Open a 3D view to render. In the View Control Bar, click (Show Rendering Dialog).
2. In the *Rendering* dialog box, in the *Lighting* area, select a *Scheme* that includes artificial lights.

   Note: *This option is only available if a Scheme with artificial lights has been selected.*

3. Click **Artificial Lights...**.

4. In the *Artificial Lights* dialog box for the view, the lists of grouped and ungrouped lights display. Clear the groups and ungrouped lights that you do not need for the rendering, as shown in Figure 4–28.

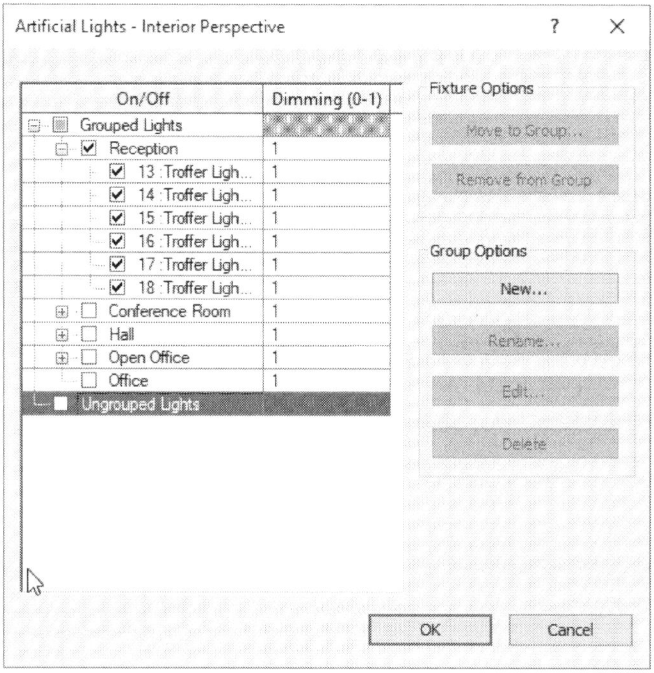

Figure 4–28

- You can also dim a light or light group using this dialog box. Set the value for *Dimming* to either **0** (off) or **1** (not dimmed).

Hint: Section Boxes and Rendering

Section boxes are another way to limit the geometry viewed and calculated when creating a rendering.

In a 3D view, in the *Extents* area in Properties, click **Section Box**. The default size is the extents of the view. Resize the section box using the controls, as shown in Figure 4–29, before rendering the view.

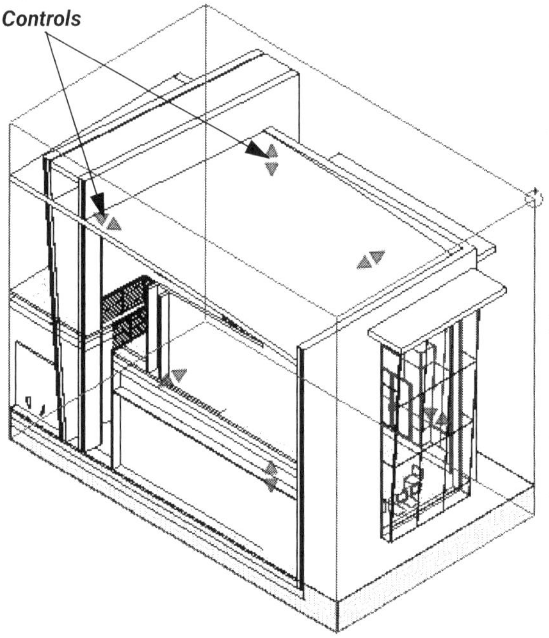

Figure 4–29

Practice 4b
Work with Lighting

Practice Objectives

- Set up light groups for a specific room and add light fixtures.
- Render a view using light groups.

In this practice, you will set up light groups, add a light fixture, view the light source, and render a region. Once the rendering is finished, you will adjust the exposure, as shown in Figure 4–30.

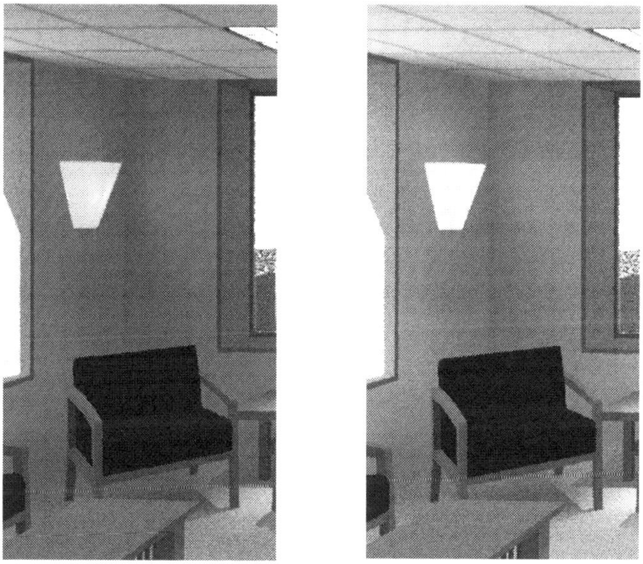

Original rendering ***Exposure adjusted***

Figure 4–30

Task 1: Set up light groups.

1. Continue working in **Midrise-Rendering.rvt**.

2. Open the Ceiling Plans: **Level 1** view. Notice the light fixtures in the ceiling, as shown in Figure 4–31.

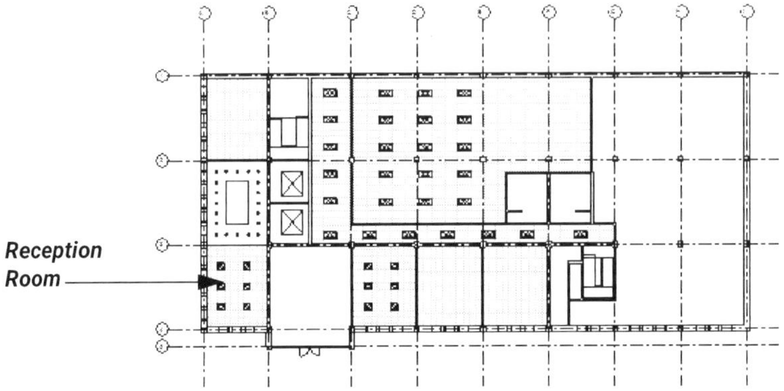

Figure 4–31

3. Zoom in on the Reception Room in the lower-left corner of the building (as shown previously in Figure 4–31).
4. Select one of the lights. In the Options Bar, in the *Light Group:* drop-down list, select **Edit/New**.
5. In the *Artificial Lights* dialog box, in the *Group Options* area, click **New**. Set the name to **Reception Room** and click **OK**. Click **OK** to close the dialog box.
6. Select all six lights in the Reception Room and set the *Light Group* to **Reception Room**, as shown in Figure 4–32.

Figure 4–32

7. Click **OK** to move the lights to the Reception Room light group. Click in an empty space in the view to clear the selection of the lights.

Task 2: Add light fixtures.

1. Open the Floor Plans: **Level 1** view and zoom in on the Reception room.
2. In the *Architecture* tab>*Build* panel, click (Component).
3. In the *Modify | Place Component* tab>*Mode* panel, click (Load Family).
4. In the *Load Family* dialog box, navigate to the practice files *Families* folder, select **Floor Lamp - Arm Extension.rfa**, and load it into the project.

5. Place the two lamps behind the chairs near the outside corner of the wall. Rotate it as shown in Figure 4–33.

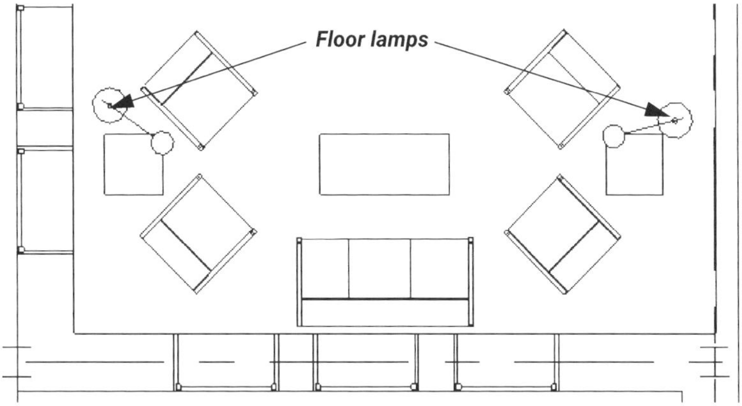

Figure 4–33

6. Select the floor lamp. In the Options Bar, set the *Light Group* to **Reception Room**. Click **OK** to accept moving the light to the Reception Room light group.
7. Open the **3D Views: Interior Perspective** view.
8. View the light sources. Type **VG** and expand the *Lighting Fixtures* category. Select **Light Source** and click **OK**.
9. In the View Status Bar, click (Shaded). The light sources display similar to those shown in Figure 4–34.

Figure 4–34

Task 3: Render a view.

1. In the View Control Bar, click (Show Rendering Dialog).
2. In the *Rendering* dialog box, in the *Lighting* area, set the *Scheme* to **Interior: Sun and Artificial**.
3. Beside *Sun Setting*, click (Choose a sun location).
4. In the *Sun Settings* dialog box, *Solar Study* area, select **Still**.
5. In the *Settings* area, set the *Time* to early morning. This keeps the light coming in from the windows from being too bright. Click **OK**.
6. In the *Rendering* dialog box, click the **Artificial Lights...** button.
7. In the *Artificial Lights* dialog box, verify that **Reception Room** is toggled on and **Ungrouped Lights** is cleared so that they do not display in the rendering, as shown in Figure 4–35.

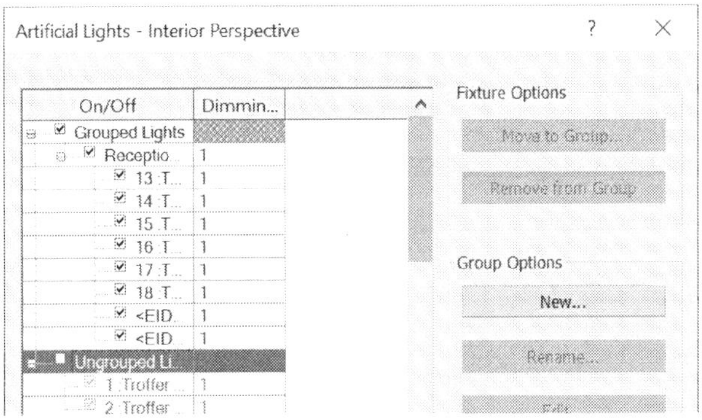

Figure 4–35

8. Click **OK**.
9. In the *Rendering* dialog box, select **Region**. Modify the region so that it shows the floor lamp and some other light fixture.
10. Set the *Quality Setting* to **Draft** and click **Render**.
11. When the *Rendering Progress* dialog box opens, check the number of Artificial Lights it is calculating.
12. When the rendering displays, click **Adjust Exposure...** and modify the various exposure controls, then click **Apply** to see the changes. Click **Reset** to go back to the original settings.
13. Click **OK**.
14. Close the *Rendering* dialog box.
15. Save the project and keep it open for the next practice.

End of practice

4.3 Enhancing Renderings

Many components provided in Revit are ready to be rendered. Although furniture has a specific wood pattern, lights include light sources, and windows have transparent glass material in the panes, this is often not enough. You can further enhance renderings by splitting faces and applying different materials to elements such as walls and floors. You can also add Rich Photorealistic Content (RPC) components, such as trees and people, that are specifically created for adding to renderings, as shown in Figure 4–36.

Figure 4–36

Applying Materials

You may want to apply information that is not in the model element, such as different materials on the face of a wall, as shown in Figure 4–37. The **Split Face** command divides an element face into smaller separate faces. You can then use the **Paint** command to apply different materials to the faces.

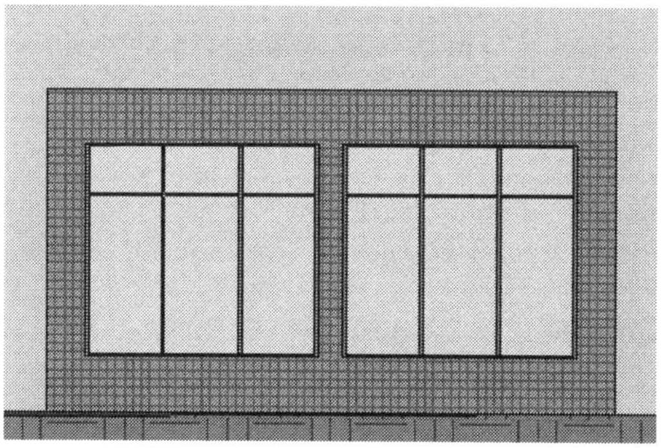

Figure 4–37

- The changes made with **Split Face** and **Paint** are displayed in elevations and 3D views.
- **Split Face** and **Paint** do not alter the structure of the wall.
- The area and other information about the materials can be used in a Material takeoff schedule.

How To: Create a Split Face

1. Switch to an elevation view (a 3D view works as well).
2. In the *Modify* tab>*Geometry* panel, click (Split Face).

   ***Note:** If the (Select elements by face) option is toggled on in the lower left corner of the Status Bar, you can click directly on the face.*

3. Select the edge of the face that you want to modify. Use <Tab> to toggle through the available faces.
4. In the *Modify | Split Face>Create Boundary* tab>*Draw* panel, use the sketch tools to create a sketch to define the split, as shown in Figure 4–38.

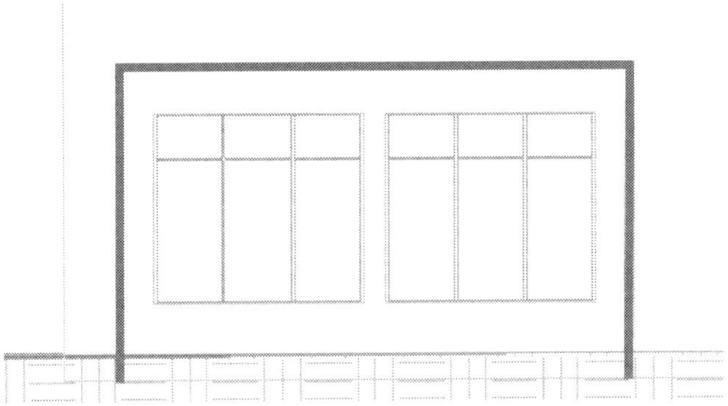

Figure 4–38

   - The split must be a closed shape completely inside the face, or an open shape that touches the face edges.
   - Windows are cut out of faces automatically.

5. Click (Finish Edit Mode).

- Before you begin working with split faces, ensure that the walls are mitered. By default, the walls are butted to each other. This creates a problem when you select faces.
- To save time, use a wall style that includes the primary material you want to use on the split face. For example, if you are working with brick, set the wall to a type that has a brick face. This way, you can work with the brick courses when creating the split face.

- When using a material, such as brick, you can snap to the pattern and even lock the split lines to the pattern, as shown in Figure 4–39.

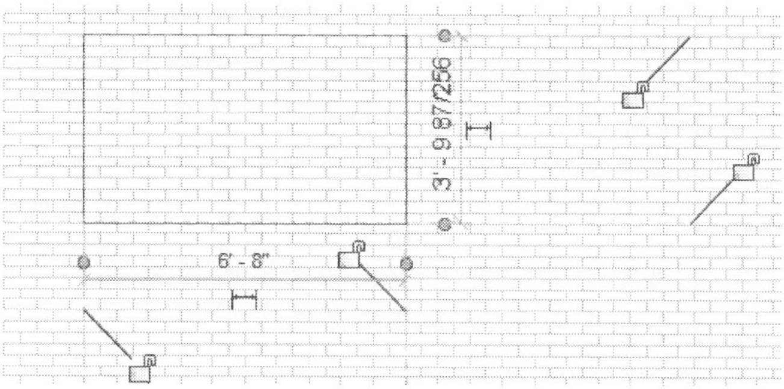

Figure 4–39

You can double-click on the edge of the split face lines to switch to the Edit Boundary mode. If you double-click on the wall face (with the **Select elements by face** option toggled on) it switches to the Edit Profile mode, which impacts the entire wall, not just the split face boundary.

How To: Apply Material with Paint

1. In the *Modify* tab>*Geometry* panel, click (Paint), or type **PT**.
2. In the Material Browser, select a material. You can run a search or filter the list using specific types of materials, as shown in Figure 4–40.

   Note: *The browser remains open as you apply the paint.*

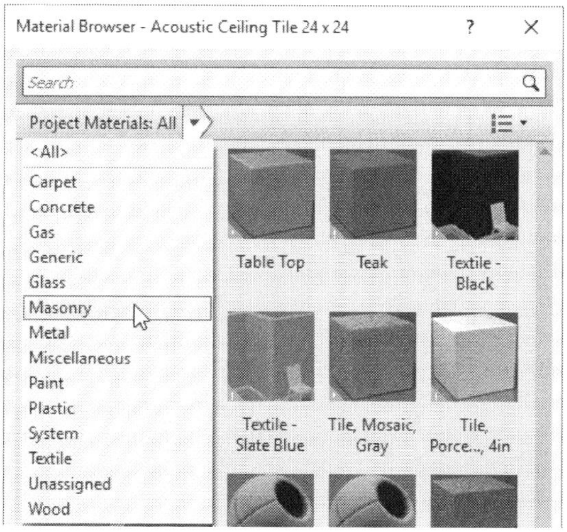

Figure 4–40

3. Hover the cursor over the face you want to paint. It should highlight, as shown in Figure 4–41. Click on the face to apply the material.

Figure 4–41

4. Continue selecting materials and painting other faces if needed.
5. In the Material Browser, click **Done** to finish the command.

- Some material patterns display as shaded when you zoom out. Zoom in to display the pattern. Other material patterns only display when you are in the (Realistic) visual style or when you render.
- To remove the material applied to a face, in the *Modify* tab>*Geometry* panel, expand (Paint) and click (Remove Paint). Select the face(s) from which you want to remove the material.

Adding People and Other Components

Rich Photorealistic Content (RPC) is a specific type of component that helps to make renderings more lifelike. The Revit libraries include RPC people and plants, as shown in Figure 4–42, as well as office items and vehicles. To place signs, paintings, and other flat graphics such as the picture in Figure 4–42, you can add decals.

Figure 4–42

Adding RPC Elements

RPC elements are added using the **Component** command. Samples of vehicles, people, and office objects are available in the Revit Library in the *Entourage* folder. Once you load them into the project, you can select them from the Type Selector, as shown in Figure 4–43.

> ***Note:*** *You can purchase additional objects from ArchVision™.*

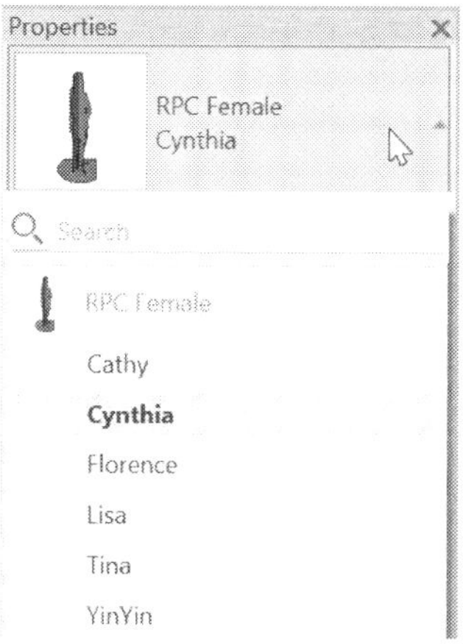

Figure 4–43

- You need to be in a 3D orthographic view or floor plan view to place components.

In a plan, the person displays with a point indicating the direction in which they are facing. In a 3D view, they display in outline. In a rendering, they display as they have been created, as shown in Figure 4–44.

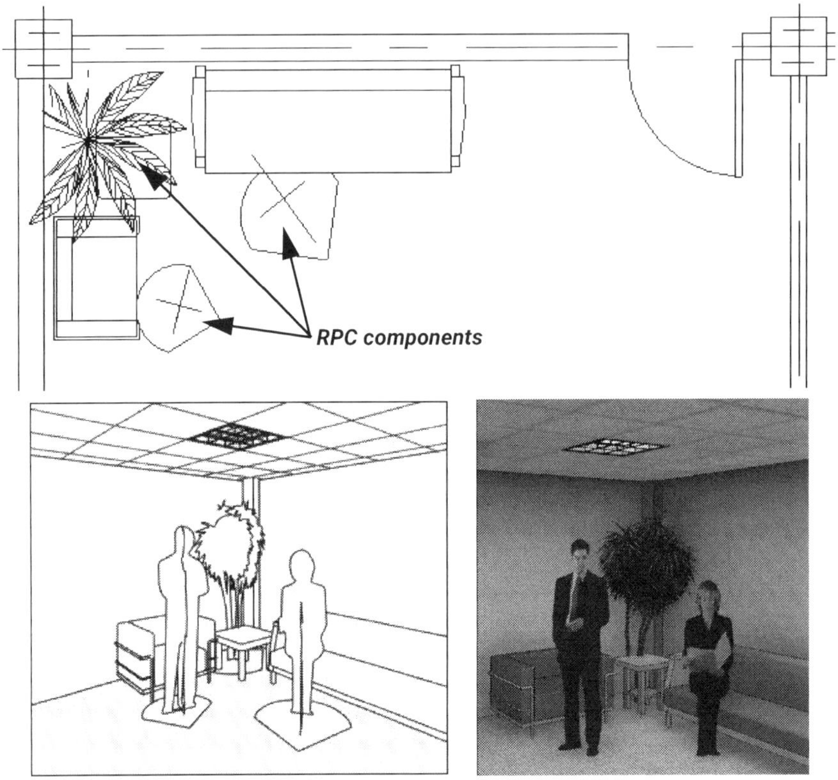

Figure 4–44

- If you are working with Revit topography element components such as trees and shrubs, you can use a different command that places the element directly on the toposurface. In the *Massing & Site* tab>*Model Site* panel, click (Site Component).

Adding Decals

Decals are links to images that you can place on flat or cylindrical surfaces. They are used for signs, pictures, or other flat surfaced elements. Decals display an outline in most visual styles (as shown in Figure 4–45); however, they display in full when rendered or in the Realistic visual style, as shown in Figure 4–46.

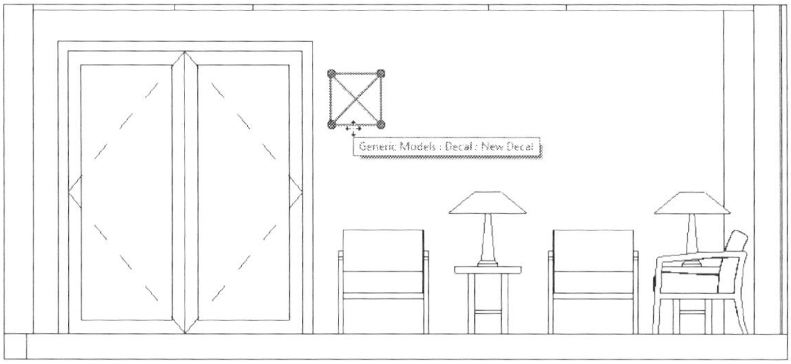

Figure 4–45

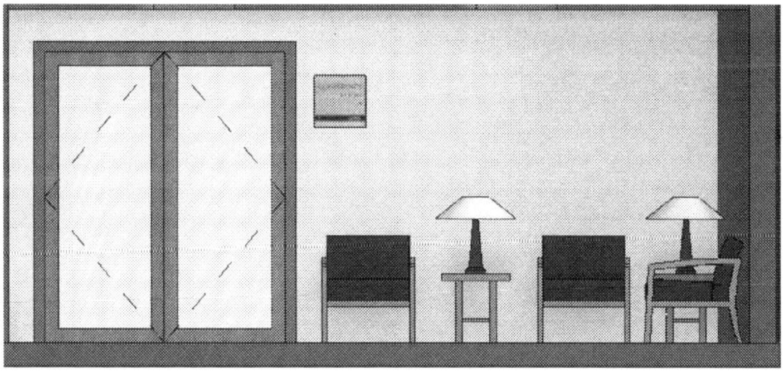

Figure 4–46

How To: Create a Decal Type

1. Start the **Decal** command.
   - If no decal exists in the project, the *Decal Types* dialog box will open. Click (Create New Decal), set a name for it, and skip to step 6.
2. In the Type Selector, select a Decal and click **Edit Type**.
3. In the *Type Properties* dialog box, click **Duplicate...**.
4. In the *Name* dialog box, enter a name for the decal and click **OK**.
5. Beside the **Decal Attributes** parameter, click **Edit...**.

6. In the *Decal Types* dialog box, click (...) beside *Source*.

   Note: *If you are adding the first decal in a project, you will work in the full Decal Types dialog box.*

7. In the *Select File* dialog box, select the image and click **Open**. The new image displays and you can modify the other settings, as shown in Figure 4–47.

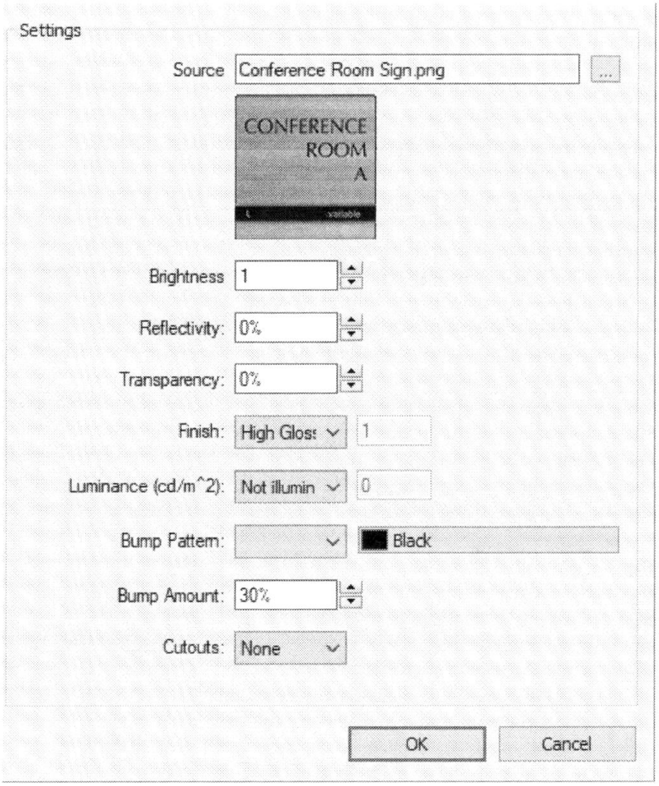

Figure 4–47

8. Click **OK**.

- To open the full *Decal Types* dialog box, in the *Insert* tab>*Link* panel, expand (Decal) and click (Decal Types).

How To: Add Decals

1. Open a 2D view such as a section or elevation.
2. In the *Insert* tab>*Link* panel, expand (Decal) and click (Place Decal).
3. In the Type Selector, select from the loaded decals.
4. Place the decal on the face of an element.
5. In the Options Bar, specify the *Width* and *Height*. Click **Lock Proportions** to lock the aspect ratio of the decal, as shown in Figure 4–48. Click **Reset** to return to the original size.

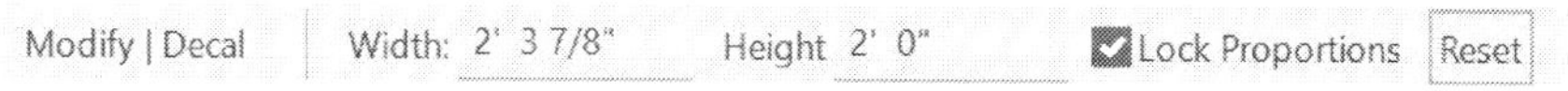

Figure 4–48

- You can also use the *Drag* controls to resize the decal.

Practice 4c
Enhance Renderings

Practice Objectives

- Modify the floor materials by splitting the face and painting a new material on part of it.
- Add a decal to a wall.
- Add people and plant components in a room and render it.

In this practice, you will split the face of the floor and apply a different material to a part of it. You will also add a sign next to the conference room door and add people and trees. You will then render the reception room, as shown in Figure 4–49.

Figure 4–49

Task 1: Modify the floor material.

1. Continue working in **Midrise-Rendering.rvt**.
2. Open the **Floor Plans: Level 1** view.
3. Zoom in on the reception room in the lower-left part of the building.
4. In the *Modify* tab>*Geometry* panel, click (Split Face).
5. Hover the cursor over the interior edge of one of the exterior walls and select the floor.

6. In the *Modify | Split Face>Create Boundary* tab>*Draw* panel, use the draw tools to split the reception room floor into two faces, as shown in Figure 4–50. Click (Finish Edit Mode) when you are done.

   Note: *The sketch must be closed or touch existing boundary lines to make the closed shape.*

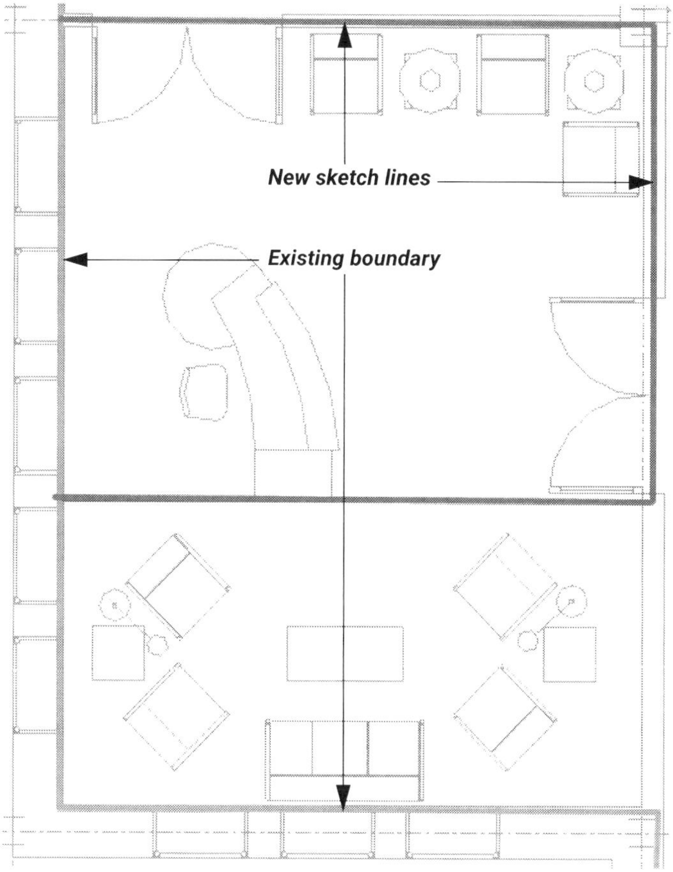

Figure 4–50

7. Click (Modify).
8. Set the *Visual Style* to **Realistic**. The existing floor type is carpet.
9. In the *Modify* tab>*Geometry* panel, click (Paint).

10. In the Material Browser, select a material for part of the floor. A variety of carpet styles are available in the project. Select the portion of the floor to apply the material, as shown in Figure 4–52.
    - There are also a number of *Wood* project materials that you can chose from, as shown in Figure 4–51.
11. The flooring will update in real time with the material you select, as shown in Figure 4–52.

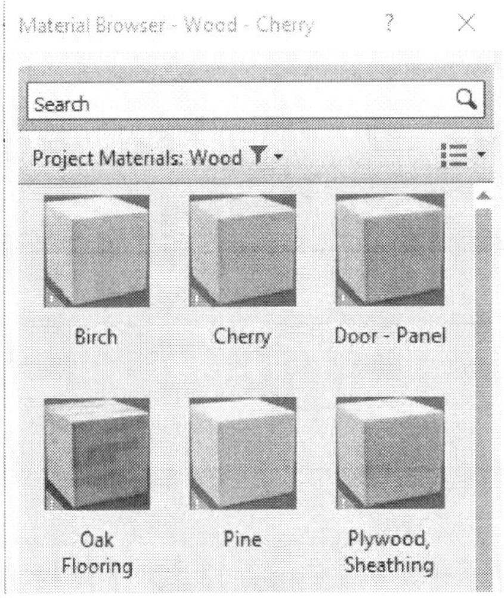

Figure 4–51

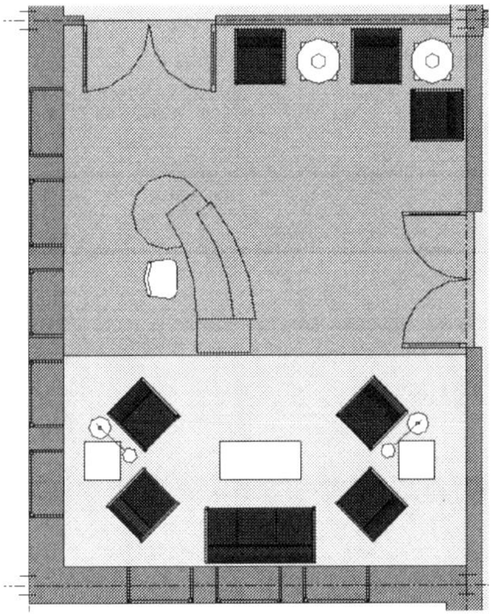

Figure 4–52

12. Click **Done**.
    - If you want to change the other half of the flooring and keep the Paint command from changing the rest of the carpeting in the building, you need to create a second split face.
13. Open the **Interior Perspective** view and test out the flooring change by setting the *Visual Style* to **Realistic**.
    - Adjust the graphic display options as needed.
14. Modify the view angle, if needed, to show the floor.
15. Save the project.

Task 2: Add a decal.

1. Return to the **Floor Plans: Level 1** view and set the *Visual Style* to **Hidden Line**.
2. Add a section that will display the double doors to the right of the reception desk.
3. Modify the section cut plane if needed, as shown in Figure 4–53.

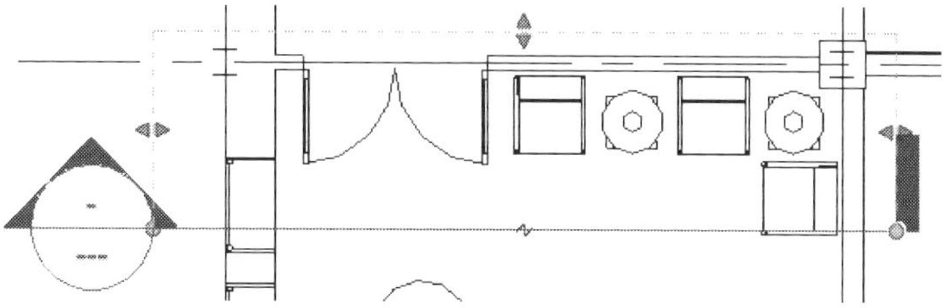

Figure 4–53

4. Open the section view, adjust the crop region (as shown in Figure 4–54), and set the *Detail Level* to **Fine**.

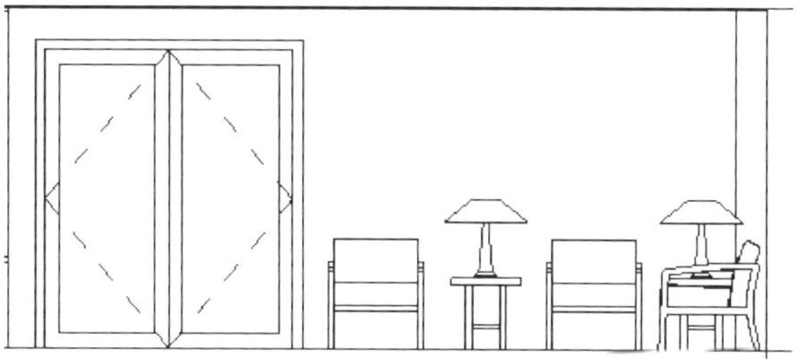

Figure 4–54

5. In the *Insert* tab>*Link* panel, click (Decal).
6. In the *Decal Types* dialog box, click (Create New Decal) and name it **Conference Room Sign**.
7. In the *Decal Types* dialog box, click beside *Source*.

8. In the *Select File* dialog box, navigate to the practice files *Images* folder and select **Conference Room Sign.png**. Click **Open**. The new image displays and you can modify the other settings, as shown in Figure 4–55.

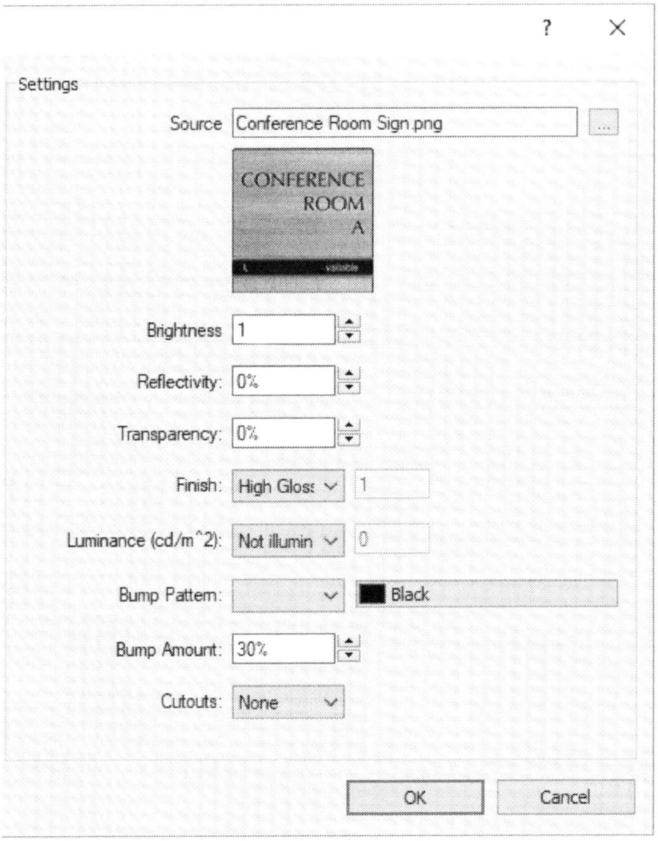

Figure 4–55

9. Click **OK**.
10. Click on the wall next to the double door to place the sign on the face of the wall.
11. Click (Modify) and select the new decal.
12. In the Options Bar, verify that **Lock Proportions** is selected. Change the *Height* to **1'-0"**, as shown in Figure 4–56.

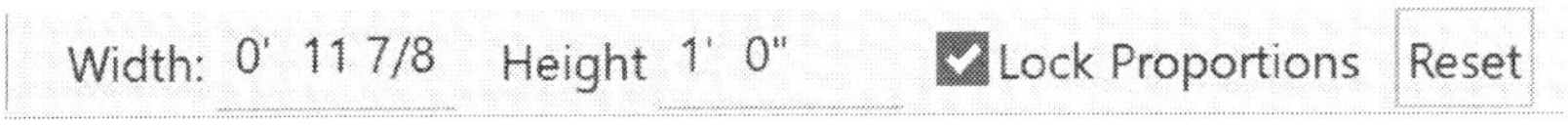

Figure 4–56

13. Click in the *Width* edit box to apply the change.

14. Change the *Visual Style* to **Realistic** to see the final image. Move the decal where you want it on the wall, such as that shown in Figure 4–57.

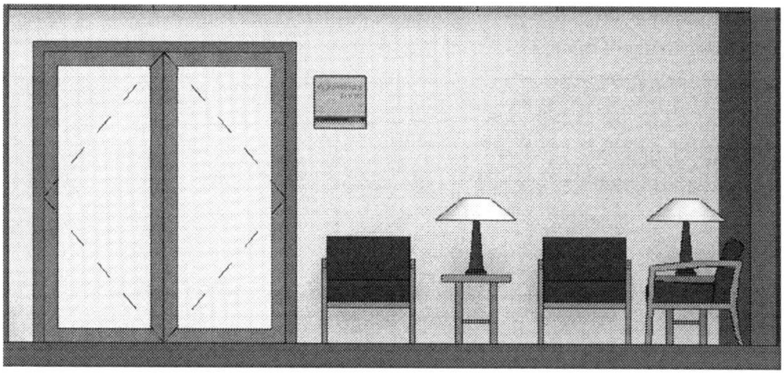

Figure 4–57

15. Save the project.

Task 3: Add people and plants.

1. Return to the **Floor Plans: Level 1** view.
2. In the *Architecture* tab>*Build* panel, click (Component).
3. In the *Modify | Place Component* tab>*Mode* panel, click (Load Family).
4. In the practice files *Families* folder, select **RPC Male.rfa** and **RPC Female.rfa** and load them into the project.
5. Place several people inside the Reception Room in the floor plan. Rotate them as required. The pointed end is the front of the person, as shown in Figure 4–58.

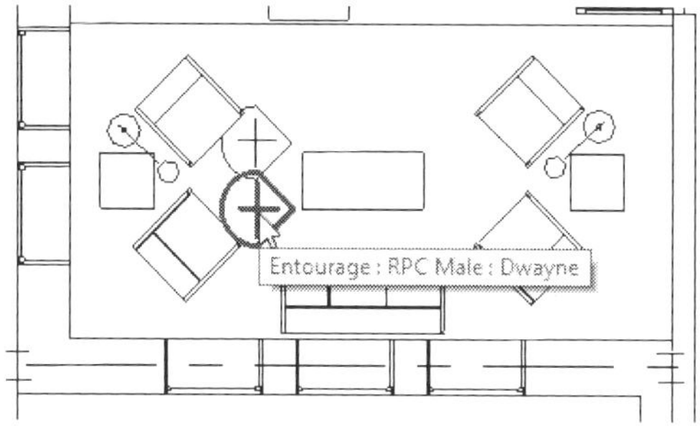

Figure 4–58

6. In the *Massing & Site* tab>*Model Site* panel, click (Site Component). Click **Load Family**. Navigate to the practice files *Families>Planting* folder and select and load **RPC Tree - Conifer.rfa** and **RPC Tree - Deciduous.rfa**.

   Note: *There is a toposurface in this project.*

7. Add trees outside the windows so that they can be seen in the perspective view.
8. Switch to the **Interior Perspective** view and change the *Visual Style* to **Hidden Line**. You should see outlines of the people and possibly some of the trees through the window, similar to that shown in Figure 4–59.

Figure 4–59

9. Switch to the  (Realistic) visual style to test the direction of the people.
10. Render a region or, if time permits, the entire scene.
11. Save and close the project.

End of practice

Chapter Review Questions

1. What should you do to prepare a view for rendering?
    a. Toggle on the Sun Path.
    b. Lock the view.
    c. Add lights.
    d. Set the *Visual Style* to  (Realistic).

2. What is the purpose of the **Region** option in the *Rendering* dialog box, as shown in Figure 4–60?

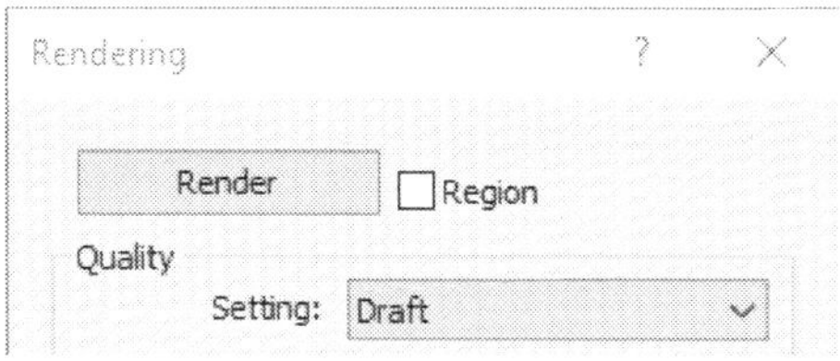

Figure 4–60

    a. It only toggles on lights in a specified region.
    b. It only displays materials in a specified region.
    c. It only includes shadows in a specified region.
    d. It only renders in a specified region.

3. If a rendering is darker than expected, how do you make it lighter?
    a. Add more light fixtures.
    b. Adjust the exposure.
    c. Modify the location of the sun.
    d. Change the Lighting Scheme.

4. How do you limit the number of lights used in a rendering?
   a. Hide any lights that you do not want to use.
   b. Isolate the lights that you want to use.
   c. Set up a light group.
   d. Delete the additional lights.

5. How can you display the light sources?
   a. Set the *Visual Style* to **Shaded**.
   b. In the *Visibility/Graphic Overrides* dialog box, select **Light Source**.
   c. In Properties, select **Light Source**.
   d. It depends on the type of light fixture family used.

Command Summary

Button	Command	Location
	**Component**	• **Ribbon:** *Architecture* tab>*Build* panel • **Shortcut:** CM
	**Decal Types**	• **Ribbon:** *Insert* tab>*Link* panel, expand Decal
	**Load Family**	• **Ribbon:** *Modify | Place Component* tab>*Mode* panel
	**Place Decal**	• **Ribbon:** *Insert* tab>*Link* panel, expand Decal
	**Site Component**	• **Ribbon:** *Massing & Site* tab>*Model Site* panel
	**Show Rendering Dialog**	• **View Control Bar**
	**Transfer Project Standards**	• **Ribbon:** *Manage* tab>*Settings* panel

Appendix A

Additional Tools for Massing

There are many other tools available in the Autodesk® Revit® software that can be used when creating massing studies for your models. This appendix provides details about tools and commands that are related to those covered in this guide.

Learning Objectives

- Review the process of creating a conceptual mass family, including dimensions, labels, and family types.
- Work with reference-based forms.

A.1 Conceptual Mass Families

Conceptual mass families can be used to create massing studies that can then be used in a project. This is useful if you are creating multiple copies of one building design on a site, as shown in Figure A–1. As with other families, you can use reference planes, dimensions and labels, and types to make the mass elements parametric.

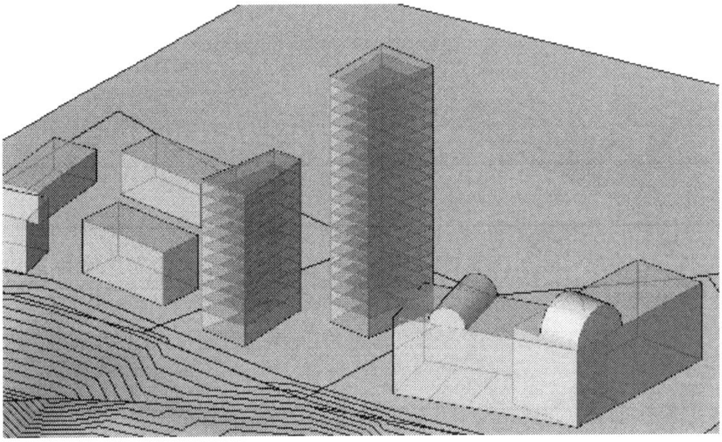

Figure A–1

How To: Create a Conceptual Mass Family

1. In the Home screen *Families* area, click **New...**, or in the *File* tab, expand  (New) and click  (Conceptual Mass).
2. In the *New Conceptual Mass - Select Template File* dialog box, in the *Conceptual Mass* folder, select the **Mass.rft** template and click **Open**.
3. In the Conceptual Mass Environment, use the *Create* tab>*Draw* panel (shown in Figure A–2) to add reference planes, reference lines, dimensions, labels, and other parameters.

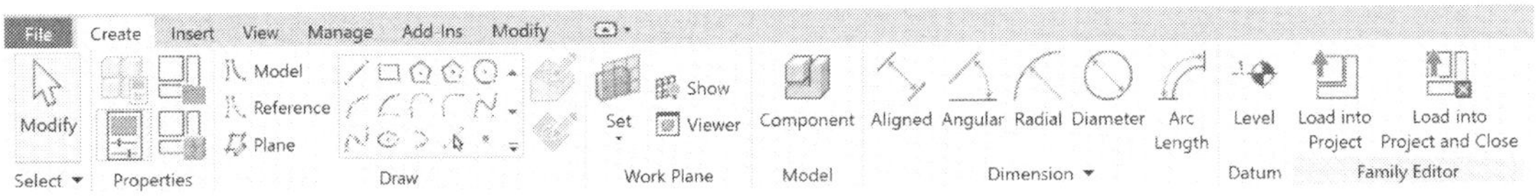

Figure A–2

4. Use the drawing tools to draw the profiles and paths that will make up the solid.
5. Select the sketched linework.
6. In the *Modify | Lines* tab>*Form* panel, click  (Create Form). Revit creates a 3D mass based on the selected linework.

7. Use the dimensioning tools to add additional labels, as shown in Figure A–3.

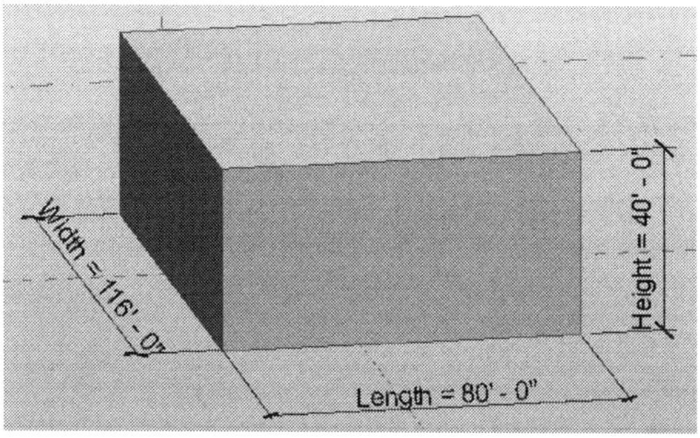

Figure A–3

8. In the *Modify* tab>*Properties* panel, click (Family Types). In the *Family Types* dialog box (shown in Figure A–4), set up formulas, additional parameters, and family types.

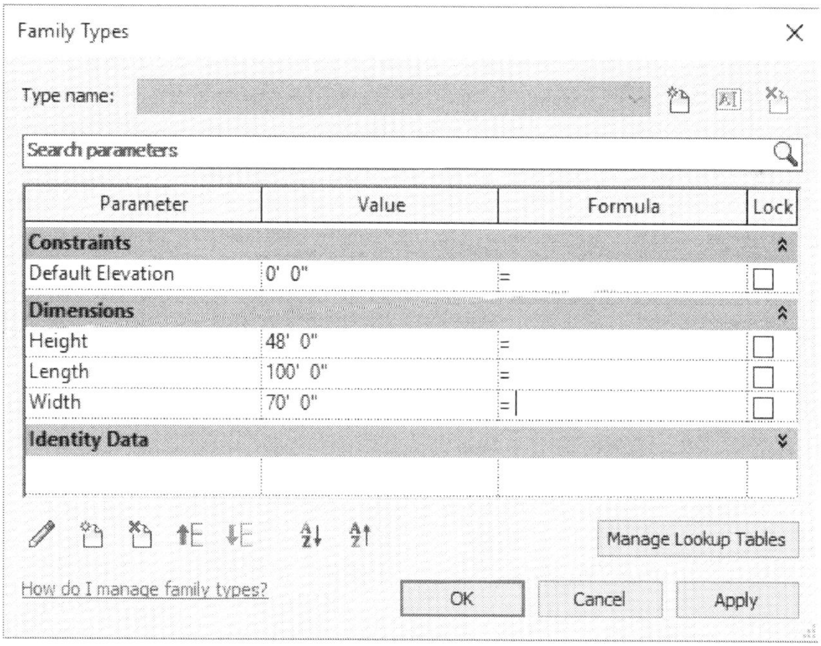

Figure A–4

9. Click (Save).

- In the *Family Editor* panel, you can click (Load into Project) to load the new mass into an open project.
- Information about creating sketches and forms is covered in ***Chapter 1 Massing Studies***.

- The conceptual mass family template contains one level and two reference planes, as shown in Figure A–5.

  Note: *You can click on the edge of the levels or reference planes to set the work plane.*

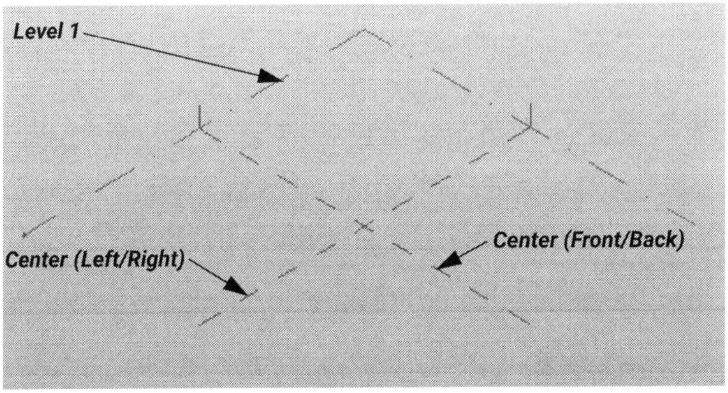

Figure A–5

  - To select another level by default, open its plan view. Alternatively, select the level marker in a 3D view, as shown in Figure A–6.

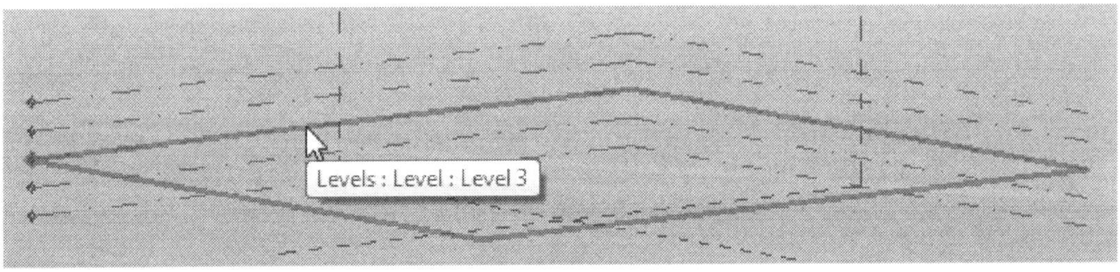

Figure A–6

- The background of 3D views in the conceptual mass family file displays as a light gray gradient.

Reference Based Forms

If you want an extruded form or a sweep to retain its shape along the path when the related parameters are flexed, you can make the profile lines a reference. Select the profile lines as though you are going to make a form. Before selecting the Form command, in Properties, in the *Identity Data* category, select **Is Reference Line**.

Before you set the profile as a reference, the lines display as shown in Figure A–7.

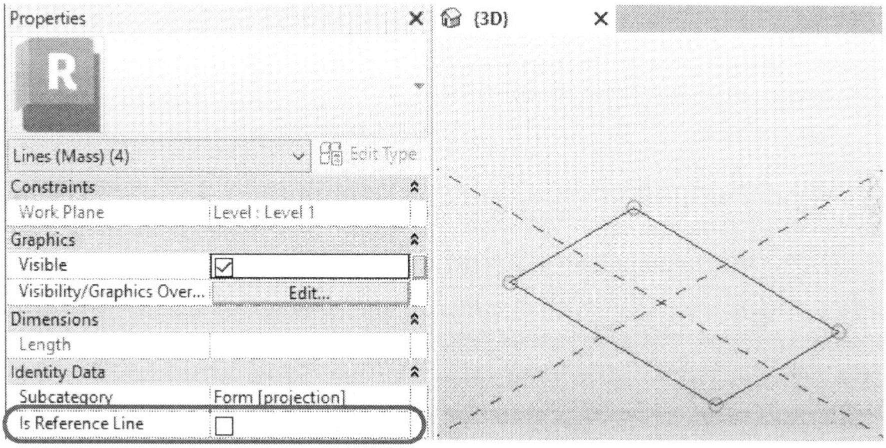

Figure A–7

Once you have set them as a reference, the Properties change and you see reference planes along the edges of the profile, as shown in Figure A–8.

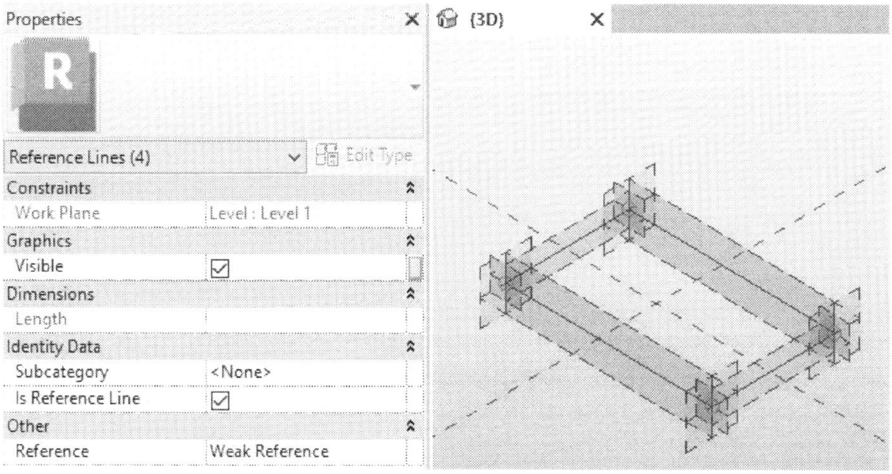

Figure A–8

Practice A1
Advanced Conceptual Massing

Practice Objectives

- Create reference planes and dimension and label them.
- Create a mass form using reference lines.
- Insert the mass family into a project and place instances of it using different parameters.

In this practice, you will create a conceptual mass family with dimensions and parameters, as shown in Figure A–9. You will then place two copies of the mass family into a project and modify them using the parameters set up in the mass family, as shown in Figure A–10.

- This practice requires an understanding of conceptual massing and parametric family concepts.

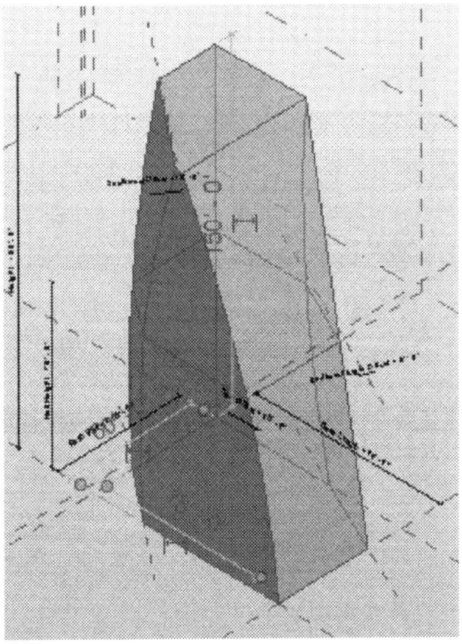

Figure A–9

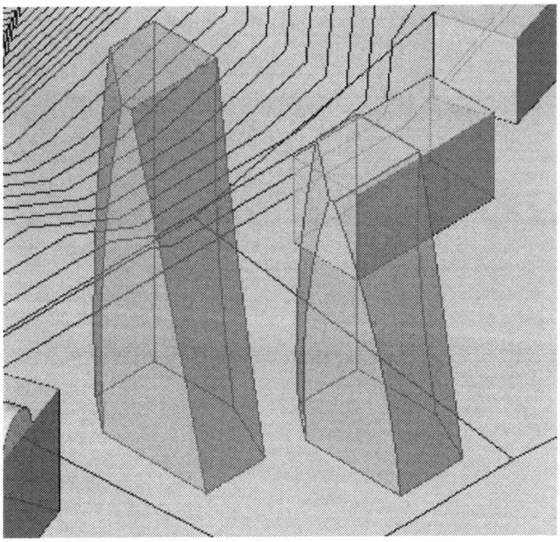

Figure A–10

Task 1: Create the base parametric framework.

1. From the Home screen, select **New** under *Families*. Navigate to the practice files *Families\Conceptual Mass* folder, select **Mass.rft**, and click **Open**.
   - Alternatively, in the *File* tab, expand (New) and select (Conceptual Mass). In the *New Conceptual Mass - Select Template File* dialog box, navigate to the practice files *Families\Conceptual Mass* folder, select the **Mass.rft** template, and click **Open**.
2. Save the family as **Edmon-Towers-Model.rfa** in the practice files *Families* folder.

3. Verify that you are in the **3D Views: {3D}** view and that no other views are open.
4. Open the **Floor Plans: Level 1** view.
5. Type **WT** to tile the two views and then **ZA** to fit the view in the windows.
6. Working in the 3D view, in the *Create* tab>*Draw* panel, click (Reference Plane).
7. In the *Properties* panel, *Constraints* section, set the *Work Plane* to **Level: Level 1.**
8. Draw the four reference planes shown in Figure A–11. The two angled reference planes should be at different angles.

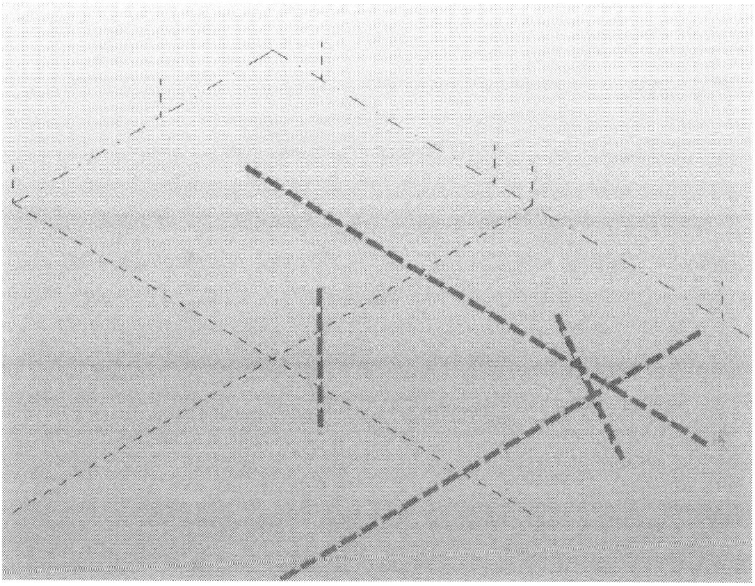

Figure A–11

9. In the plan view, dimension the horizontal and vertical reference planes, label them (instance parameters), and set the values, as shown in Figure A–12.
10. Move the angled lines, if needed, to fit inside the footprint of the building. Dimension, but do not label them. Select the reference plane and set the values, as shown in Figure A–12.

    Note: *Flexing the angles creates additional complexity. Once the rest of the mass works as expected, you can try adding labels and flexing the angles.*

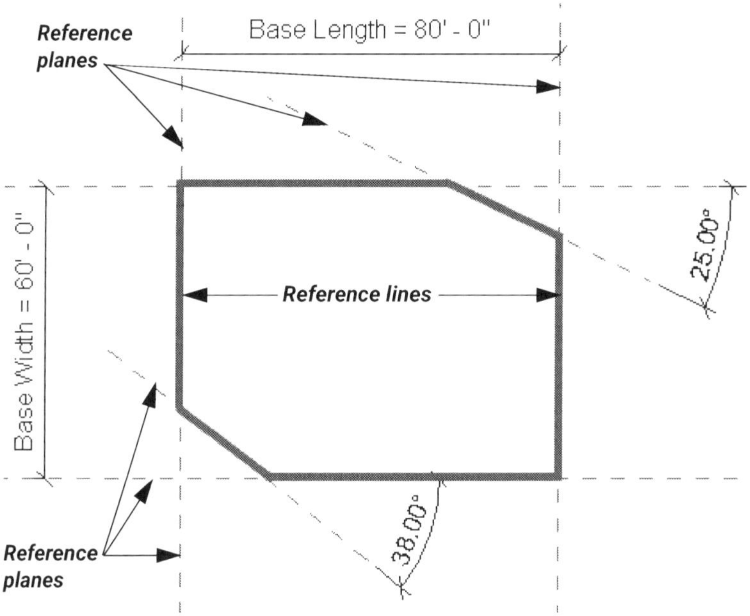

Figure A–12

11. In the *Create* tab>*Draw* panel, click  (Reference Line).
12. In the *Properties* panel, verify that *Work Plane* is still set to **Level: Level 1** and in the Options Bar, select **Chain**.
13. Draw the reference lines shown above in Figure A–12. Ensure that you snap to the intersections of the reference planes.
14. Flex the width and length to ensure that everything works.
15. Save the family.

Task 2: Create levels and additional profiles.

Note: *Remember that levels in massing families are not the same as levels in projects. These are for setting heights.*

1. Open the **Elevations: South** view.

2. Add two levels and dimension and label them (instance parameters), as shown in Figure A–13. The exact height does not matter at this time.

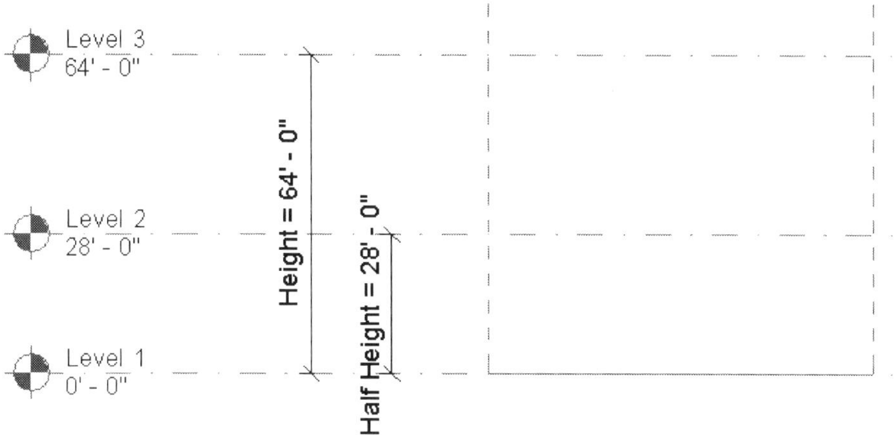

Figure A–13

3. In the *Create* tab>*Properties* panel, click (Family Types).
4. Add a formula to the *Half Height* parameter as shown in Figure A–14. Set the *Height* parameter to **150'-0"** and click **OK**.

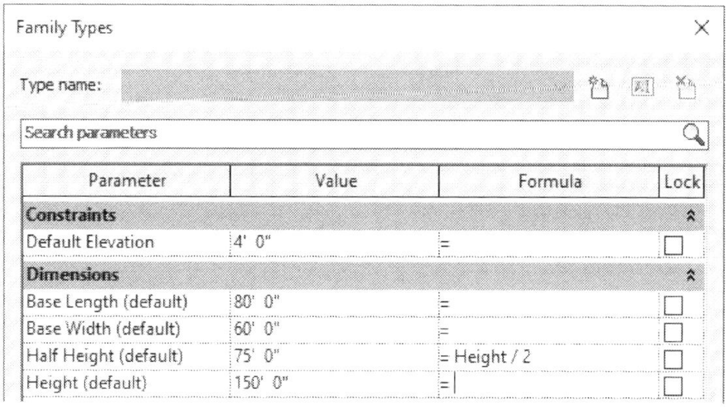

Figure A–14

5. Open the **Floor Plans: Level 2** view.

6. Add two reference planes, then dimension them, label them (instance parameters), and set the values, as shown in Figure A–15.

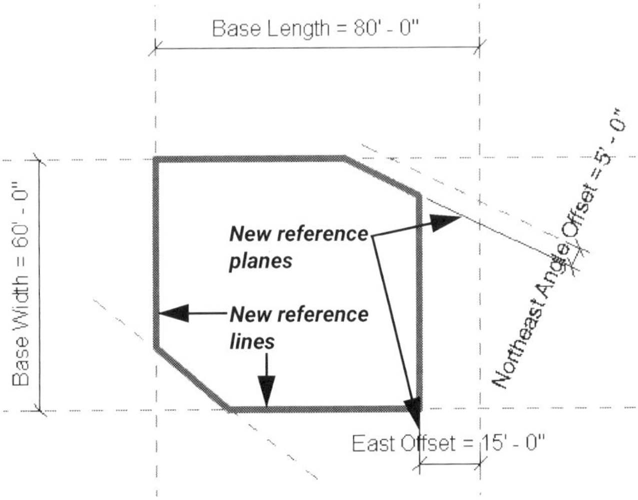

Figure A–15

7. Add reference lines on the *Placement Plane:* **Level: Level 2** using the boundary shown above in Figure A–15.
8. Flex the parameters to ensure that they work.
9. Open the **Floor Plans: Level 3** view.
10. Add the reference plane, label, and reference line boundary, as shown in Figure A–16.

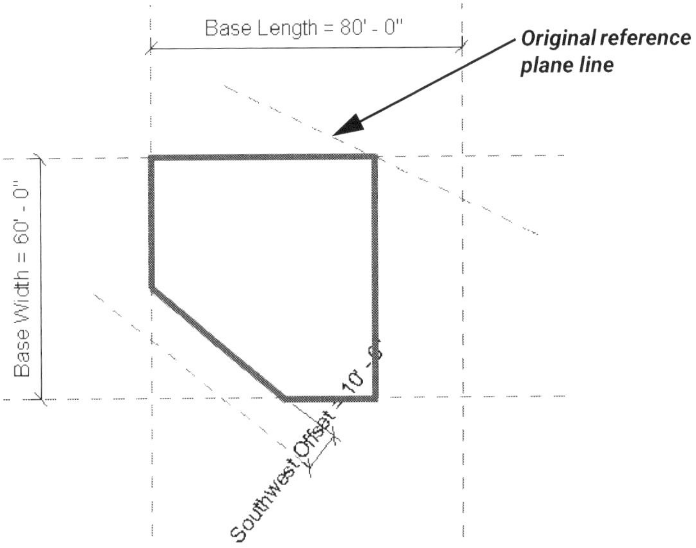

Figure A–16

11. Flex the parameters to test the framework.
12. Save the family.

Task 3: Create a mass form.

1. Open the default 3D view and select the three profiles made of reference lines that should be similar to Figure A–17.
2. In the *Modify | Reference Lines* tab>*Form* panel, click (Create Form). A new mass element should display, as shown in Figure A–18.

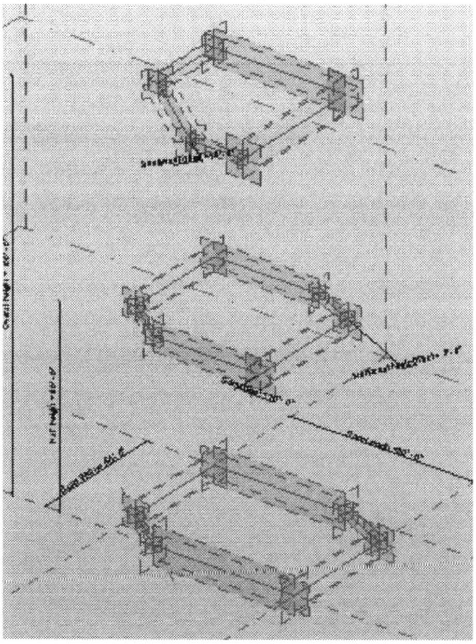

Figure A–17

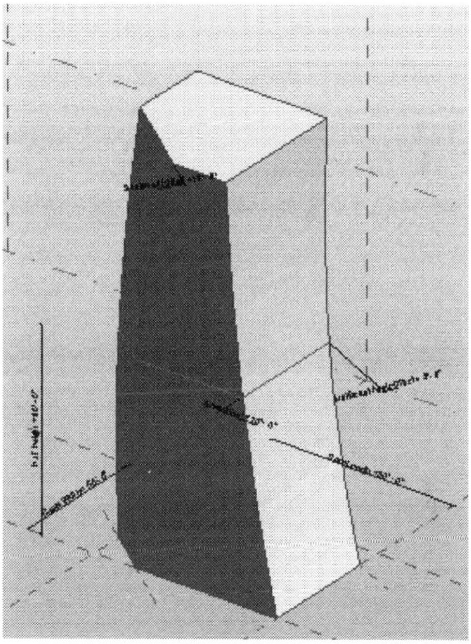

Figure A–18

3. Use the *Family Types* dialog box to flex the parameters.
4. While in this dialog box, verify that all of the parameters are instance parameters so they can be modified in a project easily. They should have (default) after the parameter name.
   - If they are not, you can change them one at a time by selecting a parameter and clicking (Edit Parameter) to change it to an instance parameter.
5. In 3D view with nothing selected, from Properties, clear the check from the *Work Plane-Based* field.
6. Save the family.

Task 4: Use the mass family in a project.

1. Open the project **Edmon-Towers-Study.rvt**.
2. Switch back to the mass family file and load it into the project.
3. Close the alert box.
4. In the Options Bar, verify **Place on Work Plane** is selected in the ribbon and *Work Plane* is set to **Level: Level 1**.
5. Place two mass families in the new site location, as shown in Figure A–19.

   Note: *Mass families can be placed using the* ***Component*** *or* ***Place Mass*** *commands.*

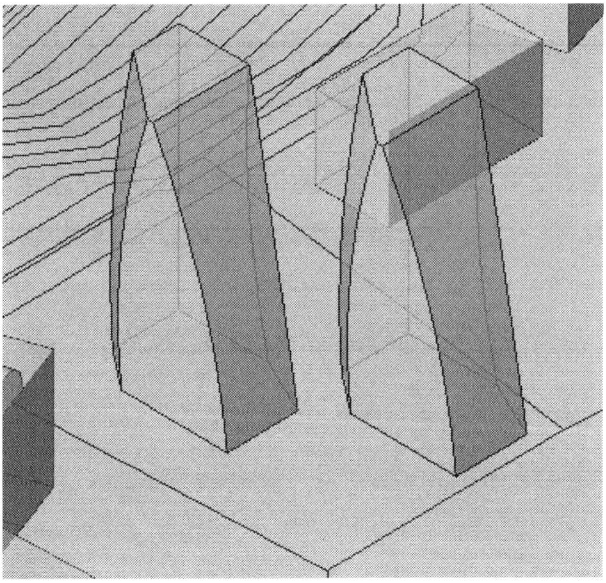

Figure A–19

6. Select one of the mass family elements and in Properties, modify the various dimensions so that the buildings are different.
   - If prompted with a warning suggesting that the type cannot be created, cancel and use a different dimension. The warning stems from Revit not being able to accommodate the given dimensions,
7. Save the project.

End of practice

Command Summary

Button	Command	Location
	**Conceptual Mass**	• **Ribbon:** *File* tab>New
	**Create Form**	• **Family Editor Ribbon:** *Modify | Place Lines* tab>*Form* panel
	**Family Types**	• **Family Editor Ribbon:** *Create* or *Modify* tab>*Properties* panel
	**Load into Project**	• **Family Editor Ribbon:** All tabs>*Family Editor* panel
	**Load into Project and Close**	• **Family Editor Ribbon:** All tabs>*Family Editor* panel
	**Place Mass**	• **Ribbon:** *Massing & Site* tab>*Conceptual Mass* panel

Appendix

B

Additional Tools for Rendering

There are many other tools available in the Autodesk® Revit® software that can be used when creating stunning visual aids of your models, like enhanced materials and walkthroughs. This appendix provides details about tools and commands that are related to those covered in this guide.

Learning Objectives

- Learn what a material is and what it contains.
- Create material libraries that can be used in multiple projects.
- Modify and create materials.
- Learn the different ways materials can be applied to elements.
- Create and edit a perspective walkthrough.

B.1 Materials and Material Libraries

3D objects help with the visualization of any design, but rendering and scheduling those objects with actual real-world material, cost, construction code, manufacturer, and other information is especially important for an interior designer.

In Revit, designers can apply materials that they have created to objects saved in project templates and save them to a custom family library for convenience. Specifying an object's appearance, including its color and surface texture, can enhance the rendering quality. Including physical properties like thermal conductivity is important for documenting the project.

When you shade or render Revit models, their appearance depends on the materials that have been associated with the elements, as shown in a rendered view in Figure B–1. Materials also include information that can be used in material takeoff schedules and in energy and structural analysis. You can use materials supplied with Revit or create custom materials.

Figure B–1

Material Browser

The *Material Browser* dialog box (shown in Figure B–2) facilitates all the materials for a project as well as existing Revit libraries. This is where you create, edit, and manage materials and material libraries through the various areas.

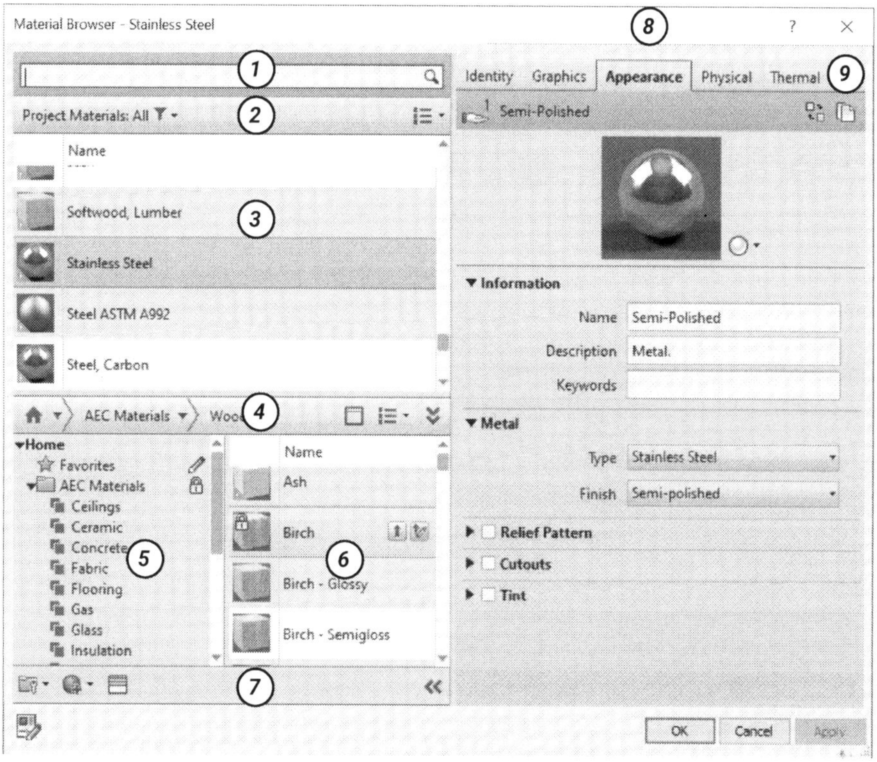

Figure B–2

Material Browser Area	Area Definition
1. Material search bar	Search for a particular material from the Project Materials list and existing and custom libraries.
2. Project Materials toolbar	You can filter the Project Materials list by class and customize how the list displays.
3. Project Materials list	The materials shown in this list are materials that are loaded in the current project.
4. Material Libraries toolbar	You can filter the library list and customize how the Library Materials list displays.
5. Library list	Displays available libraries. Within each library are multiple material categories or classes.
6. Library Materials list	When clicking on a libraries category or class, the materials saved within that category displays.
7. Material Browser toolbar	This is where you can manage, create, and edit new or existing libraries and materials.

Material Browser Area	Area Definition
8. Material Editor panel	Select a material from the Project Materials list or the Library Materials list (these are locked and cannot be edited) and review or edit the assets and properties within the Material Editor panel.
9. Asset tabs	Each material can have up to five assets assigned to it. The asset tabs are *Identity*, *Graphics*, *Appearance*, *Physical*, and *Thermal*.

- As you modify within the *Material Browser*, the changes made are automatically saved. To remove anything created, right-click on it and select **Delete**. For example, if you create a new material and decide you do not want it, you can right-click on it in the Project Materials list and select **Delete**, as shown in Figure B–3.

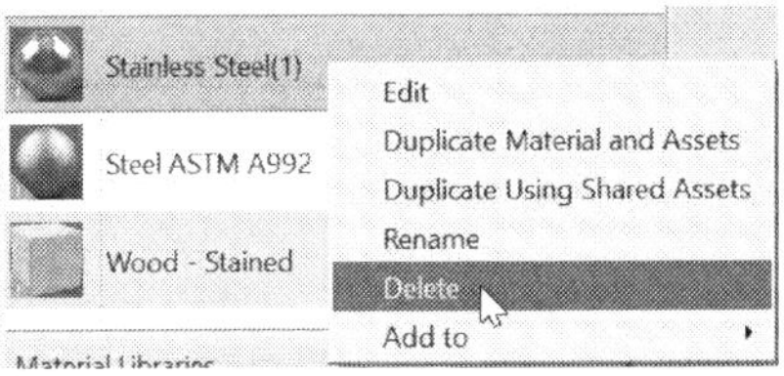

Figure B–3

- You can adjust the different panel areas in the *Material Browser* to show more information. Hover your cursor over the panel's edge until you see the icon shown in Figure B–4, then click and drag it in the required direction.

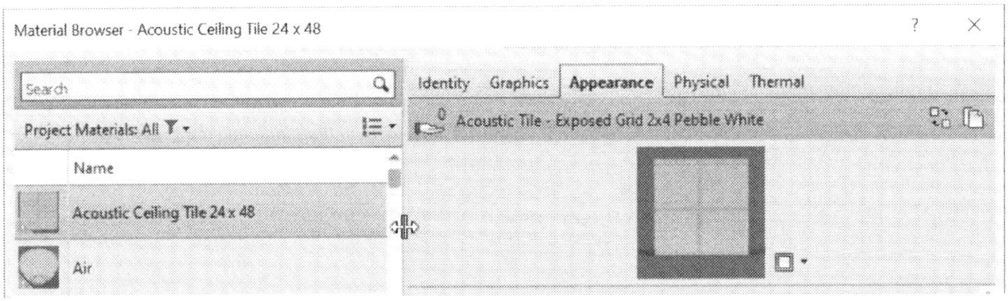

Figure B–4

About Materials

In Revit, materials represent physical building materials, such as wood, plastic, paint, and glass. In the *Material Browser*, the loaded materials for the current project are listed in the **Project Materials list** area in the left pane, as shown in Figure B–6. Additional materials can be found in the libraries in the **Material Libraries** area.

> ***Note:*** *A sample file of Revit materials can be found in the practice files folder: Autodesk_Help_MaterialGalleryPhysical-R26.rvt, as shown in Figure B–5.*

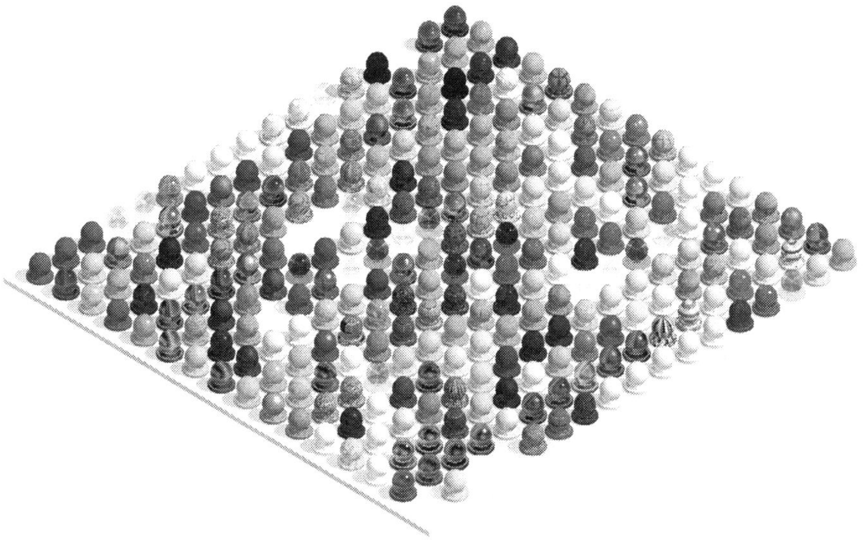

Figure B–5

Individual Revit materials store properties and assets that control various attributes of an element when they are applied to it. This information is used in various ways when designing, rendering, scheduling, and performing structural and energy analysis.

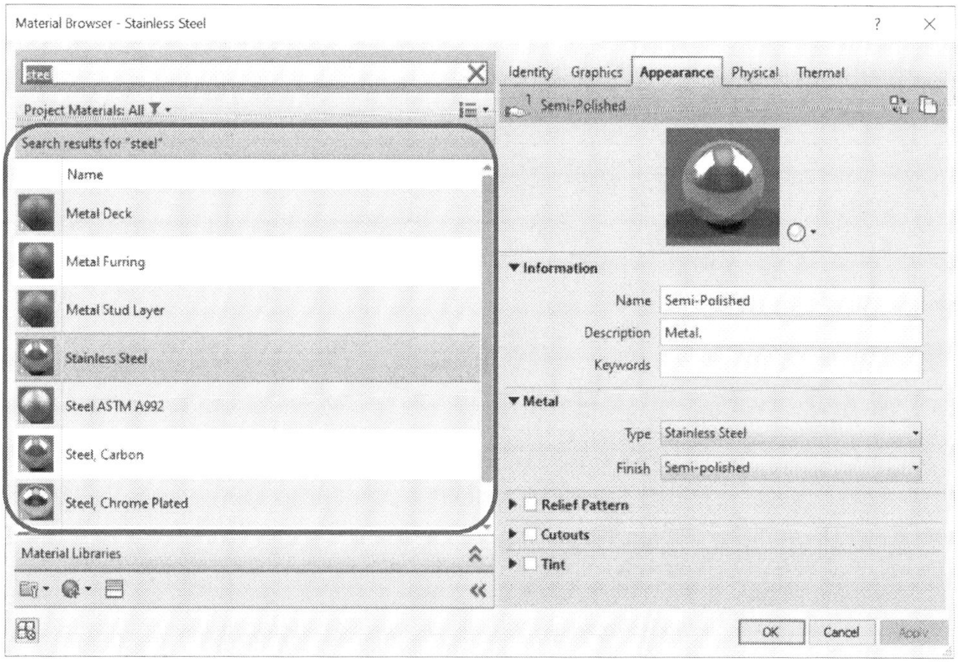

Figure B–6

- Only materials loaded into the project can be modified.
- You can use **Transfer Project Standards** to bring in all the materials from another project into the current project.

Hint: Transferring Project Standards

Some elements (such as wall types) are not accessible from a specific library. However, you can copy them from other projects.

- Transferring project standards does not transfer loadable families like custom families or families from the Revit Library.

1. Open the project from which you want to copy information.
2. Open the project to which you want to copy the information.
3. In the *Manage* tab>*Settings* panel, click (Transfer Project Standards).
4. In the *Transfer Project Standards* dialog box, select an option in the *Copy from:* drop-down list and then select the settings you want to copy into the current file, as shown in Figure B–7. Click **OK**.

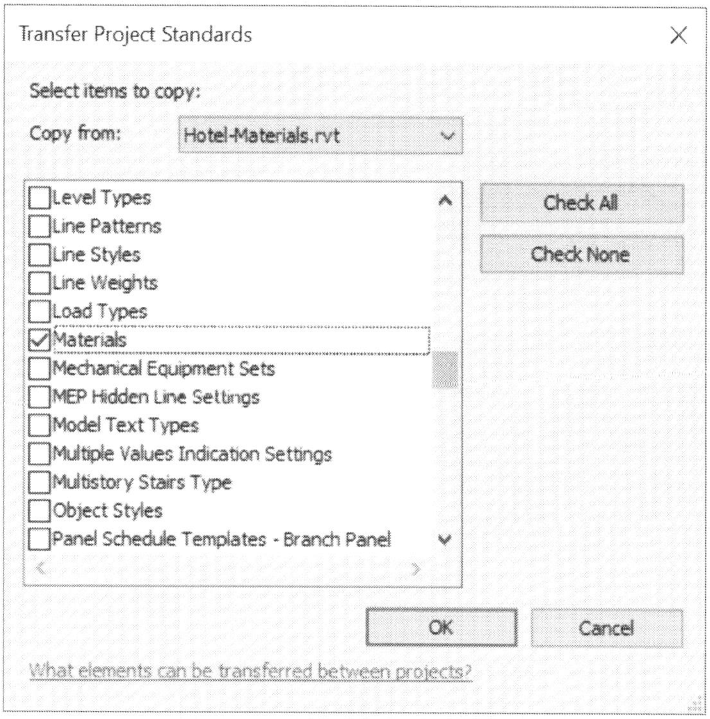

Figure B–7

5. In the *Duplicate Types* dialog box, click either **Overwrite** or **New Only** to apply the settings to the current project.

Material Libraries

Material properties and assets are stored in libraries, which can be shared between Revit projects and the Autodesk® AutoCAD®, Inventor®, Showcase, and 3ds Max® software. Before creating or customizing materials, it is recommended that you create a custom library. Materials can then be copied between the current project and the library.

- In the lower-left corner of the *Material Browser* dialog box is the **Material Libraries toolbar**.

  You can click (Show/Hide Library tree) to display the Library list and expand the library to review the different categories (e.g., Fabric, Flooring, etc., as shown in Figure B–8). Click (Changes your view) to display the materials with different thumbnail sizes for better viewing capabilities (as shown in Figure B–8).

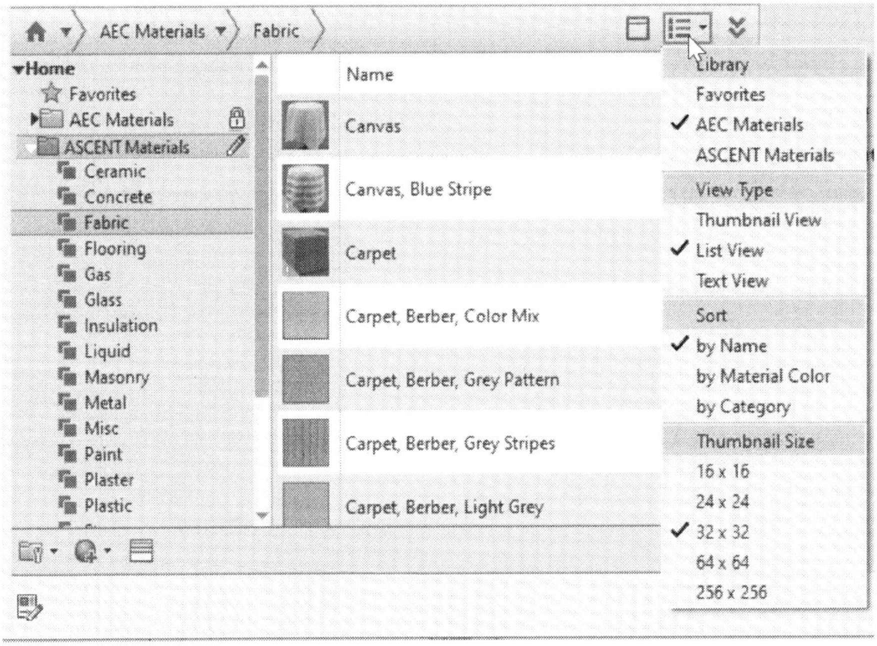

Figure B–8

- You can load materials from a library into the current project by hovering your cursor over the material in the **Library Materials list** and clicking either (Adds material to document) or (Add material to document and display in editor), as shown in Figure B–9.

Note: Libraries that come with Revit are locked and cannot be edited. You can only copy materials from locked libraries.

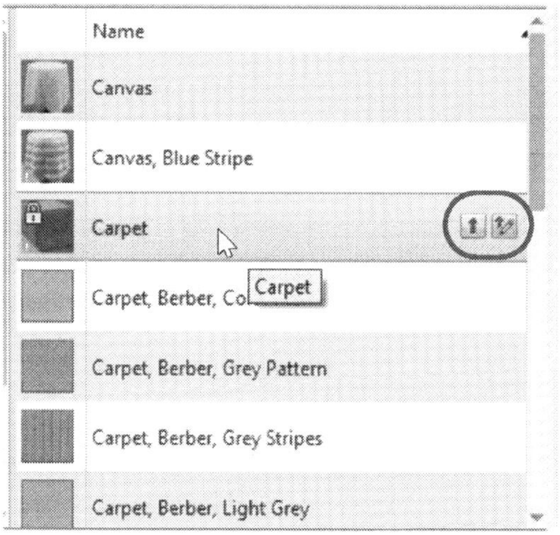

Figure B–9

- Both new and existing materials can be added to a new library.
- Older versions of materials may need to be updated with appearance assets, as shown in Figure B–10. All legacy materials still work but they may not be as complex and nuanced when rendering.

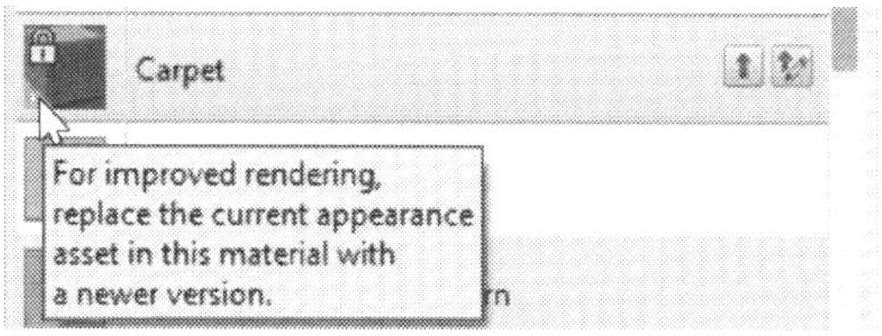

Figure B–10

- Assets that are updated have higher rendering capabilities. Figure B–11 shows the difference between an old version and a new version of the cherry wood material.

Original Cherry asset ***Updated Cherry asset***

Figure B–11

How To: Create a Material Library

1. In the *Manage* tab>*Settings* panel, click (Materials).
2. At the bottom of the *Material Browser* is the Material Browser toolbar (shown in Figure B–12). Expand (Creates, opens and edits user-defined libraries) and select **Create New Library**, as shown in Figure B–12.

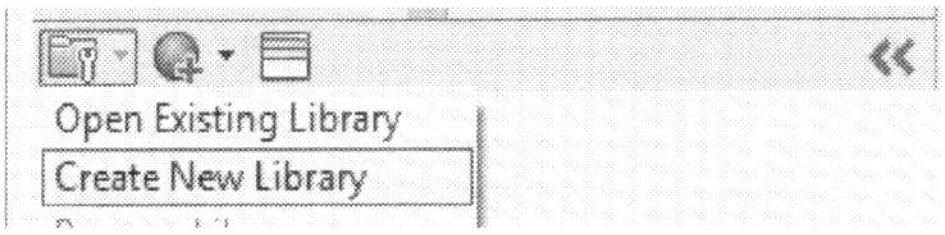

Figure B–12

3. In the *Select File* dialog box (shown in Figure B–13), navigate to the appropriate folder and type a *File name*.

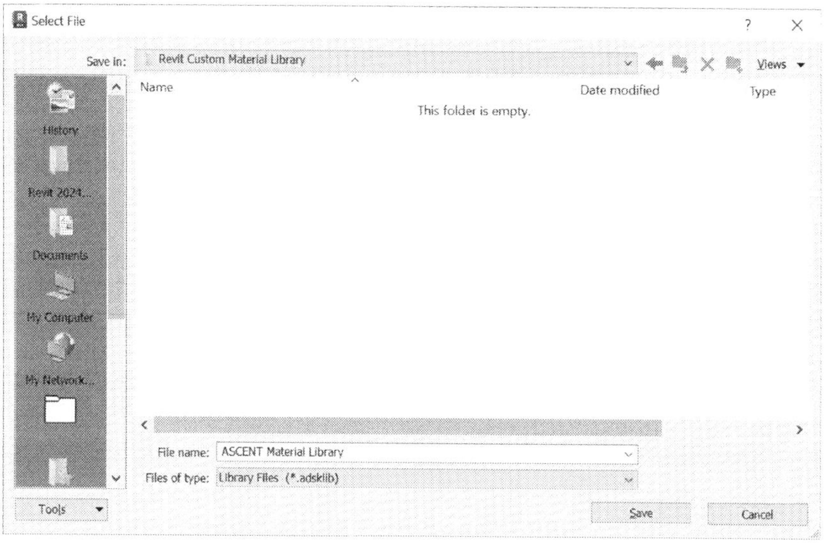

Figure B–13

4. Click **Save** to save the library.
5. The new material library displays in the **Library** list without any materials displayed, as shown in Figure B–14.

Figure B–14

6. Right-click on the new material library and select **Create Category**, as shown in Figure B–15.

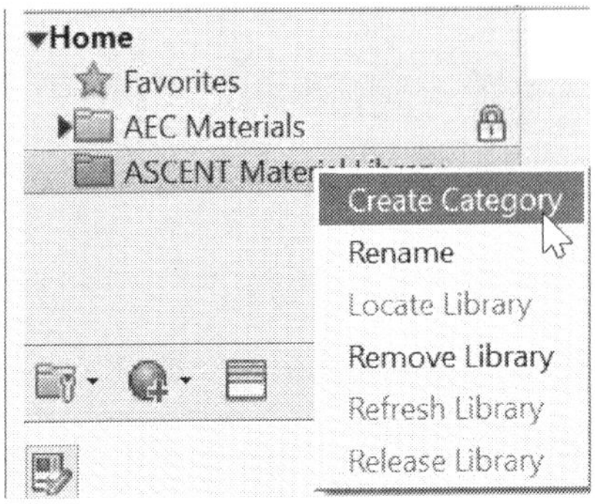

Figure B–15

7. As soon as the new category displays, you can type the name of the category or right-click on the category and select **Rename**, as shown in Figure B–16.

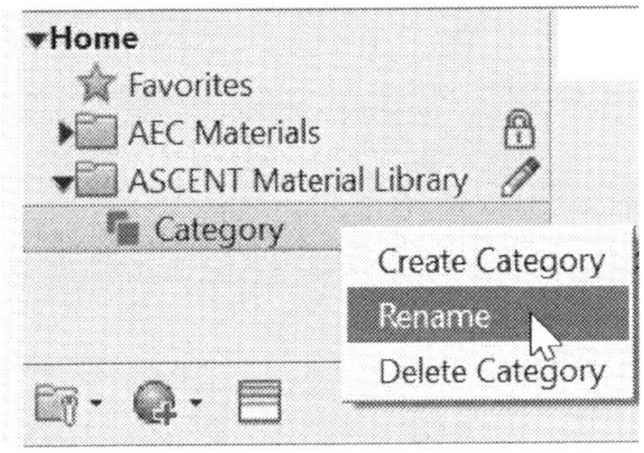

Figure B–16

8. To add materials to the category, do one of the following:
   - With the category selected, drag and drop materials from the Project Materials list to the Library Materials list (as shown on the left in Figure B–17).
   - In the Library list, expand an existing library and click on a category to display its materials. Drag and drop a material from the Library Materials list into one of the new library's categories (as shown on the right in Figure B–17).

Copy from Project Materials list ***Copy from Library Materials list***

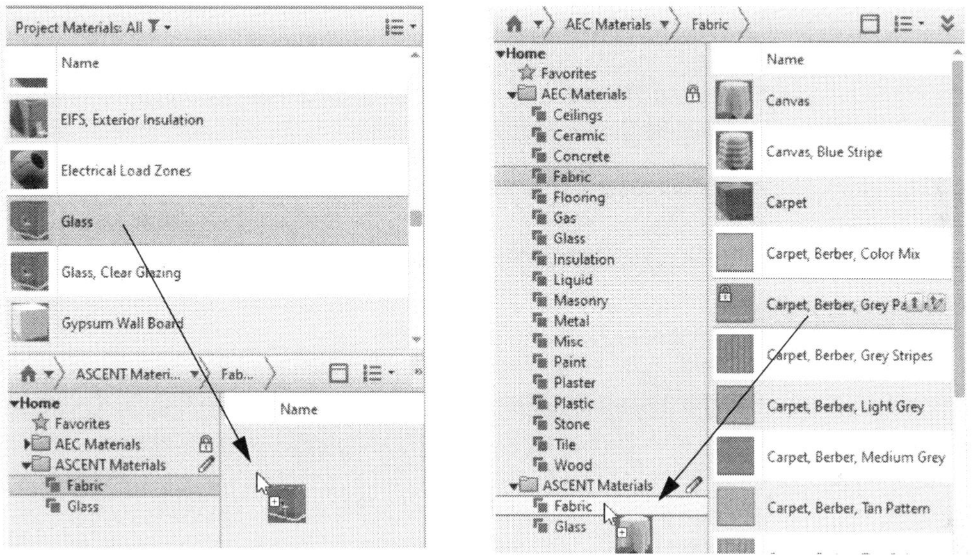

Figure B–17

Creating Materials

Sometimes the available materials are not exactly what you need and you have to create and modify a material. From the *Material Browser* dialog box, you can create a new material or duplicate an existing material using the Material Browser toolbar (as shown in Figure B–18), then modify the name and other attributes to suit your needs. It is recommended that you find an existing material that is similar to what you want and create a duplicate of it so the majority of the properties and assets are already filled out.

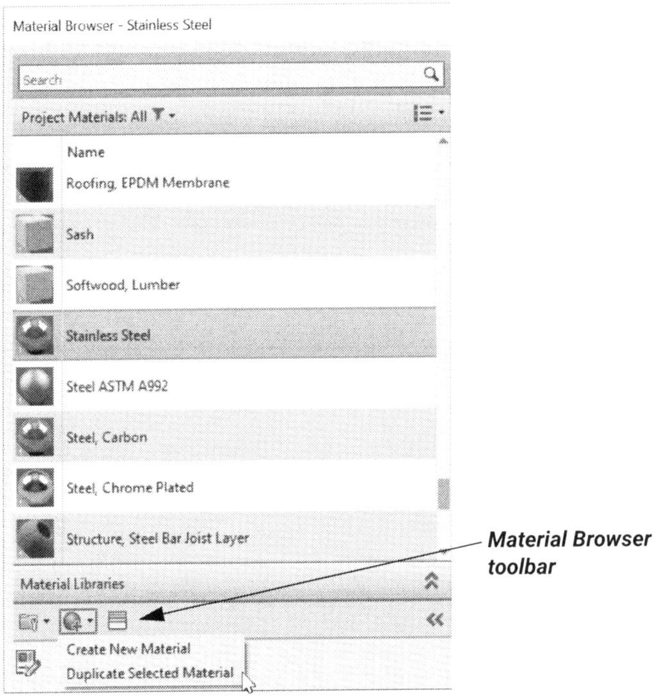

Figure B–18

- It is important when duplicating an existing material to always review the asset tabs, especially the *Appearance*, *Physical*, and *Thermal* tab information, as these tabs store assets about the material that, if modified, can affect any other material that also uses that asset. For example, the Stainless Steel material uses a Semi-Polished asset for its appearance, as shown in Figure B–19.

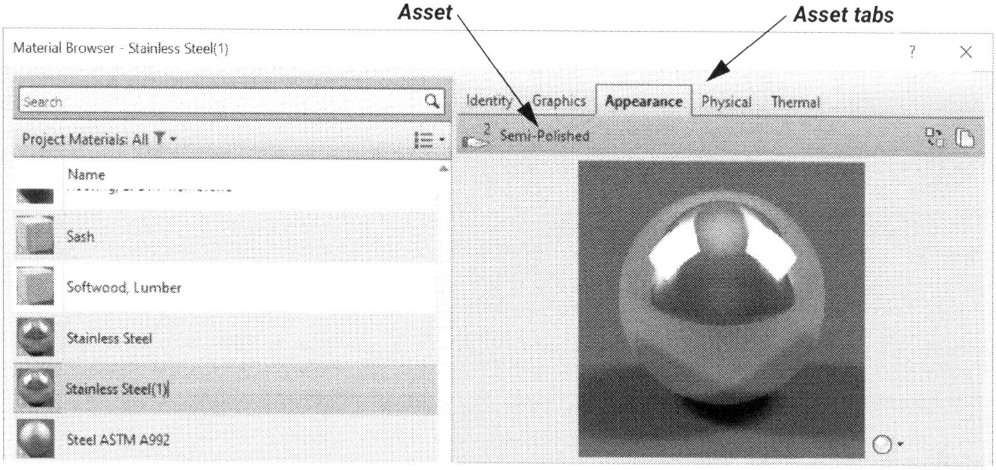

Figure B–19

- The asset will indicate if it is used by another material in the Project Materials list. The number **2** on the Semi-Polished asset indicates that this asset is used by two materials, as shown in Figure B–20.

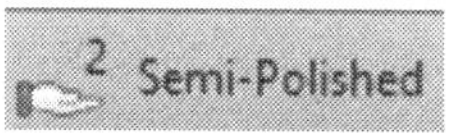

Figure B–20

- It is recommended to duplicate or replace an asset so you can further modify it without affecting any other materials.

How To: Duplicate a Material

1. In the *Manage* tab>*Settings* panel, click  (Materials).
2. Select a material from the Project Materials list.
3. In the Material Browser toolbar, expand  (Creates or duplicates a material) and select **Duplicate Material and Assets** or **Duplicate Using Shared Assets**, as shown in Figure B–21.
   - You can also right-click on an existing material in the Project Materials list and select **Duplicate**.

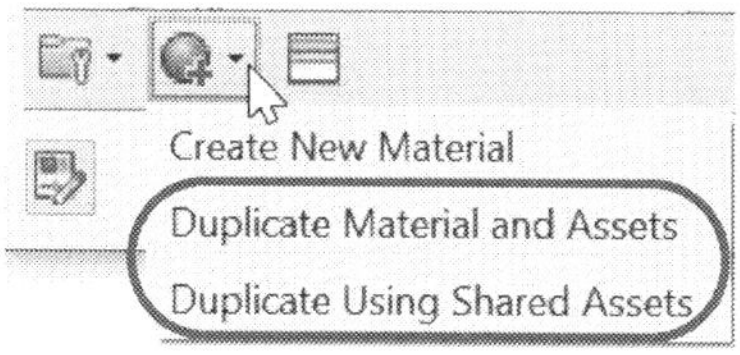

Figure B–21

4. A new material is added to the Project Materials list, typically with a **(1)** at the end of the name, as shown in Figure B–22. Modify the name of the material or right-click on the material name in the Project Materials list and select **Rename**.
    - **Duplicate Material and Assets** will duplicate the asset and source material and the material and asset will have a **(1)** at the end of the name indicating it has been duplicated.
    - **Duplicate Material Using Shared Assets** will share the asset and source material and does not duplicate anything. If the appearance of the material is modified, the duplicated material updates accordingly.

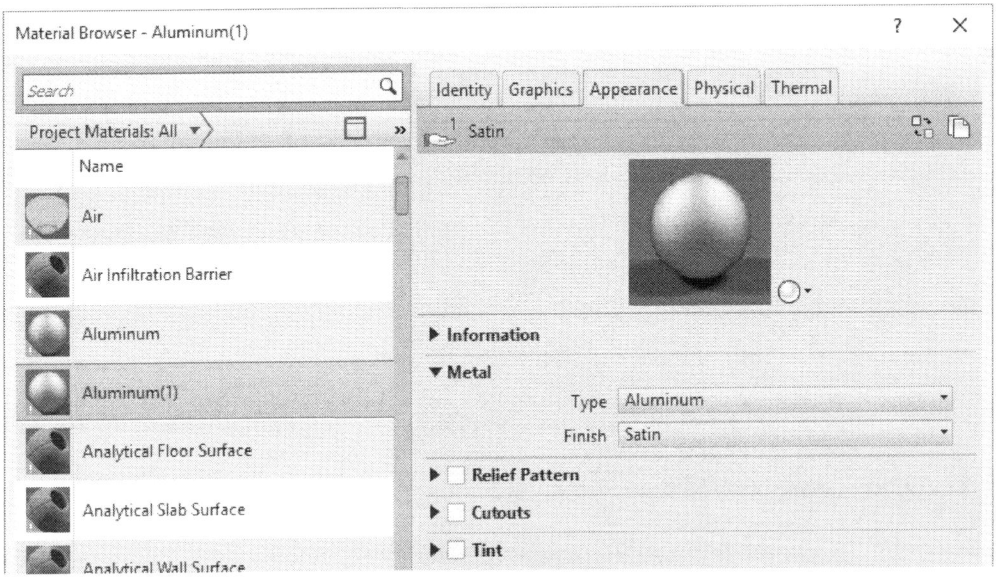

Figure B–22

5. Review and fill out the information on each of the asset tabs. On the *Appearance*, *Physical*, and *Thermal* tabs, review the asset and replace or duplicate it to avoid creating issues with other materials that use the asset.
6. Click **Apply** to save the changes and continue to add additional materials.
7. Click **OK** when you are finished adding materials.

How To: Create a New Material

1. In the *Manage* tab>*Settings* panel, click (Materials).
2. Select a material from the Project Materials list.
3. In the Material Browser toolbar, expand (Creates or duplicates a material) and select **Create New Material**, as shown in Figure B–23.

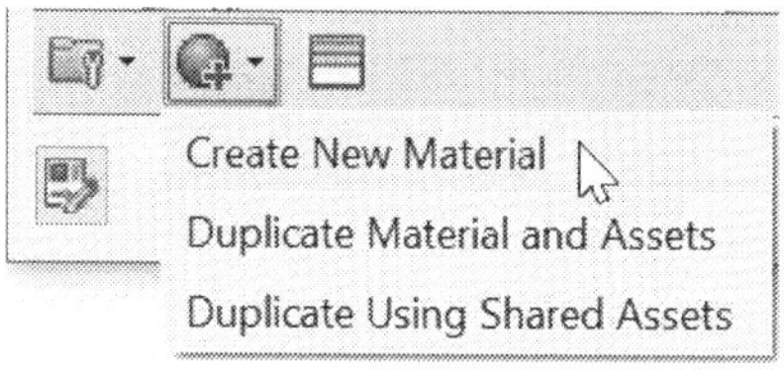

Figure B–23

4. A new material is added to the Project Materials list and is typically named **Default New Material**, as shown in Figure B–24. Enter a new *Name* and fill out the other required properties and assets in the *Identity*, *Graphics*, and *Appearance* tabs.
   * To change the name, you can also right-click on the material in the Project Materials list and select **Rename**.

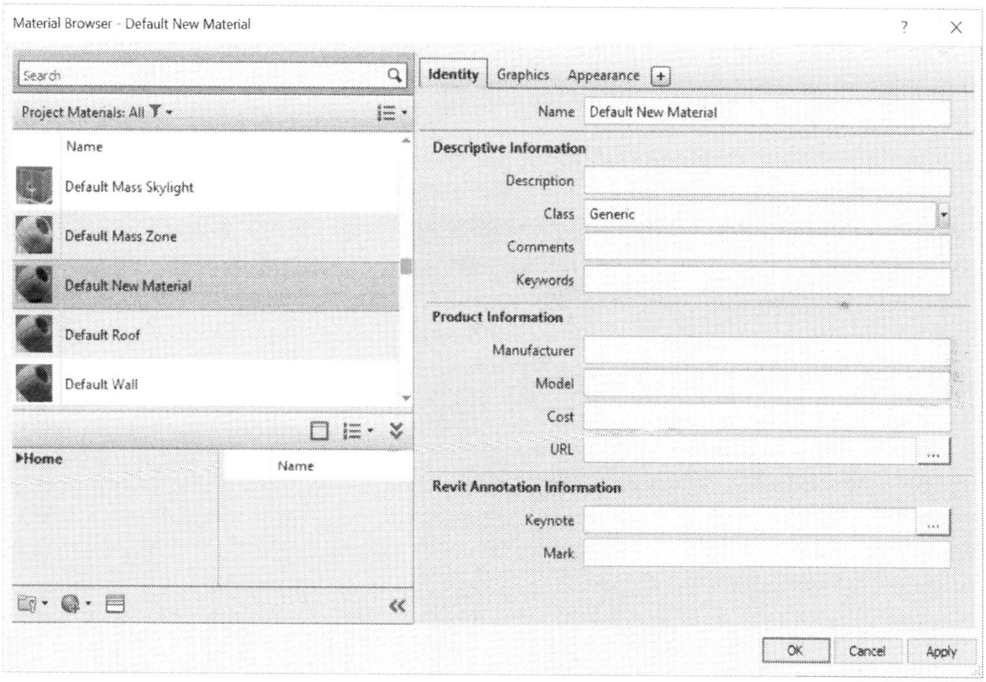

Figure B–24

5. Click **Apply** to save the changes and continue to add additional materials.
6. Click **OK** when you are finished adding materials.

Material Editor Panel

The Material Editor panel enables you to review or edit material assets and properties. You can only edit materials that are in the Project Materials list. If you select a material from the Library Materials list, the Material Editor's properties are grayed out, as shown in Figure B–25. The asset tabs at the top of the Material Editor panel are where you can review and specify the material's properties and assets.

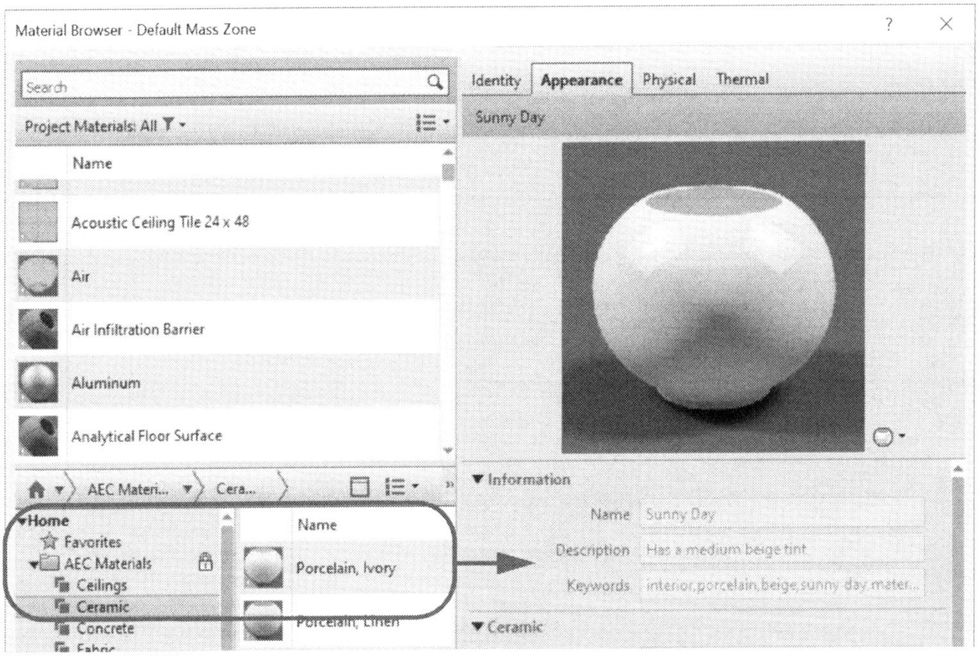

Figure B–25

Identity Tab

In the *Identity* tab, you set up the *Descriptive Information*, *Product Information*, and *Revit Annotation Information* for the material, as shown in Figure B–26. This information can be used in material takeoff schedules.

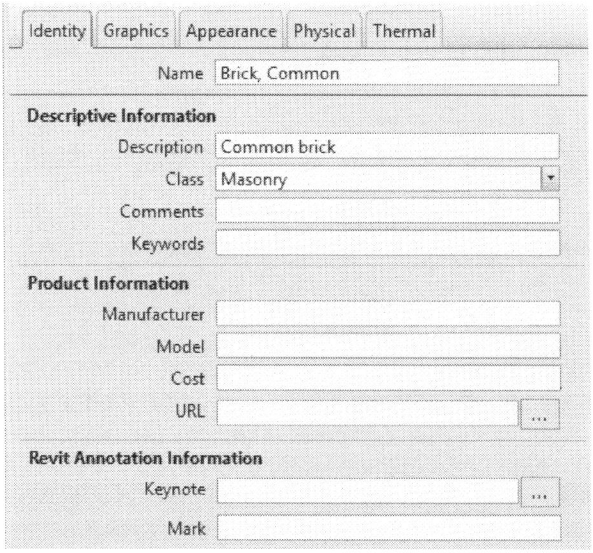

Figure B–26

Graphics Tab

In the *Graphics* tab (shown in Figure B–27), you set how a material displays in shaded or hidden line mode.

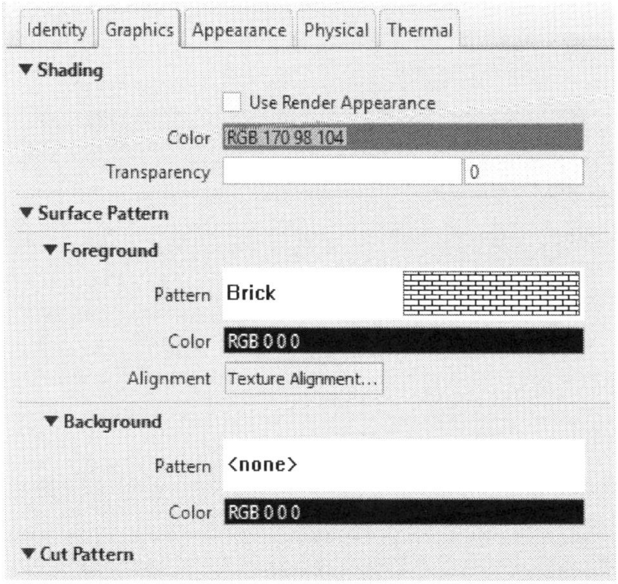

Figure B–27

- The *Shading* area controls how the material displays when an element is shaded. If you want the shaded view to resemble the rendered view, select **Use Render Appearance**. The color and other options are modified to match the render appearance selection. Alternatively, you can set up a color and transparency ratio. Only use this if the render appearance would be too dark or otherwise not suit the use.
- The *Surface Pattern* and *Cut Pattern* areas enable you to select a fill pattern and color to display on a surface or in a section cut. Surface patterns stay true to size. Cut patterns are drafting patterns, which change size according to the view scale. The *Surface* and *Cut Patterns* can be set for *Foreground* and *Background*.

Appearance Tab

In the *Appearance* tab, you can set different aspects of a rendered material, including *Information*, the type of material (in this example, **Masonry** is selected, as shown in Figure B–28), and other parameters depending on the type of material you are working with. Note that changing the asset changes all of the information, so check with your BIM manager first to confirm if that is an option before making these changes.

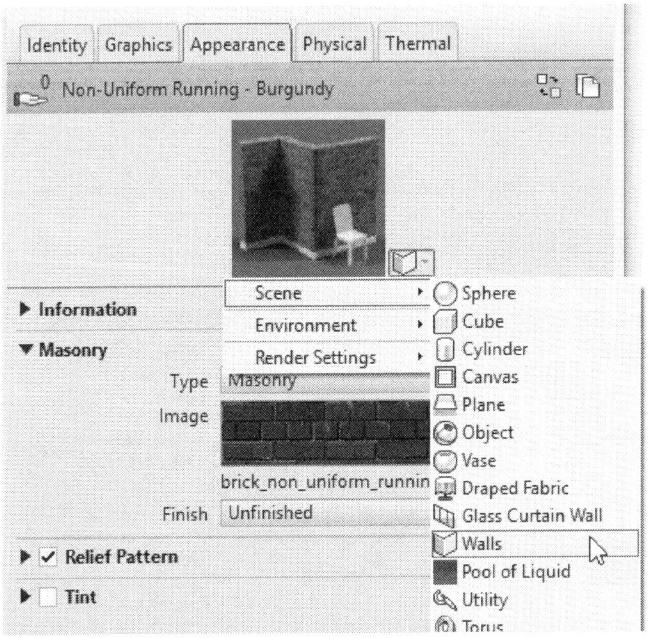

Figure B–28

- You can select how to display the preview of the material by expanding the *Scene* list next to the graphic, as shown in Figure B–28 above.
- You can modify the *Render Settings* of the preview to either **Draft Quality** or **Production Quality**.

- If you duplicate a material and then change asset-related information (such as the *Image* or *Color*), the original material also updates. To prevent this from happening, duplicate or change the asset before making changes using the buttons shown in Figure B–29.

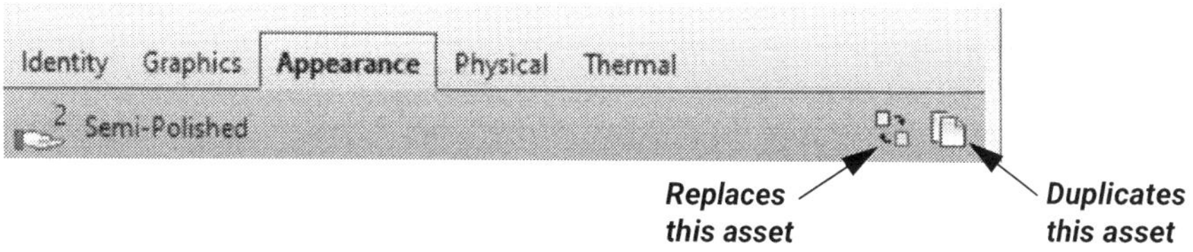

Figure B–29

Physical Tab

In the *Physical* tab, you can specify information about the physical properties of the material. The options vary by material type, as shown in Figure B–30.

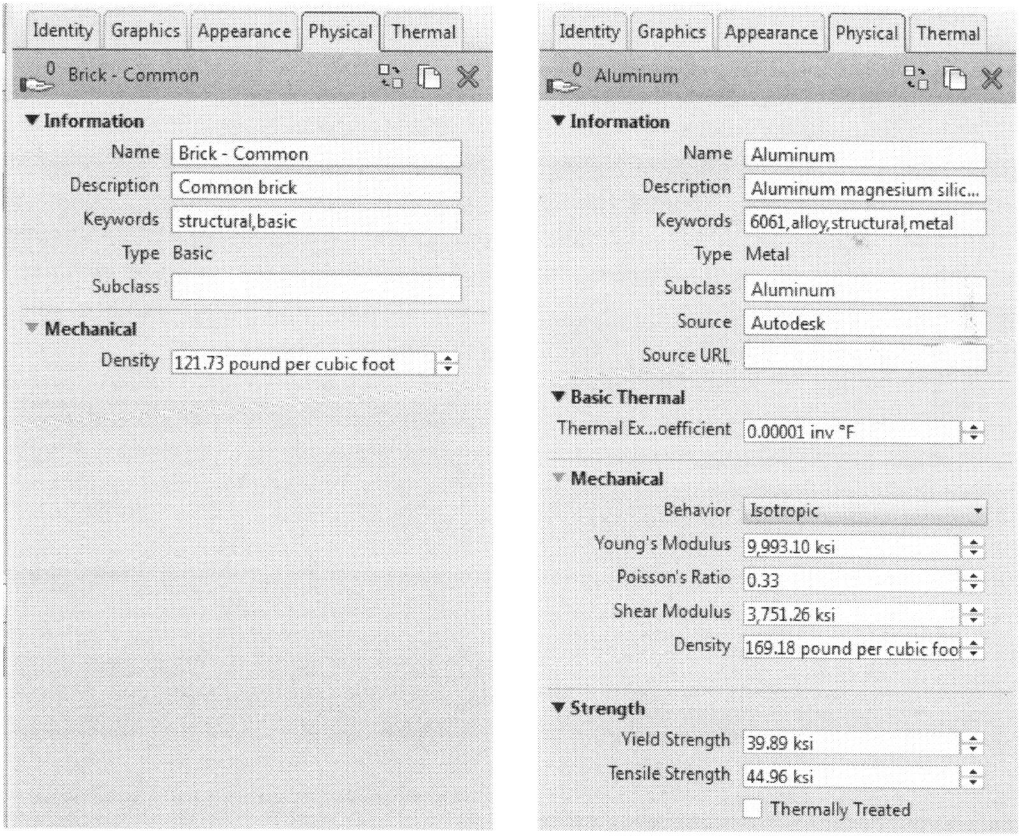

Figure B–30

- Some materials, such as **EPDM Membrane** or **Vapor Retarder**, do not have physical properties, but do have thermal properties.

- Analytical surface and default materials do not have physical or thermal properties.
- Some materials do not have **Physical** assets. They can be added by clicking the **+** symbol next to the assets tabs, as shown in Figure B–31. Note that **Appearance** is grayed out because this asset is already used in this particular material.

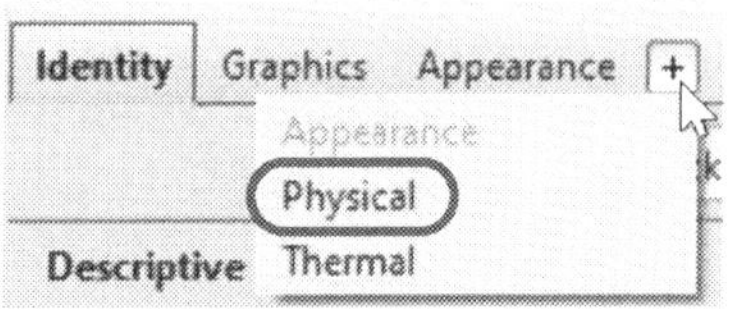

Figure B–31

- When you duplicate a material and then change asset-related information, the original material also updates. To prevent this from happening, duplicate or change the asset before making changes. If your material does not need to include the physical information, you can click the red X to remove the physical asset, as shown in Figure B–32.

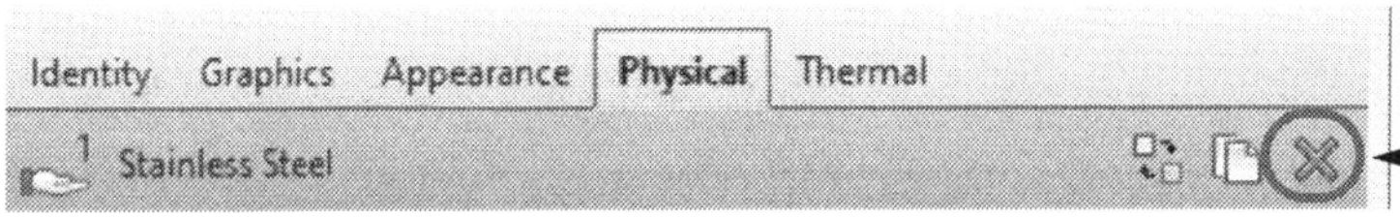

Figure B–32

Thermal Tab

In the *Thermal* tab, properties are added to be used for energy analysis, as shown in Figure B–33.

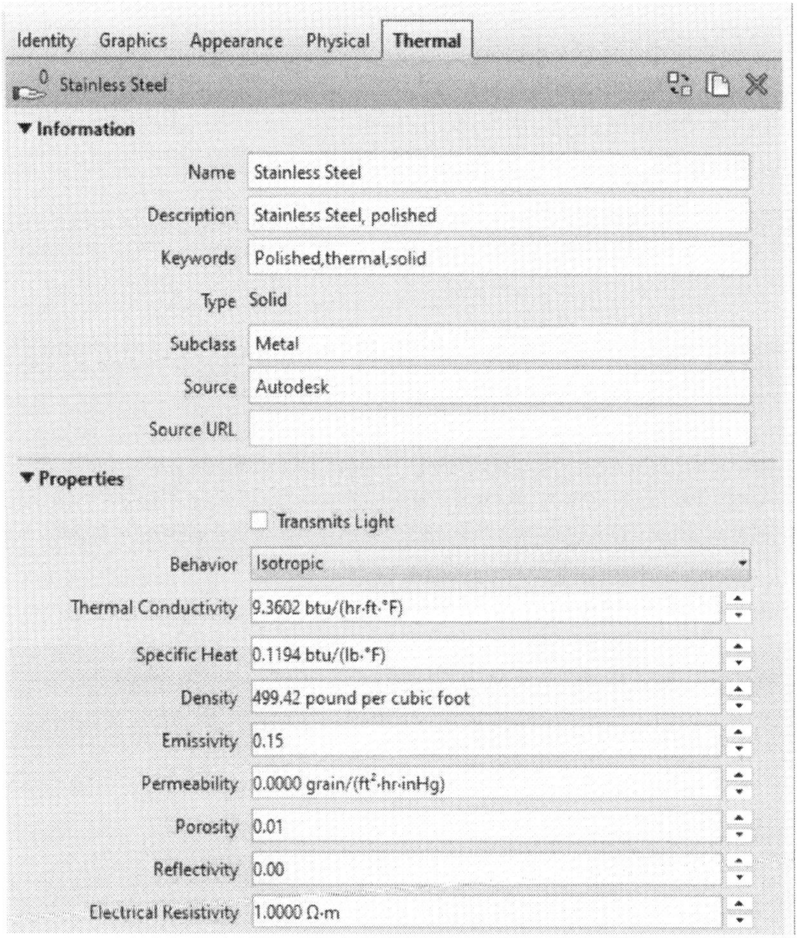

Figure B–33

- Some materials do not have **Thermal** assets. They can be added by clicking the **+** symbol next to the assets tabs, as shown in Figure B–34. Note that **Appearance** is grayed out because this asset is already used in this particular material.

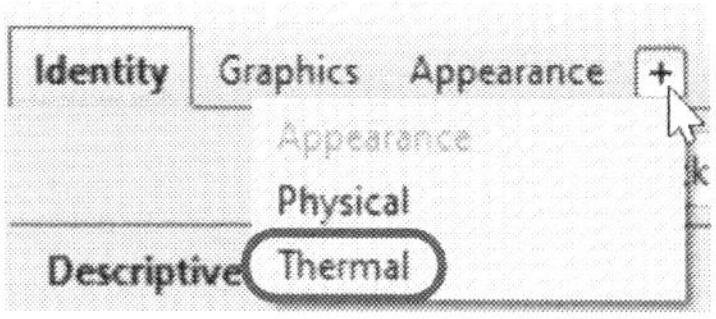

Figure B–34

- When you duplicate a material and then change asset-related information, the original material also updates. To prevent this from happening, duplicate or change the asset before making changes. If your material does not need to include the thermal information, you can click the red X to remove the thermal asset, as shown in Figure B–35.

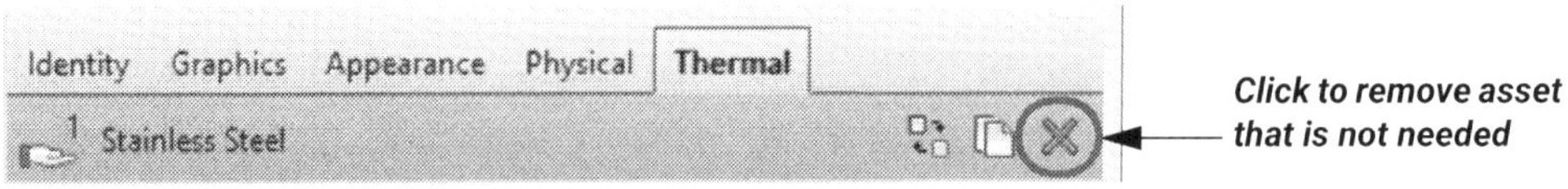

Figure B–35

Material Assets

Assets contain preset parameters that control a material's appearance in certain views, and its physical and energy analysis properties. These assets are in the *Appearance*, *Physical*, and *Thermal* tabs. Autodesk provides an extensive library of assets, as shown in Figure B–36, that are sub-divided by material categories or class. You can modify and add assets to materials depending on the variables required in the project.

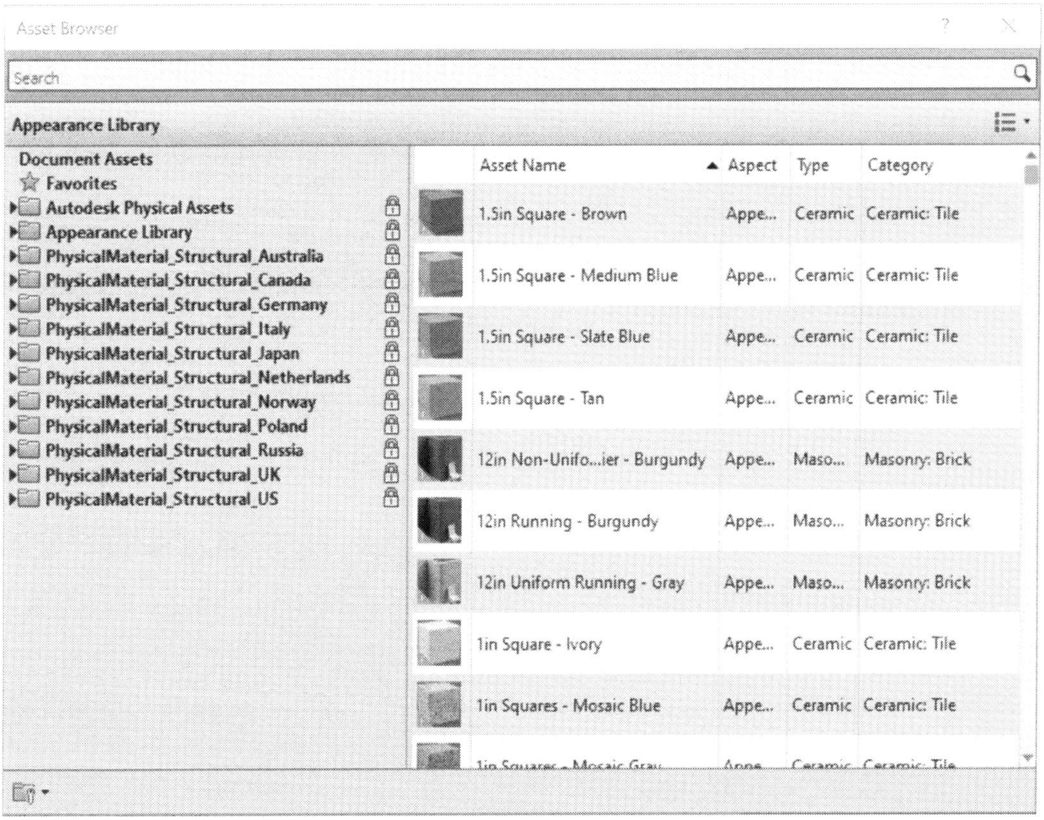

Figure B–36

- Assets can be accessed or modified in the *Asset Browser* or from within the *Material Browser*.
- The assets are filtered by type, so you need to modify the appearance asset using the *Appearance* tab, etc.
- You can create new assets by duplicating an existing one and then modifying the parameters.

How To: Replace an Asset for a Material

1. Verify that the new or duplicated material is selected in the Project Materials list.
2. Select one of the asset tabs (*Appearance*, *Physical*, or *Thermal*) and click (Replaces this asset).
3. The *Asset Browser* dialog box opens. Hover your cursor over the asset and click (Replaces the current asset in the editor with this asset), as shown in Figure B–37.

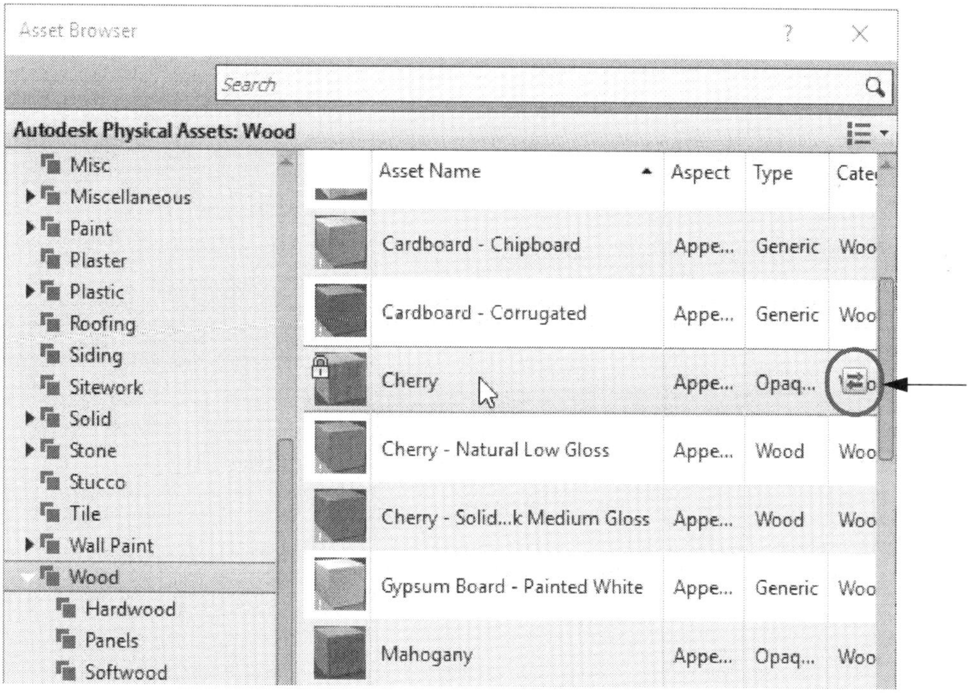

Figure B–37

4. The asset updates, as shown in Figure B–38.

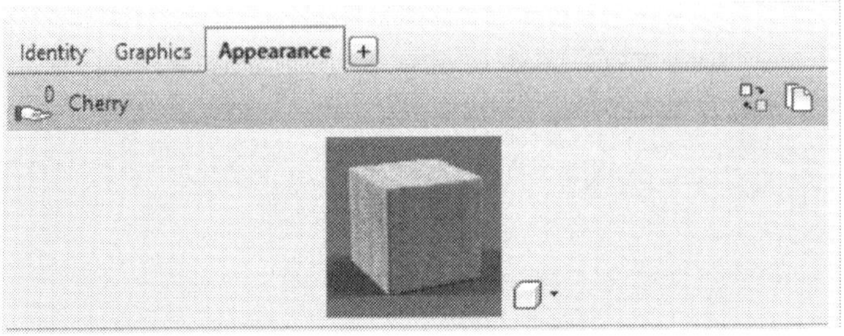

Figure B–38

5. Close the *Asset Browser* by clicking the **X** in the upper-right corner of the dialog box.
6. In the *Material Browser* dialog box, click **Apply** to save your changes.

How To: Duplicate an Asset

1. Verify that the new or duplicated material is selected in the Project Materials list.
2. Select one of the asset tabs (*Appearance*, *Physical*, or *Thermal*) and click (Duplicates this asset).
3. The asset duplicates, which is indicated by a **(1)** at the end of the asset's name, as shown in Figure B–39.

Asset name

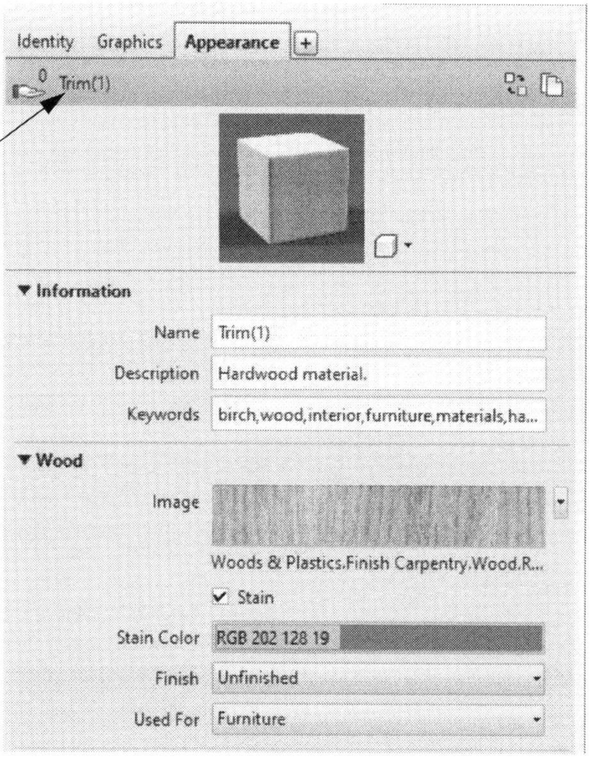

Figure B–39

4. Now that the asset is duplicated, in the *Information* area, you can change the *Name*, *Description*, and *Keywords*.

5. The area below the *Information* area is the material category or class. For example, if the asset is within the Wood category in the Library list, there will be a *Wood* area (as shown in Figure B–40) as an option to review or modify.
6. Within this area, there will typically be an image shown that the material asset uses when applied to an element. You can modify the image that is being used by clicking on it in the *Image* field, as shown in Figure B–40.

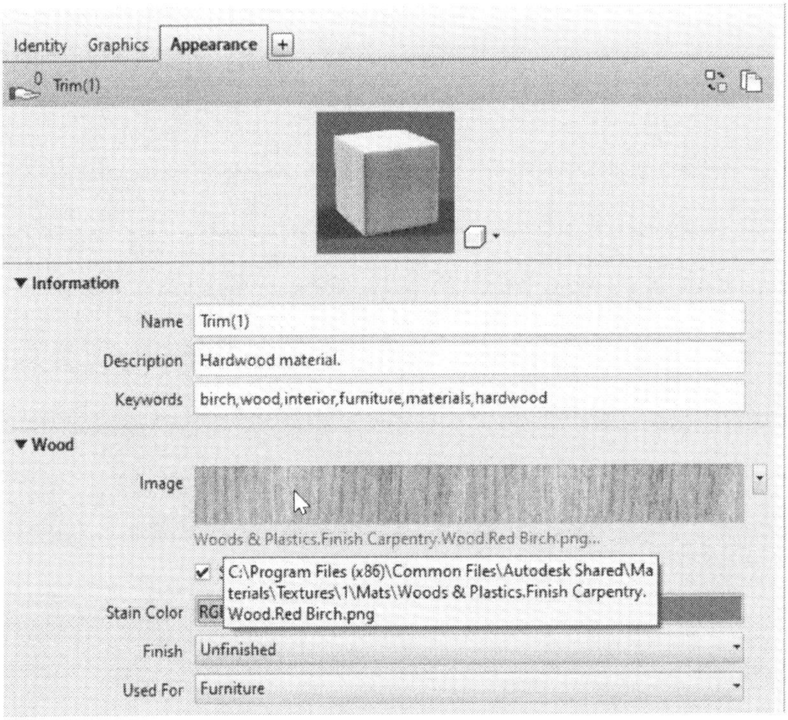

Figure B–40

7. In the *Select File* dialog box, you can search through several material textures, as shown in Figure B–41. When you find a material image that you want to use for the asset, select it and click **Open**.

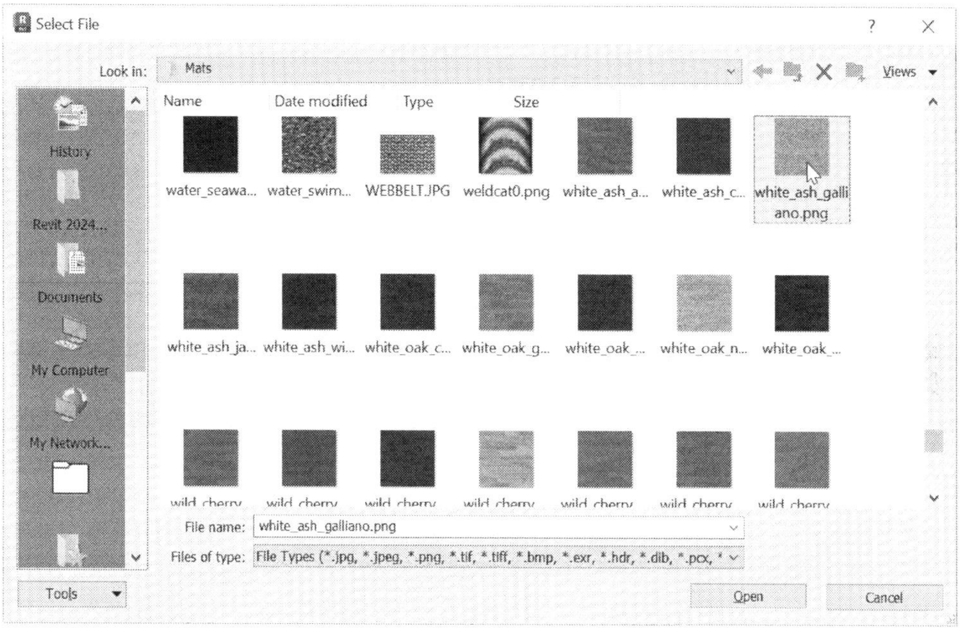

Figure B–41

8. Continue reviewing and modifying the asset properties as needed.

Apply Materials to Elements

Materials can be applied to elements in a model to display a realistic visualization of the element when it is viewed in the **Realistic** visual style or in a rendered view.

Materials can be applied to elements in a model in the following ways:

- **By Element Parameter:** Select an element in the model and, in Properties, modify the material parameter within the *Materials and Finishes* section.
- **By Face:** Apply a material to an element's surface using the **Paint** tool.

Note: For information on managing materials though object styles, refer to ASCENT's Autodesk Revit BIM Management: Template and Family Creation guide.

- **By Category:** This is managed through the **Object Styles** and modifies all elements of the same category. This is typically set up and managed by your BIM manager.

How To: Apply Material to an Element Parameter

1. In the view, select the element that you want to change the material for.
2. In Properties, modify the material parameter in the *Materials and Finishes* section in either the instance parameters or the type parameters.
   - **Instance parameter:** In Properties, if the material is an instance parameter (shown in Figure B–42), the *Materials and Finishes* section will display. By modifying the material parameter in the instance properties, it will only change on the element you have selected in the view.

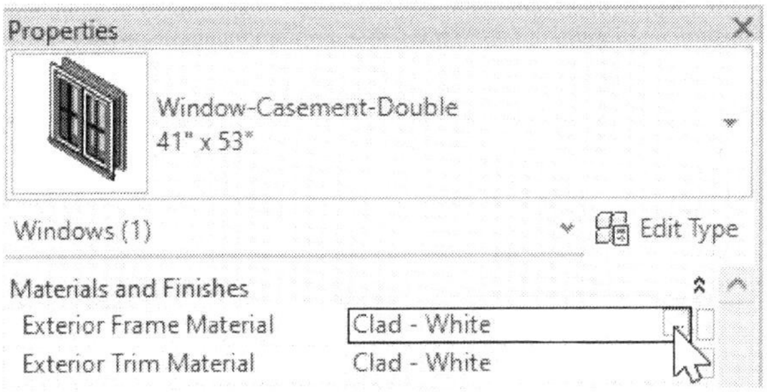

Figure B–42

   - **Type parameter:** If the material is a type parameter (shown in Figure B–43), click **Edit Type** and modify the parameter in the *Materials and Finishes* section in the *Type Properties* dialog box. By modifying the material parameter in the *Type Properties*, it will change the material for all instances of the same element in the model.

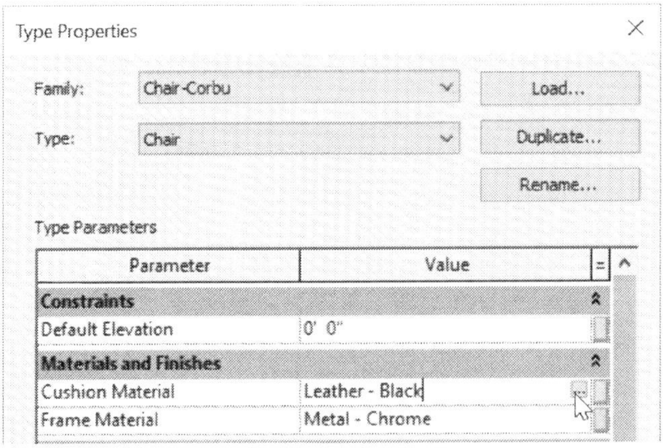

Figure B–43

Practice B1
Create Materials

Practice Objectives

- Create a new material from an existing material.
- Duplicate a material's appearance asset and modify it.
- Create a new material and apply a material appearance asset to it.

In this practice, you will create a new material based on an existing material. You will also create a brand new asset material.

Task 1: Duplicate an existing material.

1. Open the project **Multi-Use_Materials.rvt** from the practice files folder.
2. In the *Manage* tab>*Settings* panel, click (Materials).
3. At the top of the *Material Browser* dialog box, click inside the material search bar and type **Tile**.
4. Scroll through the project materials list and find **Tile, Porcelain, 4in**. Right-click on it and select **Duplicate Material and Assets**, as shown in Figure B–44.

Figure B–44

5. The new material will be highlighted in the Project Materials list. Click on the duplicate name and rename it to **Tile, Porcelain, 12in**.
6. Expand *Information*. Change the *Name* to **11in Squares - White** and change the *Description* to **11-inch square pure white**, as shown in Figure B–45. Note that after you change the name, the asset name changes as well, as shown in Figure B–45.

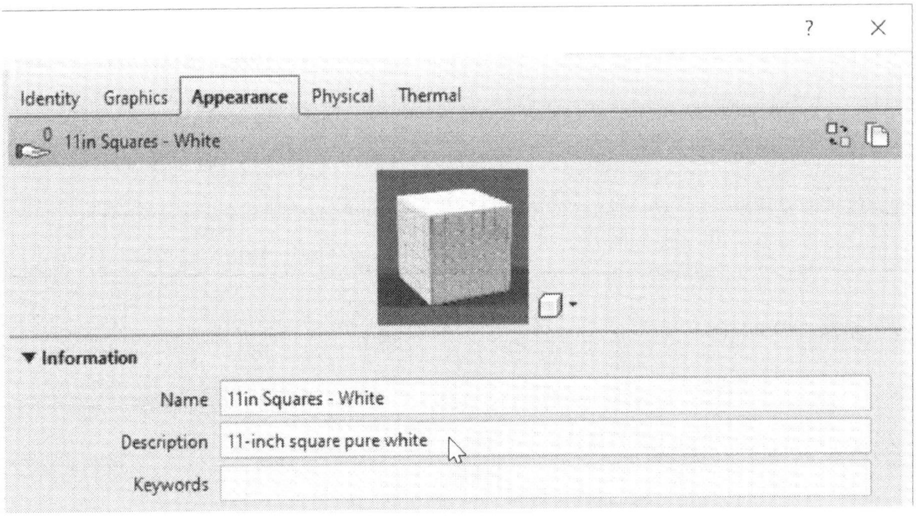

Figure B–45

7. Expand *Relief Pattern* and click on the image, as shown in Figure B–46.

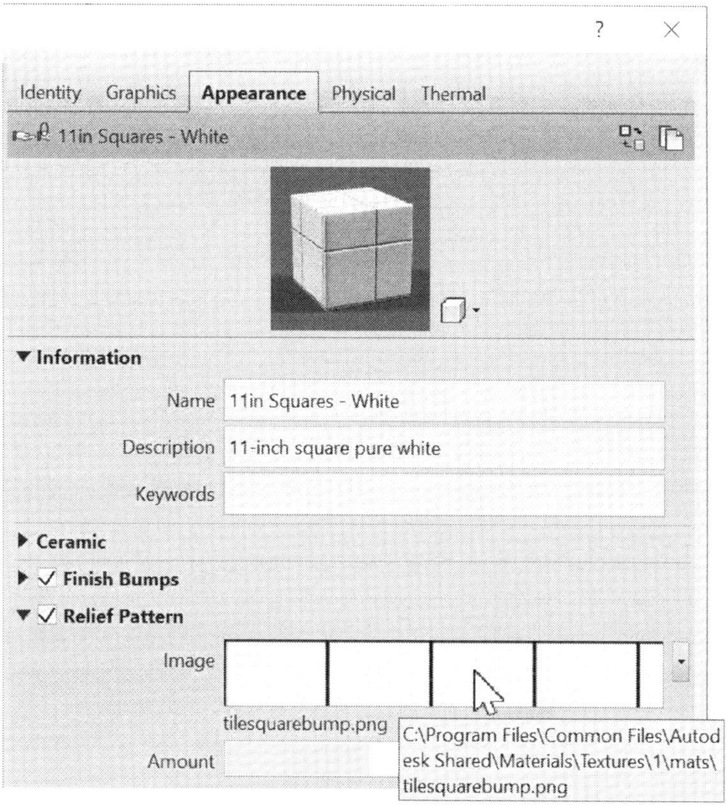

Figure B–46

8. In the *Texture Editor* dialog box, in the *Scale* area, change the *Sample Size* to **2'-0"** for the *Width* and *Height*, as shown in Figure B–47, and click **Done**.

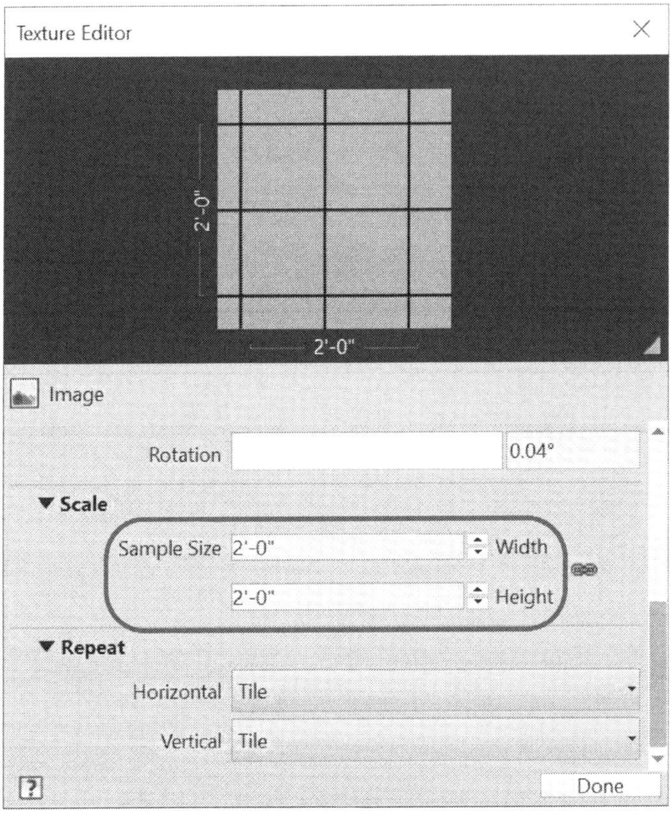

Figure B–47

9. If you want your new material to display correctly in a plan view, click on the *Graphics* tab and expand the *Foreground* area, then click on the *Pattern* image, as shown in Figure B–48.

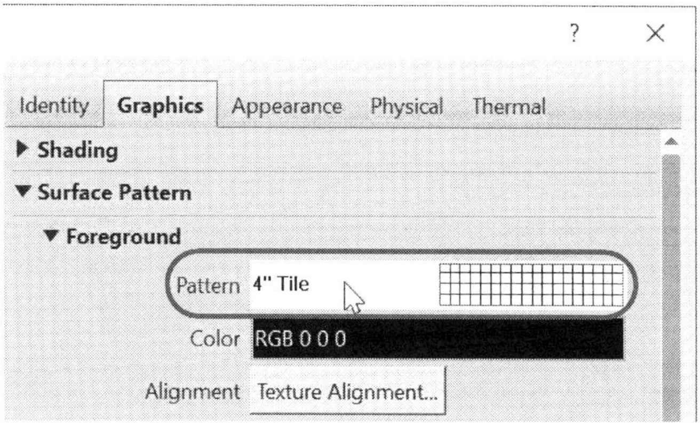

Figure B–48

10. In the *Fill Patterns* dialog box, select **12" Tile**, as shown in Figure B–49.

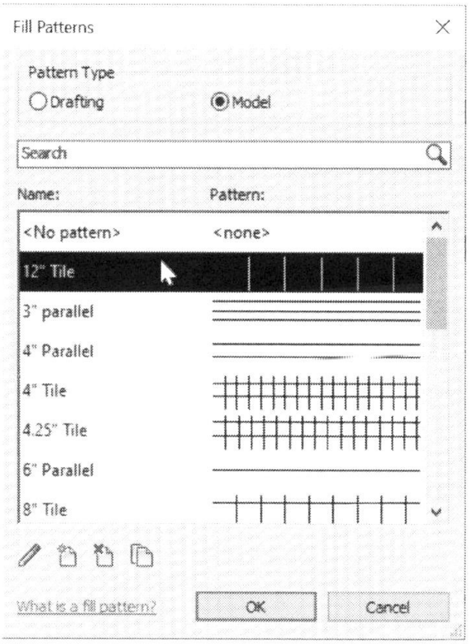

Figure B–49

11. Click **OK**.

Task 2: Create a new material.

1. While still in the *Material Browser* dialog box, expand  (Creates or duplicates material) in the Material Browser toolbar and select **Create New Material**.
2. Right-click on the new **Default New Material** in the Project Materials list and select **Rename**.

3. Type in the name **Kitchen Backsplash - Mosaic** and press <Enter>.
4. With **Kitchen Backsplash - Mosaic** selected, click the *Appearance* tab.
5. In the upper-right corner, click (Replaces this asset), as shown in Figure B–50.

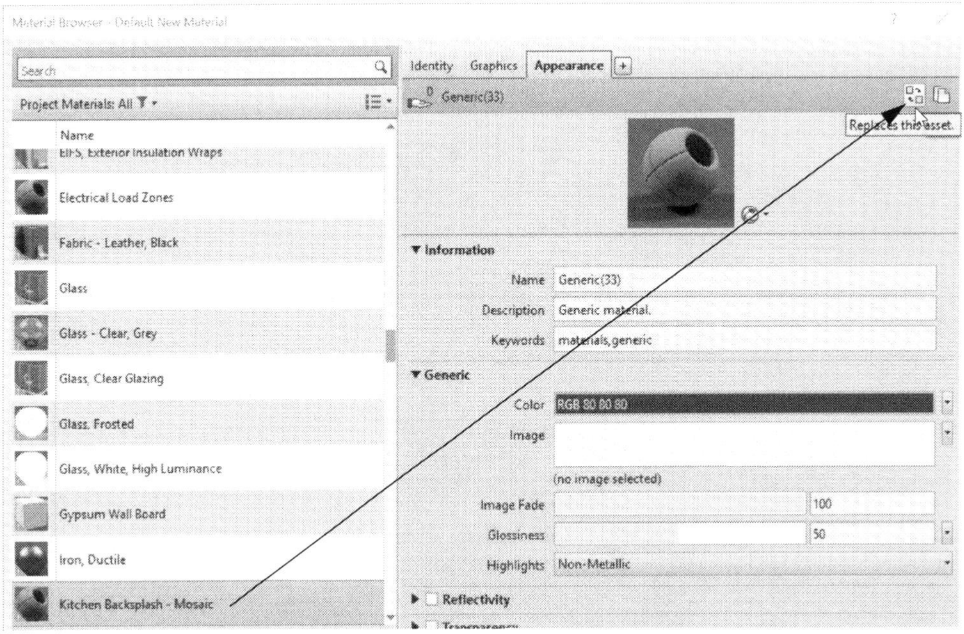

Figure B–50

6. In the *Asset Browser* dialog box, in the *Document Assets* panel, expand **Appearance Library>Ceramic** and select **Tile**, as shown in Figure B–51.

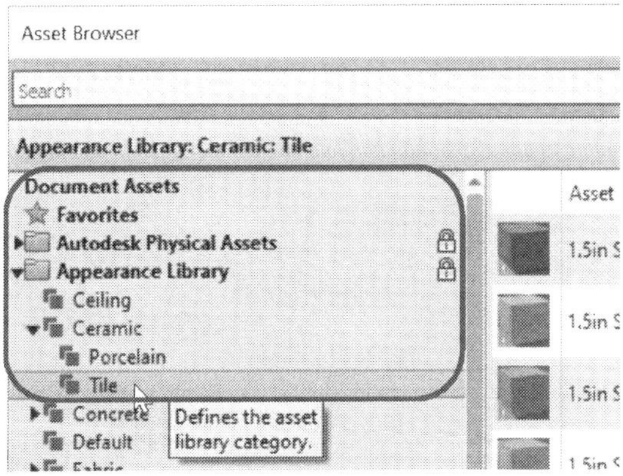

Figure B–51

7. On the right side of the dialog box, scroll through the materials and select **Circular Mosaic - Black & White**.

8. Click (Replaces the current asset in the editor with this asset), as shown in Figure B–52.

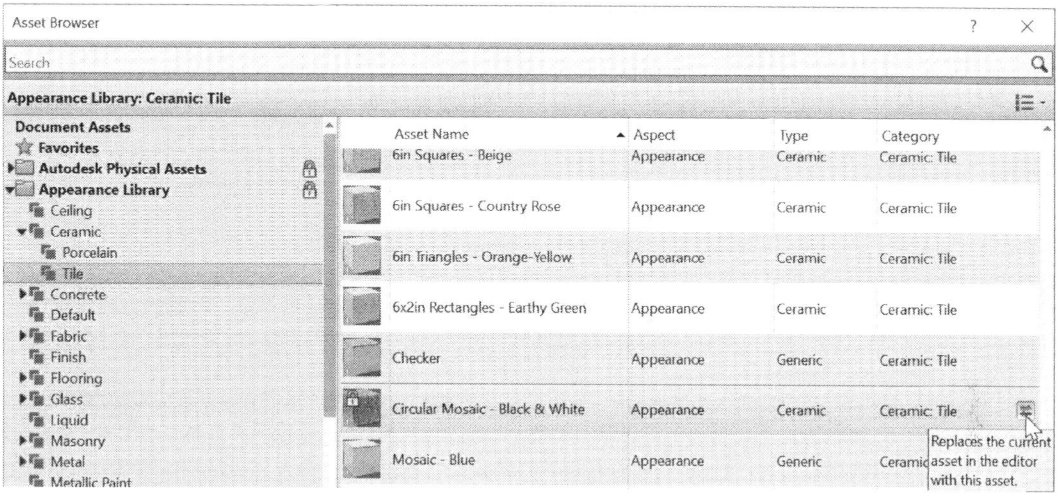

Figure B–52

9. Move the *Asset Browser* dialog box away from the *Material Browser* dialog box to see the material applied to your newly created Kitchen Backsplash - Mosaic material, as shown in Figure B–53.

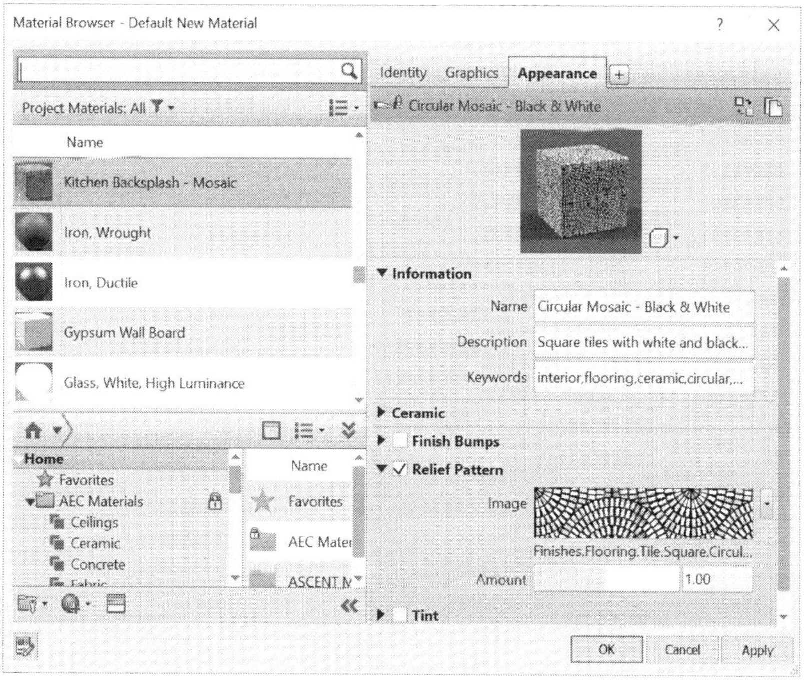

Figure B–53

10. Close the *Asset Browser* dialog box by clicking the X in the upper-right corner.
11. In the *Material Browser* dialog box, click **OK**.
12. Save and close the project.

End of practice

B.2 Creating Walkthroughs

A *walkthrough* is a series of perspective views linked together in a path. You specify the location of *key frames*—specific points in the plan that create the path of the walkthrough. Key frames are displayed as squares on the path, as shown in Figure B–54. A line shows the view direction. Once you create a walkthrough, you can edit its individual frames and export the whole sequence to an .AVI file.

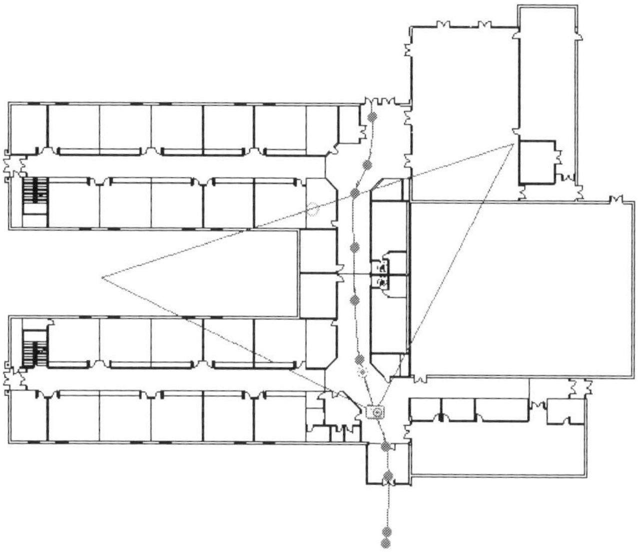

Figure B–54

How To: Create a Walkthrough

1. Open a plan view. Walkthroughs can be made in other views, but they are typically laid out in plan views.
2. In the *View* tab>*Create* panel (or Quick Access Toolbar), expand (3D View) and click (Walkthrough).
3. In the Options Bar, set the following, as shown in Figure B–55:
   - Select **Perspective**
   - *Offset*: **5'-6"**
   - *From:* **Level 1**

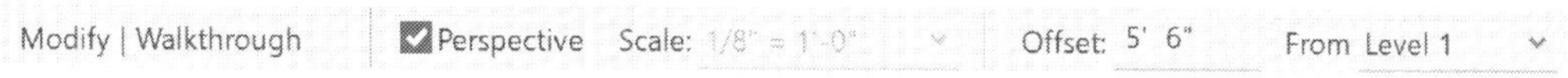

Figure B–55

4. Click on the screen to place the first key frame.
5. Continue adding key frames. You can change the offset, if required. For example, in frame locations where you are walking up a set of stairs.
6. In the *Modify | Walkthrough* tab>*Walkthrough* panel, click (Finish Walkthrough). A walkthrough view is created in the Project Browser with the default name of **Walkthrough1**.

- You can view and modify the walkthrough in either the plan view (to edit the path) or walkthrough view (to display the 3D views).

How To: View a Walkthrough

Note: To see the camera and path in a plan view, right-click on the walkthrough name in the Walkthrough section of the Project Browser and select ***Show Camera****.*

1. In the Project Browser, expand the **Walkthroughs** node and select the name of the walkthrough.
2. Click on the edge of the crop region.
3. In the *Modify | Cameras* tab>*Walkthrough* panel, click (Edit Walkthrough).
4. The *Edit Walkthrough* tab displays additional tools and the Options Bar displays the location controls, as shown in Figure B–56.

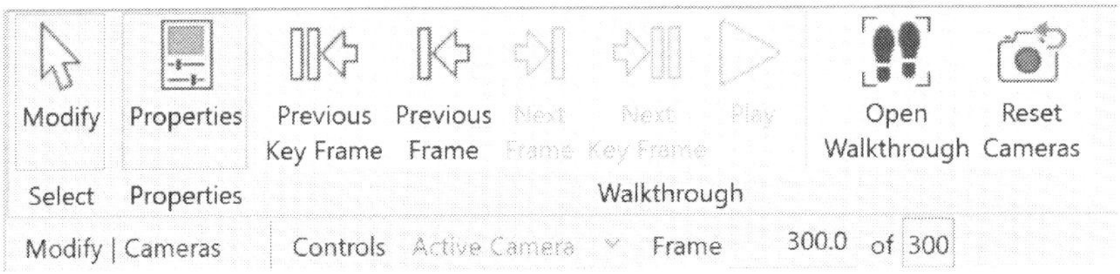

Figure B–56

5. Set the *Frame* number to **1**.
6. In the *Edit Walkthrough* tab>*Walkthrough* panel, click (Play).

Modifying a Walkthrough

When you are modifying a walkthrough, it can help to have both the walkthrough view and the plan view open at the same time. This enables you to see the 3D view and modify the path in the 2D view.

Controls	With the plan view active, select either **Active Camera**, **Path**, **Add Key Frame**, or **Remove Key Frame**. Then, modify the controls.
Frame #	Moves the cursor to the specified frame.
Arrow buttons	Use when you are viewing the walkthrough to ensure that it displays the views you are expecting. You can select from (Previous Key Frame), (Previous Frame), (Next Frame), (Next Key Frame), and (Play). To stop playing, press <Esc> or click **Cancel** in the Status Bar.
	Open Walkthrough opens the specified frame. Modify the crop window in one frame, it modifies in all frames.
	Reset Cameras. If you move the direction of the camera in a frame, clicking this button to reset all of the changed camera directions to the original path.

- If you click in a view while editing a walkthrough, an alert box opens, prompting you to decide whether to continue editing the walkthrough.

Setting Walkthrough Frames

To upgrade the performance of the walkthrough and smooth out portions where the rate of change appears to be too fast, you can change the number of frames between key frames.

In Properties, scroll down to the *Other* section and click the button next to the *Walkthrough Frames* parameter, as shown in Figure B–57.

> **Note:** *The button displays the number of frames in the walkthrough.*

Figure B–57

In the *Walkthrough Frames* dialog box (shown in Figure B–58), you can adjust the frame number, increment, or travel per frame. Clear the **Uniform Speed** option to change individual frame times.

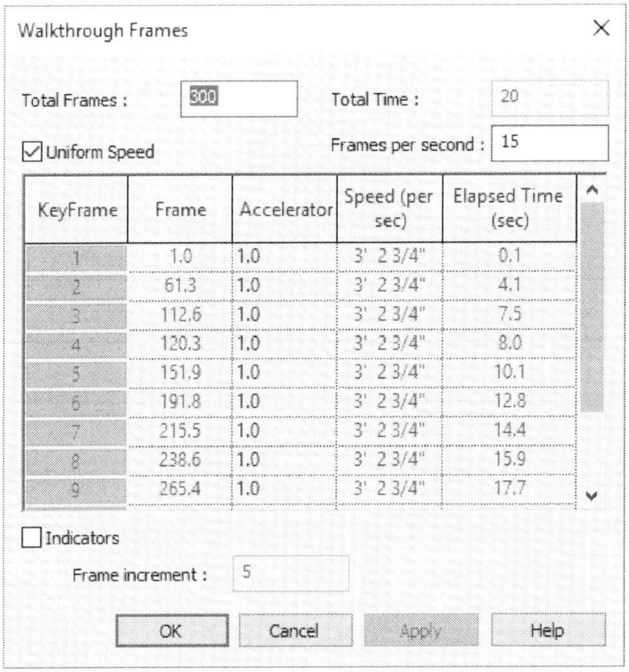

Figure B–58

How To: Export a Walkthrough

To show the walkthrough outside Revit, you need to create an AVI file.

1. Open the walkthrough.
2. In the *File* tab, click (Export)> (Images and Animations)> (Walkthrough).

3. Fill out the *Length/Format* dialog box, as shown in Figure B–59. In the *Output Length* area, specify which frames you want to include and the number of frames per second. In the *Format* area, select how you want the movie to display. You can display in **Wireframe**, **Hidden Line**, **Shaded**, **Shaded with Edges**, **Consistent Colo**r, **Realistic**, **Realistic with Edges**, and **Rendering**. Use the existing dimensions or specify a zoom scale factor.

   Note: *Autodesk Raytracer settings are used if you are in the Rendering display.*

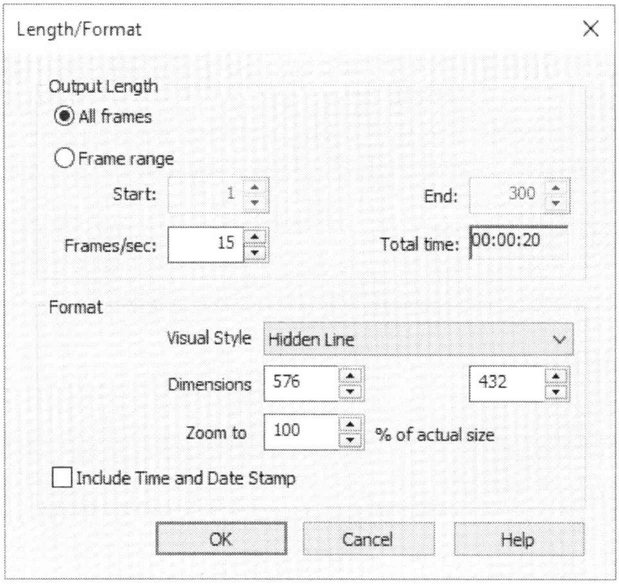

Figure B–59

4. Click **OK**.
5. In the *Export Walkthrough* dialog box, specify the folder and name for the new file.
6. Click **Save**.
7. In the *Video Compression* dialog box, select the format and quality and click **OK**. The walkthrough displays as it creates the video file.

- You need significant computer resources (CPU and RAM) to produce .AVI files.

Practice B2
Create Walkthroughs

Practice Objective

- Create an interior walkthrough and edit it to display better views along the path.

In this practice, you will create a walkthrough in a building.

Task 1: Create an interior walkthrough.

1. In the practice files folder, open **Midrise-Walkthrough.rvt**.
2. Open the **Floor Plans: Level 1** view.
3. In the *View* tab>*Create* panel (or Quick Access Toolbar), expand (3D View) and click (Walkthrough).
4. Select points to create a path that comes in through the front entrance, then goes to the left side into the reception room and conference room, in which the furniture and ceilings have been configured, as shown in Figure B–60.

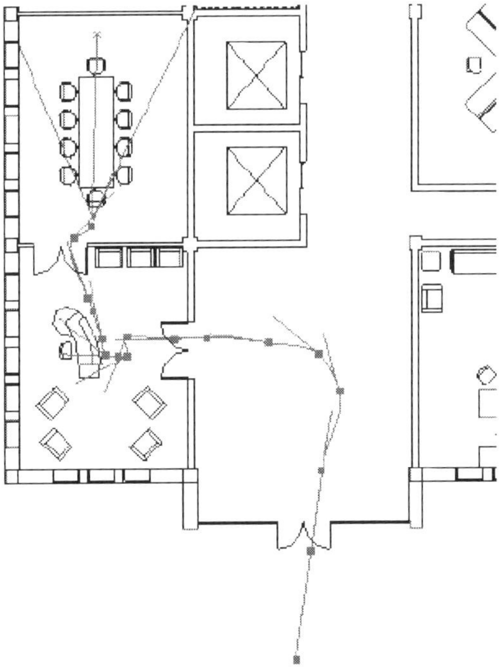

Figure B–60

5. After the last point, click (Finish Walkthrough).

Task 2: Test and edit the walkthrough.

1. Open the **Walkthroughs: Walkthrough1** view and the **Floor Plans: Level 1** view. Tile these two views.
2. In the walkthrough view, select the edge of the crop region.
3. In the *Modify | Cameras* tab>*Walkthrough* panel, click (Edit Walkthrough).
4. Click (Open Walkthrough).
5. In the Options Bar, set the *Frame* to **1** and press <Enter>.
6. Return to the *Edit Walkthrough* tab>*Walkthrough* panel, click (Play).
7. Edit the walkthrough as needed. Adjust the camera at different frames or speed up the process through some turns.
8. If you have time and computer resources, create an AVI file of your walkthrough.
9. Save and close the project.

End of practice

Chapter Review Questions

1. Within the *Material Browser* dialog box, in which area do you duplicate or create a new material?
   a. Material search bar
   b. Project Materials list
   c. Asset tabs
   d. Project Materials toolbar

2. In Revit, where are materials stored with their assets?
   a. Revit Settings
   b. Asset Library
   c. Material Libraries
   d. Material Editor panel

3. Which of the following tabs in the *Material Browser* dialog box enable you to duplicate or replace material assets? (Select all that apply.)
   a. Identity
   b. Appearance
   c. Physical
   d. Thermal

4. Materials cannot be shared to other projects.
   a. True
   b. False

Command Summary

Button	Command	Location
Materials		
	**Materials**	• **Ribbon:** *Manage* tab>*Settings* panel
	**Paint**	• **Ribbon:** *Manage* tab>*Settings* panel
Walkthroughs		
	**Edit Walkthrough**	• **Ribbon:** *Modify | Cameras* tab>*Walkthrough* panel
	**Export Walkthrough**	• **Ribbon:** *File* tab>Export>Images & Animations> Walkthrough
	**Open Walkthrough**	• **Ribbon:** *Edit Walkthrough* tab>*Walkthrough* panel
	**Walkthrough**	• **Ribbon:** *View* tab>*Create* panel, expand 3D View • **Quick Access Toolbar:** expand 3D View

Index

Made in the USA
Monee, IL
05 November 2026

67977827R00160